# Chicano Poetry

# Chicano Poetry
## A CRITICAL
## INTRODUCTION

Cordelia Candelaria

GREENWOOD PRESS
WESTPORT, CONNECTICUT • LONDON, ENGLAND

Library of Congress Cataloging in Publication Data

Candelaria, Cordelia.
  Chicano poetry.

  Bibliography: p.
  Includes index.
    1. American poetry—Mexican American authors—History
and criticism. 2. American poetry—20th century—History
and criticism. 3. Mexican Americans in literature.
I. Title.
PS153.M4C27  1986      811'.54'0986872073      85-10019
ISBN 0-313-23683-6 (lib. bdg. : alk. paper)

Library of Congress Catalog Card Number: 85-10019
ISBN: 0-313-23683-6

First published in 1986

Greenwood Press
A division of Congressional Information Service, Inc.
88 Post Road West
Westport, Connecticut 06881

Printed in the United States of America

The paper used in this book complies with the
Permanent Paper Standard issued by the National
Information Standards Organization (Z39.48-1984).
10 9 8 7 6 5 4 3 2

*Agua Negra* by Leo Romero, by permission of the author and Ahsahta Press, Boise State University. During the Growing Season and Celso by Romano, by permission of the author.

*Hijo del Pueblo: New Mexico Poems* and *Sangre* by Leroy Quintana, by permission of the author.

*Con Razón Corazón* by Inés Hernandez Tovar, by permission of the author and Caracol Press, San Antonio.

*Whispering to Fool the Wind* by Alberto Ríos, by permission of Sheep Meadow Press.

*Survivors of the Chicano Titanic* (1981) by Reyes Cardenas, by permission of Place of Herons Press, Austin, Texas.

*Canto y Grito Mi Liberación* by Ricardo Sánchez, by permission of the author.

*HechizoSpells* by Ricardo Sánchez, by permission of the author and Chicano Studies Research Center Publications.

*Spik in Glyph?* by Alurista, by permission of the author.

*Timepiece Huracán* by Alurista, by permission of Pajarito Press, Albuquerque.

Poems by Alurista in *Return: Poems Collected and New,* edited by Gary Keller, by permission of Bilingual Press/Editorial Bilingüe, Office of the Graduate School, SUNY-Binghamton, Binghamton, New York 13901.

*Restless Serpents* by Bernice Zamora, by permission of the author and José Antonio Burciaga.

*Flor y Canto IV and V,* edited by the Festival Committee, by permission of Pajarito Publications, Albuquerque.

Every reasonable effort has been made to trace the owners of copyright materials in this book, but in some instances this has proven impossible. The publishers will be glad to receive information leading to more complete acknowledgments in subsequent printings of the book and in the meantime extend their apologies for any omissions.

To my parents
Addie Trujillo Chávez and Ray Chávez

# Contents

# Introduction

The poetic imagination is as persistent as a cactus flower. Despite the awesome strength of the forces that challenge it, that would deny its central place in human discourse, the poetic imagination persists in expressing its specific truths ánd impressions about our complex planet. The forces of the modern age—both pre- and post-industrial—have greatly undermined the intensity of popular interest in poetry. The increased literary importance of prose fiction, for example, was an especially powerful detractor from poetry in the early modern period, and the ubiquity of the electronic media in the post-industrial period has further eroded its primacy as a prevailing art form. But like the cactus flora that transforms months of blistering heat and random drops of water into vibrant blooms, the poetic imagination persists in transmuting mundane experience and bare being into lyrical insight.

Nowhere is this noble persistence more clearly visible than in Chicano poetry, a body of American literature that has lived, and even flourished, quietly for over a century. Not only has Chicano poetry suffered the blistering hostility of a U.S. literary tradition that would deny the legitimacy of non-British origin, non-English language forms, but it has also had to endure the indifference of a publishing industry content to promote literature patterned in recognizable Yankee forms, however esoteric and avant-garde they might be. But although Mexican-American poets and their audiences may properly be seen as victims of a harsh literary environment, Chicano poetry itself is neither victim nor loser. Like the Old Testament tales of faith that outlived ancient Zion's oppressors, like the Christian parables that survived their Creator's crucifixion, like, in short, all the persecuted forms of expression and art forms that appear throughout human history—Chicano poetry has survived and in many instances, surpassed the challenges of its national environment.

Because of its emergence in recent years as a significant part of the literary landscape in the United States, Chicano poetry now demands a sustained, comprehensive, and systematic critical analysis. It deserves both the rigorous scrutiny valued by well-informed appreciators of the material and the interpretive guidance required by those readers not well acquainted with the field. An exhaustive analysis of Chicano poetry is also timely because, like the mountain, it is there. *Chicano Poetry* is an attempt to meet these mostly contradictory needs—an attempt that, given the contradictions, must admittedly fall short of the scholar's, the novice's, and the metaphorical mountain climber's ideals. In view of these factors, then, this study limits itself to three objectives.

1. To present an overview of Chicano poetry from 1967 to the present.

2. To apply salient critical theories and methodologies to a largely neglected universe of texts.

3. To apply a bilingual, multicultural perspective to a literary movement that is at once ethnic minority in its roots and articulation even as it is prototypically U.S. American in its promulgation of cultural pluralism.

The year 1967 was selected as the starting point for a number of reasons relating to Chicano literary history. In that year Rudolfo "Corky" Gonzales began distributing his poem, *I Am Joaquín*, a remarkable piece of nationalistic protest poetry. *Joaquín's* impact was immediately felt by Mexican-Americans in the Denver area and, later, by activists throughout the country who saw the poem as a seminal consciousness-raising vehicle for *el pueblo**  and the larger U.S. society. By experiencing *I Am Joaquín* either in a reading or through the film, many young Chicanos for the first time felt the possibilities inherent in a genuine Chicano literature. Another reason for selecting 1967 is that in that year *El Grito*, the vastly important "journal of contemporary Chicano thought," began publishing in Berkeley. *El Grito's* singular role in the promotion and dissemination of Chicano literature is well established, and despite its demise in 1974 it has a lasting place in contemporary letters because of its early recognition of such writers as Rudolfo Anaya, Alurista, Rolando Hinojosa, José Montoya, and Estela Portillo Trambley.[1] Like Charles Olson and the *Black Mountain Review* of an earlier era, *El Grito's* founding editors, Octavio Romano-V. and Nick Vaca, demonstrated courage, originality, and faith in venturing to publish a Chicano journal where none had existed and in risking the journal's future by publishing hitherto unpublished talent, some of whom insisted on experimenting with bilingual language forms before they were even recognized as legitimate poetic idioms.

---

*A short lexicon of terms appears on p. xv below, and a Spanish/English glossary follows the last chapter on p. 253.

Relative to the non-literary world, 1967 marked the establishment of a variety of forums which became central to the promulgation of the multifaceted message of the Chicano Movement. For example, MALDEF (the Mexican-American Legal Defense and Education Fund), the Southwest Council of La Raza (now the National Council of La Raza—NCLR), the Brown Berets, and other significant Mexican-American groups were formally organized that year. Many of these organizations have since become important institutions for social change in the United States, whereas others have disappeared, leaving a legacy of counterculture activism behind them.[2] In addition, in 1967 both the Courthouse Raid took place in Tierra Amarilla, New Mexico, and the United Farm Workers' (UFW's) national boycott of table grapes began in California.[3] Looking back, then, the appearance of both *I Am Joaquín* and *El Grito* in one year signaled a watershed in the literary history of *la raza*: between an era of Mexican-American consciousness and the emergent era of *chicanismo*, as well as between Mexican-American writing submerged in an ocean of so-called mainstream literature and the emerging Chicano literature buoyed by a vigorously developing sociopolitical movement.[4]

It must be remembered, however, that Mexican-Americans were writing and publishing long before 1967. As a result of the painstaking work of a number of scholars, we know that Mexican-Americans consistently published their work in the past, most often in Spanish and frequently in established presses, even in the nineteenth century.[5] Nevertheless, before the mid-1960s the literature produced by these writers was neither widely disseminated nor read by the majority of either *raza* or the non-Chicano population in the twentieth century. Thus, its influence as a shaping force of Chicano aesthetics and ideology—in short, of a Chicano consciousness—was only minimal. This observation is not intended to diminish the value of that body of work—for its rediscovery and reinterpretation by scholars reveals a vitality and quality that cannot be facilely denied—but only to acknowledge the history realistically.

One final point about the time frame of this book. Any calendar demarcation is to some extent arbitrary when considered from a broad historical perspective. During the course of my research, however, it became clear that to be fair toward and respectful of the large quantity of published Chicano poetry and the equally large number of Chicano poets actively publishing and reading their work would require a tight focus to keep the study workable. I chose to concentrate on contemporary Chicano poetry because in teaching literature I have found that all contemporary poetry has suffered the most critical neglect. The contemporary period is also a natural area for study because a significant gap of both time and tone separates it from the Mexican-American poetry written in earlier periods.

Just as the time frame for this study derives from literary and historical bases, so the criteria for text selection emerge from similar contexts. However, the selection process was based on a desire to achieve comprehensiveness for the period 1967 to the present—that is, to strive to mention every significant Chicano poet writing in that fifteen-year span and to shed light on both the broad contours of Chicano poetry and how the poets contributed to its shape and texture. Obviously not every poem or poet published in that period could be mentioned in *Chicano Poetry*. Accordingly, in addition to the principle of comprehensiveness, three other general principles have been followed:

- To include writers consistently writing, publishing, and reading their work between 1967 and the present.

- To include writers receiving serious critical attention either through published criticism of their work or through juried literary awards.

- To include writers whose works are of high quality and/or historical significance.

Fortunately, these three principles together accounted for the great majority of the selections, but given the nature of literary criticism and taste, another reader might present different selections with different emphases.

Because the book's critical approach (which also bears on my selection process) is discussed in detail in Chapter One, a few general remarks about that approach will suffice at this point. In view of the wonderful multiplicity of thought and belief, of custom and lifestyles defining the Chicano experience in the past two decades, it is entirely consistent with *raza* culture to find that Chicano poetry is comparably multiplicitous, wide ranging, and dynamic. The diversity of voices, styles, idioms, images, and personas examined in this book is striking, if not altogether magnificent. To best appreciate that magnificent diversity demands that the critical approach applied be sufficiently flexible to accommodate the subject's range. In this book that challenge has been addressed by applying a theory that allows for an eclectic synthesis of approaches, one that mirrors the fundamental synthesis of values existing in the culture itself. This synthesis of values encompasses such basic *raza* concepts as *mestizaje*, *chicanismo*, *la familia*, and *flor y canto*. As explained in Chapter One, these *raza* concepts yoke together widely disparate elements of experience, and the actual process of yoking itself produces a harmony that transcends the constituent parts. This book's critical method strives to attain a similar harmonious tension between a response to the text and the text itself. Ultimately, I seek a dialectical reciprocity between the poetic text and the critical methodology, just as there is dialectical reciprocity between poet and society.

The final introductory task here is to define terms. Because a glossary appears at the end of this book, definitions are given here for only those specialized terms that are used so frequently that an extended definition is appropriate early in the book.

*American* is used either as a noun or an adjective to refer to persons or things of the Western Hemisphere. Thus, "an American writer" could be from Mexico, Brazil, the United States, or any other country in the Americas. Similarly, "American literature" distinguishes writing from, say, European or Oriental literatures and is used generically for any literature of the Americas.

*Chicano* is common to many regional Spanish dialects in the United States and refers to Mexican-Americans—that is, U.S. citizens of Mexican ancestry. Its exact etymology is not known, though published speculation on the subject traces its origin either to an early linguistic corruption of the Spanish word *méjicano* or to a variation on the Nahuatl (Aztec) pronunciation of *mexicano*: MESH - ee - KAHN - o. *Chicano* or *Chicanos* is used in a generic sense to refer to Mexican-Americans or in a particular sense to refer to Mexican-American males. In Spanish grammar it is a masculine noun. *Chicana* or *Chicanas* refers to Mexican-American women, singular and plural forms; grammatically, they are feminine nouns. Occasionally, the forms *Chicano/a* or *Chicanos/as* are used to denote the total Mexican-American people regardless of (grammatical) gender.

*Mestizaje* refers to the mixture of Native American and European blood, as in the interbreeding of Mexican Indians with Spaniards. The term has increasingly been used in the United States by Chicanos to refer to the intermingling of cultural elements within Chicano culture—that is, the presence of indigenous pre-American sociocultural features as well as European, Moorish, and U.S. American traits. In this sense, *mestizaje* provides a prideful understanding of the blended Mexican heritage which contrasts with the racist view of that blendedness as, for example, in the term "mongrelization."

*Pre-American* is used synonymously with the term "pre-Columbian" or "pre-Cortesian" in this book. It refers to indigenous things, people, and life in the Americas before the Europeans arrived and renamed the Western Hemisphere.

*Raza* refers to the *Hispanic* community in a broad sense, but is most frequently used in this book to refer to the *Chicano* community. Used synonymously with *el pueblo*, it is an insider's self-reference to his/her primary social matrix (cf., the Jewish use of *goyim*). It is literally translated as the "race." That translation is inaccurate, however, because it does not capture the subtle connotations of community implicit in the term; "folk" or, simply, "community" would be better translations. "La Raza is all the Indoafrohispanic people, over 20 million of whom live in the United States—the fastest growing and most dynamic minority—from the sprawling city of Los Angeles to the metropolis of New York, from the grapevines near San Francisco to the beaches of Florida."[6]

*Yankee* refers to U.S. American people, things, and life as distinct from other Americans, say from Mexicans or Argentines. The term is disparaging only in context and almost always when spelled *Yanqui*. Used non-pejoratively, consistent with modern colloquial usage, it is the most recognizable term for U.S. Americans conveniently available that does not communicate the hemispheric chauvinism implicit in the term "American" used to denote only the United States or U.S. citizens. The United States is the only major country in the world that does not have a specific term to identify its people.

## NOTES

1. Arnulfo D. Tréjo, *Bibliografía Chicana—A Guide to Information Sources* (Detroit: Gale Research Co. 1975), 133; and Bruce-Novoa, *Chicano Authors: Inquiry by Interview* (Austin: University of Texas Press, 1980), 10.

2. MALDEF was founded to protect the legal rights of Chicanos and to promote the education of Chicano attorneys. The NCLR is a national affiliate organization that specializes in providing technical assistance to local Hispanic groups, in making public policy analysis, and in monitoring the legislative process on behalf of all Latinos. MAYO, the Mexican-American Youth Organization, was formed to help stimulate solidarity and political activism among Chicanos in Texas. The Brown Berets were members of a Los Angeles organization dedicated to the preservation of Chicano rights through any means necessary, including physical force. See the Prologue for further sociohistorical information.

3. The Raid was led by Reies Lopez Tijerina on behalf of his land grant struggle, and César Chávez led the grape boycott on behalf of the United Farm Workers Union which he founded. See the Prologue for further sociohistorical information.

4. Many revisionist scholars find the expression "American mainstream" too narrow and distorting to be of much academic value. Usually used as a synonym for WASP America, the "mainstream" in the United States has changed a number of times throughout history and should not be confused with the numerically largest subpopulation in the country. In fact, the U.S. mainstream is more accurately described as pluralistic and multi-ethnic. See the footnote on p. 76.

5. Raymund A. Paredes, "Mexican American Authors and the American Dream," *MELUS* 8:4 (Winter, 1981), 71–80; Tino Villanueva, *Chicanos: Antología histórica y literaria* (México, D.F.: Fondo de Cultura Economica, 1980), passim; and Luis Leal, "Mexican American Literature: A Historical Perspective," in Joseph Sommers and Tomás Ybarra-Frausto, eds., *Modern Chicano Writers* (Englewood Cliffs, N.J.: Prentice-Hall, 1979), 18–30.

6. Unsigned editorial, *El Diario La Prensa* (July 21, 1982), 4.

# Chicano Poetry

# Prologue: Summary of Chicano History

To fully understand the rich and complex multiplicity that constitutes the Chicano experience, it is essential to understand the pre-1900 history of Hispanics in the New World[1] and especially in the U.S. Southwest. Key to that understanding is the period 1848 to 1900 when Yankee colonization flourished in the Southwest after Mexico ceded the territory to the United States. During those five decades, all the traditions, quotidian habits, laws, language, religious and social values—in short, all the myriad components of a 250-year old civilization—were disrupted and irrevocably changed. In a sense, the history of Mexican-Americans officially began in 1848, though its earliest origins extend much farther back in time.

One caveat is in order before continuing. Capsule summaries of times past usually have a neatness about them which seems to deny that they reflect a living past in all its lively, sprawling messiness. Looking backward and telling in only limited space what is seen demands condensation and conciseness, and it is essential to note that any recapitulation of history is by definition incomplete and selective. Hence, throughout this book when historical sketches are required the emphasis is on context rather than causality and on ambience rather than objectivity. By seeking to evoke a feeling for the general effects of a given historical context, the aim is to convey the atmospheric *truth* of the times rather than to communicate a catalog of discrete *facts* about the period.

American history as we know it began with Christopher Columbus in 1492. While the pre-1492, pre-American history of indigenous societies has had marked influence on contemporary conceptualizations of *chicanismo*, limited space precludes a review of that history beyond pointing out that the pre-American—that is, Indian—aspect is essential to the *mestizaje* that defines the Chicano ethnic character.[2] Certainly, Chicanos recognize the crucial importance of the indigenous element to *raza* heritage, and that recognition is clearly present in the literature. When, for example, Luis

Valdez and El Teatro Campesino invoked the pre-Columbian past in their farmworkers theatre in the sixties, they were demonstrating the importance of being conscious of one's ancestral myth long before Alex Haley's *Roots* made the premise a national fad. When Alurista integrates Mexican mythology with Eastern and Christian lore in his poetry, he is confirming the universality of *mestizaje*. When Rudolfo Anaya weaves indigenous science and religion into *Bless Me, Ultima* and his other novels about modern Chicano experience, he is reasserting the persistence of the past in shaping the present. When Ron Arias' *Road to Tamazunchale* describes the living presence and undeniable efficacy of adopting an autochthonous consciousness in struggling with the Space Age, he, like the others, is doing nothing less than redefining truth and knowledge for a Yankee public.

Even though the Indians were defeated in the Conquest, their indigenous influence survived and adapted itself to the post-Conquest exigencies of the new Spanish order. Occurring in 1519–1521, the Conquest itself had generally cataclysmic effects on world history. However, its most important consequences were (1) the subjugation of all the indigenous peoples of the Western Hemisphere, (2) the emergence of new racial and ethnic groups of people, (3) the introduction of the European personality to Mesoamerica, and (4) the exportation of that personality throughout the Americas by Spanish explorers and settlers. Long before the English and other Northern Europeans came to the Western Hemisphere, the Spanish colonized the Americas. Spanish settlements in Florida (from 1563) and in Texas and New Mexico (from 1598) preceded the landing of the Pilgrims at Plymouth Rock and all subsequent Anglo settlements. Indeed, most of what is now the U.S. Southwest was a part of Mexico until 1848 when Mexico ceded it and most of its northern lands to the United States at the end of the U.S.-Mexico War. The document spelling out the terms of the war's end was the Treaty of Guadalupe Hidalgo, which to Chicanos is as significant as the Declaration of Independence. The cultural implications of the treaty were immense and, for the ancestors of present-day Chicanos, nearly as socially revolutionary as the Conquest was to the natives of Mesoamerica.

The Treaty of Guadalupe Hidalgo brought the imposition of an alien culture—the U.S. American or Yankee—on the deeply rooted Indo-hispanic/Mexican civilization with its laws and traditions in the Southwest. Only fifty years later the Southwest was almost entirely annexed by statehood into the union (only New Mexico and Arizona were added later, in 1912). Remarkably, the imposed alienness did not destroy Mexican-

Summary of Chicano History                                                                    5

American culture. The resilience of that culture stems largely from three factors: the established rootedness of the Mexican culture in the Southwest; its inherent strength and viability; and the proximity of Mexican-Americans to the original *patria*. To be sure, the imposition of U.S. laws and the immigration of hordes of Anglo-Americans brought radical changes to the region, especially to the land-based economic order. At first the new settlers' takeover of the native Southwesterners' land was gradual, but before long the takeover became large scale as Mexican-Americans were denied access to governance in their communities.[3] This land grab continued even until World War II when many farms, ranches, federal grazing permits, and oil/gas rights were sacrificed by *raza* leaving their natal homes in search of improved economic conditions in cities booming with war industries.

The tradition of hostile interaction between the natives and the newcomers thus began with their earliest encounters. Put another way, the hostility can be seen as a continuation of the Mexican-American conflict which the Treaty of Guadalupe Hidalgo was supposed to have settled. From today's perspective, we can see that the chasm of distrust between the two groups was deepened primarily because the alien leadership controlled all significant centers of political and economic power in the Southwest. As a result, change that would affect everyone in the new territory was initiated and executed by the new immigrants into the region, the Anglo minority, who did not seek or want the cooperation of either the *méjicanos* with their 250-year traditions and experience in the area or the Native Americans whose culture was even more antecedent. Although the Treaty of 1848 contained safeguards to assure the rights of the conquered native peoples, the white conquerors did not officially respect or implement those protections.

Nevertheless, while the United States was establishing itself in the West following 1848, Mexican-Americans were adapting to the changes occurring around them. Part of that adaptation was a vigorous struggle for social equity and civil rights. The struggle included resisting assimilation to the alien Anglo lifestyles, insisting on the continued use of Spanish, seeking economic and social alliances with the Indians, and adapting Anglo America's democratic process to Southwestern customs and perspectives. For instance, native New Mexicans were able to preserve relatively strong political and economic influence in their territory's governing structure, and in California, *El Clamor Público*, a Spanish-language newspaper, was influential in promoting a pro-*raza* position.[4] Accordingly, the Chicano

Movement of the 1960s is directly linked to historical activities like these which are deeply rooted in *raza* traditions which antedate that most recent decade of turbulent social change. Considered another way, the 1960s Chicano Movement represents but another wave of the antinomianism which is so central to and characteristic of the U.S. heritage dating back to the Pilgrims, to Anne Hutchinson, Thomas Paine, Henry David Thoreau, and to all the other individuals and movements that have challenged a narrow, rigid, and exclusionary interpretation of democracy.

On the other hand, not all events of major significance to Mexican-Americans originated in the United States. The Mexican Revolution of 1910, the century's first major social upheaval, had singular impact on the United States in general and Chicanos in particular. During the early years of the Mexican Revolution, masses of Mexican citizens escaped the horrors of civil war in their country by crossing the border into this country. That the great migration from Mexico began with the Revolution does not mean that it ceased with the end of the conflict, for thousands have continued to migrate, both legally and without documents, into the United States to the present time. The greater numbers of people of Mexican origin in the United States brought to this country new problems and new variations of old problems. Fortunately, they also brought fresh energy, talent, and resolve to a population still forced to function as a second-class citizenry, and these strengths were especially vital to the Chicano Movement to come four decades later. The great Mexican migration occurred at a time when the U.S. need for labor was intense. The demand for labor was equally great in urban industry and in the vast agricultural regions of the West and Midwest. Coincidentally, this period also saw the politicization of labor throughout the United States. Although the birth of the labor movement occurred in the nineteenth century, it peaked in the 1920s and 1930s and much of the labor union activity was spearheaded by Mexican-Americans, especially in the Southwest.[5] Thus, as a willing and capable workforce and as a determined and persistent union-organizing force, Mexican-Americans were actively engaged in one of this century's most significant phenomena in North America.

Along with union organizing, Mexican-Americans of the early twentieth century were active in organizing self-help groups—called mutual aid societies or *los mutualistas*. This activity emerged in the 1920s to serve a variety of needs and purposes. Although most *mutualistas* were middle class in their values and goals, they also exhibited a powerful desire for demo-cratic autonomy within the dominant society. Interestingly, these groups often held conflicting philosophies simultaneously in that they sought both assimilation into the U.S. mainstream and retention of their ethnocultural uniqueness.[6] One of the most well known of these organizations was LULAC, the League of United Latin American Citizens formed in 1927 and still active today. Although not politically militant in a contemporary sense, LULAC promoted ethnic awareness and the application of constitutional rights to all, especially those, like Chicanos, who were consistently denied them.[7]

By 1940 *raza* in the United States had begun to identify more closely with their Yankee homeland as time contributed to a natural evolution of attitudes. Thus, with the breakout of World War II Mexican-Americans did not hesitate to serve the United States and Allied powers. In fact, they volunteered and were drafted in disproportionately high numbers, and they served with outstanding distinction, earning disproportionately higher numbers of awards for valor than other groups, including overrepresentation among Congressional Medal of Honor recipients. Ironically, although the war was a time of sacrifice for everyone, for Mexican-Americans it was a time of even harsher persecution. It was the era during which *pachucos* (zoot suiters) were targeted for abuse by law enforcement officials in particular, though many others, including a shockingly biased press, shared in their mistreatment.[8] Nevertheless, the wartime economy enabled countless Mexican-Americans to enter occupations hitherto closed to them. In addition, because of the great demands for labor created by the war, the government instituted the Bracero Program which legalized the use of large numbers of Mexican nationals as "guest workers" in this country. Even after the return of the veterans at the war's end, the Bracero Program continued, primarily because it was an easy source of cheap labor for U.S. business. As expected, the program encouraged extensive immigration and led to the exceedingly large presence in the United States of Mexican workers without proper long-term documents—a result which today is described as the chronic undocumented worker problem. Here, as with other chronic social ailments in this country, this one was caused and nurtured by the government's kowtowing to the desires of powerful business interests.[9]

The war and its aftermath had a decisive impact on the lives of Mexican-Americans and produced dramatic changes in the ways *raza* perceived themselves both as individuals within the ethnic group and as citizens of the larger nation. Returning home with a new self-confidence generated by their war experiences coupled with their interaction in the armed services with *raza* from other parts of the nation, Chicano GIs found themselves victims of some of the most blatant racist discrimination ever.[10] Coming as it did on the heels of valorous service to the nation in the war, the returning veterans and their families viewed the continued racism with disgust. With the steely determination born of the rightness of the cause, however, *raza* turned to their old mutual aid societies and formed new ones for support in the fight against their second-class status. For example, the American GI Forum joined LULAC and other organizations in providing support, means, numbers, and strong ethnic identification in the growing militancy for civil rights. Thus, even though the Black Movement is credited in the public mind with heralding the start of the civil rights movement, Mexican-Americans also contributed substantially to it. Whether in labor organizing, in law courts, in united efforts against unfair practices in politics, business, and education, Mexican-Americans contributed to advancements in social justice and economic equity. For example, the 1948 Delgado Case in Texas resulted in a school desegregation ruling six years before *Brown vs. Topeka Board of Education*, and the Confederation of Unions of Mexican Workers established in the 1920s antedated the AFL-CIO by over thirty years in the amalgamation of separate unions.[11] These advancements—rooted in the post-1848 period and originating even before that time—explain why the sixties' Chicano Movement was so quick to catalyze and even quicker to spread across the nation. It emerged from within a ready context of heightened consciousness and grass-roots political experience, as well as from a refusal to conform to socially mandated inequalities.

A new era for Mexican America began in 1965 in California when what was to become the National Farm Workers Organizing Committee called a strike against growers near Delano. The strike eventually led to the famous nationwide boycott of table grapes in 1967, which in turn led to the emergence of the United Farm Workers Union (UFW). With its founder César Chávez, a proponent of non-violence as a means of effecting social change, the UFW became synonymous with "the Chicano Movement" in the mainstream news media, and national publicity proved beneficial to the UFW's cause as millions of consumers participated in the boycott, assuring its success. To informed Mexican-Americans, however, *el Movimiento* extended far beyond the *campesinos* and their just cause, as the closing years of the decade saw other grass-roots issues and *raza* leaders emerge. Accordingly, in 1966 Rodolfo "Corky" Gonzales organized the Crusade for Justice in Denver, an organization still in existence and which militantly agitated on behalf of Chicano rights, particularly in public education. The Crusade also promulgated the famous Plan de Aztlán, a document of nationalistic *raza* objectives for Chicano self-determination. Looking back, we can see that 1967 was a landmark year for *el Movimiento Chicano*. In 1967:

- The UFW called for a nationwide boycott of table grapes.

- Reies Lopez Tijerina and his Alianza Federal de Mercedes (founded in 1963) attempted the takeover of the County Courthouse in Tierra Amarilla, New Mexico. The Courthouse Raid was planned to call attention to the history of broken land treaties and fraudulent contracts which since 1848 had left Mexican-Americans virtually bereft of their land in the Southwest.

- In Los Angeles the Brown Berets formed and promoted militant action, including physical means, to overcome the social inequities suffered by Chicanos.

- MAYO, the Mexican-American Youth Organization, was organized in Texas by José Angel Gutiérrez. An activist advocacy organization, MAYO was instrumental in the political success of *raza* in Crystal City in 1969 and was in many ways a precursor to La Raza Unida party (RUP) which Gutiérrez founded in 1970.

- The Ford Foundation provided start-up funds for MALDEF, the Mexican-American Legal Defense and Education Fund, an organization comparable to the American Civil Liberties Union and the National Association for the Advancement of Colored People in its strong pursuit of civil rights through the judicial system and in its active promotion of the education of Chicano attorneys.

- Scholars Ernesto Galarza and Julian Samora and business executive Herman Gallegos began an important study of Mexican-Americans in the Southwest out of which eventually came significant grants for the advancement of Chicanos from the Ford Foundation. This work also led to the formation of the National Council of La Raza.

- In Ignacio, Colorado, Chicanos organized the Chicano and Southern Ute populations for the first time, an effort that culminated in the following year's unseating of the town's Anglo political power structure and the election of Ignacio's first non-Anglo mayor.

- Protesting deficient public education for Mexican-Americans, Chicano students organized a nationwide boycott of classes which was especially successful in California, Texas, and Colorado.

- In Berkeley, three Chicano professors began publication of *El Grito*, a journal devoted to contemporary *raza* issues and creative literature, which had impact on the conceptualization of *chicanismo* in the Movement's early years.

These seminal events and activities revealed the great extent of energy, commitment, and political power that existed within the Mexican-American community. Even though there had been consistent pro-*raza*

activism since 1848, the late 1960s for the first time saw a coalescence of
Chicano grass-roots causes, national journalistic coverage, and sophisticated
leadership within the community. The groups and individuals mentioned
here along with a host of others in every Southwestern state and key parts
of the rest of the country united to form—sometimes systematically, most
often loosely and spontaneously—what we know today as the contemporary
Chicano Movement.[12] That the Chicano Movement crystallized at a time
when other popular causes (like the Student Movement and the Anti-
Vietnam War Movement) were at their prime is probably not coincidental,
but it is beyond the scope of this prologue to explain their shared
characteristics. Suffice to observe that from these other leftist liberal efforts
came a measure of the support, leadership, research, and numbers needed
for public protest demonstrations which were required to sustain the
Chicano Movement beyond its infancy.

The *Movimiento* tapped its members' historical roots, mestizo heritage,
and wide variety of *raza* experiences for its inspiration. At the time its goals
were sometimes vague and its methods sometimes desultory but overall the
heart of the Movement (as opposed to some of its ideological fringes) sought
(1) to better the group's socioeconomic condition, (2) to heighten its
participation in the political process, and (3) to increase its members' access
to effective education. To do this required active consciousness-raising both
among *raza* and within U.S. society as a whole. As the cultural awareness
developed, the Movement's breadth and scope expanded geographically,
numerically, and in its representation of all socioeconomic classes. Eventually, even some of the most conservative Hispano assimilationists had
their consciousness raised enough to permit, say, open use of the progressive term "Chicano" without alarm, something which previously had
created considerable polemic.

Accordingly, one by-product of the extensive consciousness-raising
among Chicanos was an intense debate concerning the nature of Chicano
identity and the appropriate use of group identification labels. The reason
for both the discussion and its intensity derived for the most part from three
circumstances. The first had to do with the discrepancies between how *raza*
perceived (and, to some extent, still perceive) themselves and how the
dominant society perceives them. Because of the antagonisms generated on
both sides by the war between Mexico and the United States, Anglos
generally considered "Mexican" a derogatory label and, thus, they most
often used it in conjunction with defamatory terms like "Mexican greaser"
or "dirty Mexican." The people themselves, however, most often used

"Méjicano" as an objective, positive self-referent because it accurately reflected the *raza* heritage. In addition, the U.S. government had great difficulty deciding how to officially designate *raza*, and its changing application of official labels further confused the issue of ethnic identification. At various times Chicanos were identified by the U.S. Census Bureau as Spanish-American, Spanish-speaking, Spanish-surnamed, Mexican-American, Mexican-origin citizens, and/or Hispanic-American.[13]

A second reason for the intense debate concerning the use of group identification labels related to the distinct differences in cultural identity between those people who had a centuries-old history in the Southwest and those who were twentieth-century immigrants from Mexico. The recent immigrants most often held more intimate ties with the original *patria* than did the long-established Southwestern families, who often viewed the new immigrants with only slightly less disdain than they did their alien Anglo counterparts. Frequently, *raza* with deep roots in the United States distinguished themselves from other Mexicans by employing "Spanish" or "Hispano" as a self-referent.[14] Third, Chicanos disagreed about whether or not there should be only one label of ethnic identification for the group or whether, like Native Americans with their distinct tribal names, self-identification by regional preference should be favored. Ultimately, influential leaders and segments of the Movement saw that the evolution of attitudes within the community would resolve the issue and that that resolution would ramify beyond the ideologically engagé. Accordingly, today the widespread use by both Mexican-Americans and others of "Chicano" and *"raza"*—terms which at one time were relegated to in-group usage only—indicates one aspect of the issue's resolution. Signifying the cultural bonds of a people of common heritage as well as an ideology of democratic self-determination, the term "Chicano" is now widely accepted, for it aptly refers to the complex combination of *raza* and U.S. American characteristics which form the Mexican-American experience. Of course, there are still some, primarily those descendants of deep-rooted Southwestern families, who do not rely on "Chicano" as a principal self-identifier, preferring "Spanish" or "Spanish-American." Nevertheless, if they happen to be fluent Spanish speakers, the most common self-identifier in the Spanish language even for them is still *"méjicano."*

In recent years the Chicano community has grown considerably. Demographers even predict that by the turn of the century the Hispanic population will constitute the largest ethnic minority in the United States with Chicanos forming its largest subset. Such numerical growth brings natural changes of major proportions to society, and it has already had profound impact on the country's socioeconomic and political system. Recent years have also seen the beginning of a new unity among Hispanics, and Chicanos, Puerto Ricans, Cubans, and Central and South American Latinos have begun to see themselves as part of a single *raza* minority. This attitudinal shift in group perception will have dramatic effect in the future as Hispanics join together to pursue economic, educational, and political empowerment and social advancement. U.S. society in general will, of course, reap the greatest benefits of such progress.

## Notes

1. The so-called New World was, of course, not new at all to its millions of indigenous inhabitants. The term refers to the European perception of this hemisphere in that period.

2. For more information on the pre-American *raza* heritage, see Miguel León-Portilla, *Aztec Thought and Culture: A Study of the Ancient Nahuatl Mind* (Norman: University of Oklahoma Press, 1963), 74–75 and passim; and R. C. Padden, *The Hummingbird and the Hawk* (New York: Harper Colophon Books, 1967).

3. Rudolfo Acuña, *Occupied America: A History of Chicanos*, 2nd ed. (New York: Harper & Row, 1981), 29–33 and 52–64.

4. Ibid., 109–10.

5. Ibid, 190–298; and Ernesto Galarza, *Merchants of Labor: The Mexican Bracero Story* (Santa Barbara Calif.: McNally & Loftin, 1964), 17–45.

6. Acuña, *Occupied America*, 303.

7. Ibid., 191–92 and 313–15.

8. Carey McWilliams, *North from Mexico* (New York: Greenwood Press, 1968), 227–43.

9. There is a long list of post-Watergate exposés of the U.S. government's misuse of official authority on behalf of the private sector; see Daniel Ford, *The Cult of the Atom: The Secret Papers of the Atomic Energy Commission* (New York: Simon & Schuster, 1982), for an excellently researched recent study of the government's "sweethearting" of the nuclear industry.

10. Acuña, *Occupied America*, 329–30.

11. Matt S. Meier and Feliciano Rivera, eds., *Dictionary of Mexican American History* (Westport, Conn.: Greenwood Press, 1981), 118 and 100–1.

12. For more information on the contemporary Chicano Movement, see Acuña, *Occupied America*, 352–427; and Meier and Rivera, *Dictionary of Mexican American History*, 239–40.

13. Meier and Rivera, *Dictionary of Mexican American History*, 74–75. Also see Manuel Gamio, *The Life Story of the Mexican Immigrant* (New York: Dover, 1971 [1931]) in which the subjects of the autobiographical oral histories continually refer to themselves and their people as "Mexican" (translated from "méjicano").

14. Frances L. Swadesh, *Los Primeros Pobladores: Hispanic Americans of the Ute Frontier* (Notre Dame, Ind.: University of Notre Dame Press, 1974), 206–7.

# 1

# The Literary Context of Chicano Poetry

---

## CHICANO LITERARY HISTORY

Contemporary Chicano poetry emerged out of a context of grass-roots political activism and heightened *raza* literary sensitivity. The political context and key historical factors affecting Chicano literature were sketched in the Prologue. This chapter summarizes the salient literary background, based on the chronology below which outlines the macro literary context out of which Chicano literature evolved.[1] That macrocosm spans approximately three millennia and comprises four major civilization types—the indigenous Western Hemispheric, the Southern European (primarily Spanish), the Northern European (primarily English), and the African.

### American Literature of the United States

I. Pre-American Period
   A. Indigenous Oral Traditions from 1000 B.C.*
   B. Columbus' Mistake of West Indies for India, 1492*
II. Colonial Period
   A. Hispanic, 1521–1810*
   B. British, 1607–1765
   C. African Slave Oral Tradition, 1619–1847
III. National U.S. Literary Period
   A. Anglo-American: 1776–Nineteenth Century
   B. Mexican-American: 1848–Twentieth Century*
   C. Negro Emancipation: 1862–Twentieth Century
IV. Modern Period

A. Nineteenth-Century Rise of Realism and Criticism
["American Renaissance" in mid-1800s]
B. Twentieth-Century Rise of Counter Literatures: Jewish, Afro-American, Feminist, Chicano,* Native American, etc. ["Harlem Renaissance" in 1920s and "Chicano Renaissance" in late 1960s]

*Designates link to Chicano literature.

The year 1000 B.C. was used as a starting date in the accompanying outline because by that time Mesoamerica appeared to have been well settled by immigrants from the north and Asia and the beginnings of established civilizations in the Western Hemisphere appeared. The Hispanic Colonial Period spans the end of the Conquest and the start of the Mexican revolt against Spain; the British Colonial Period starts with the settlement at Jamestown, Virginia, and ends in 1765 with the passage in England of the Stamp Act which so infuriated the colonists that an independence movement and nationalism emerged. The African Slave Oral Tradition begins with the introduction of slaves in Virginia and ends with the first publication of Frederick Douglass' abolitionist newspaper, *North Star*, the first national publication by and on behalf of Negroes. In section III of the outline, 1776 marks the signing of the Declaration of Independence; 1848 the signing of the Treaty of Guadalupe Hidalgo; and 1862 the issuance of the Emancipation Proclamation by Lincoln.

In broad strokes the outline represents approximately 3,000 years of human civilization scattered over the North American continent prior to European exploration. More than half the outline's time span comprises the pre-American period during which hundreds of tribes native to the land[2] passed along their history, religion, lore, and culture in oral form. Not until the Spanish *conquistadores* and the *pobladores* (pioneers) who followed them began colonizing Central and South America were alternatives to the oral tradition introduced. Nevertheless, inasmuch as Chicano literature reflects a mestizo quality, its cultural (if not literary) roots began in the oral tradition of the aboriginal pre-American age. The essential character of Chicano literature's ancestry lies, however, within the colonial period. The centuries between the Conquest and the *Grito de Dolores* of 1810 which signaled the start of Mexico's revolution against foreign domination saw the transformation of Mesoamerica from its aboriginal state to the birth of Mexico, a Spanish-speaking colony which for another century was to be the only center of European and Christian values in this hemisphere. Accordingly, the habits and values of this age were the ones exported into northern Mexico by Spanish/Mexican *pobladores*, and as historians and linguists have observed, the vestiges of this colonial era are still manifest in many Chicano communities, especially in northern New Mexico.[3]

If Chicano literature's ancestral character lies in the Hispanic colonial period, its ideological foundation may be traced to the national U.S. Literary Period when the Mexican revolutionary spirit strengthened and spread beyond the intelligentsia to the entire peasantry. That spirit of liberation, equality, and brotherhood symbolized by *el Grito de Dolores* underlies the basic theme of early Chicano literature, and it emerged in the turbulent years after 1810. The gap in the outline between 1810 and 1848 represents the early turbulence before a true and undeniable Mexican nationalism took hold.[4] Another aspect of Chicano literature's ideological foundation appeared after 1848 and the signing of the Treaty of Guadalupe Hidalgo—the aspect of resistance to the new Yankee government and culture. In *raza* folklore, in unpublished writings (like letters and diaries), and in published written forms (like newspapers and pamphlets), the progenitors of today's Chicanos advanced an ethos of resistance to forced subjugation and of support for *raza* self-determination.

The outline thus discloses the undeniable vein of micro literary history that flows from this country's cultural genesis to today's Chicano literature. That Chicano literature is fundamentally "American" is clearly established, for its origins and influences are all part of the very basis of the macro context that constitutes the U.S. American literary tradition. In this sense, therefore, it, like other ethnic minority literatures of the United States, lies within the *mainstream* of American literature. As the Society for the Study of Multi-Ethnic Literature in the United States (MELUS) and others have long argued, the American mainstream is basically pluralistic, iconoclastic, democratic, and multi-ethnic and should be thus perceived, instead of being viewed as a solely Anglo-American stream of folklore and *belles lettres*.[5]

Although rooted in the pre-American and Hispanic colonial past, Chicano literature as a distinctive body of work grew directly out of the aftermath of the 1846–48 war between Mexico and the United States. In these years the new U.S. citizens, the approximately 80,000 *Méxicanos* who remained in the Southwest after the 1848 treaty, began to adapt their relationships to their brethren in the Mexican heartland and to accommodate themselves to the crescive Anglo-American influences of their new nation. Still, for at least a generation after the end of the war, the artistic and literary sensibility and practice of these people were not palpably different from those of Mexico. Continuing to write in Spanish, Mexican-American authors in the Southwest still reflected a Mexican literary style and addressed the same subjects they had before the political environment had been so dramatically altered. For instance, the 1855 poem "A ella,"[6] written by José Elias Gonzales, a Los Angeles editor, exhibits a wholly conventional Mexican lyrical shape and theme, just as nostalgia for the Mexican past and for the pre-Anglo homeland, a theme that was to reappear in the next century's Chicano literature, surfaces as a clash of cultures in poetry and essays published in Spanish-language newspapers of the period.[7] Nearly a generation after the signing of Guadalupe Hidalgo, around the late 1880s, Mexican-Americans began to take literary cognizance of the changed political order. They began to write about the difficulties between *raza* and their new Anglo-American compatriots and to describe, usually with considerable poignancy, the changes in their cultures and the *raza* struggle to maintain their ethnic ambience within a region that only two decades before had been foreign to the Yankees. These and other sociohistorical events and experiences following the 1846–48 tumult formed the turn-of-the-century Chicano literary sensibility.

To understand that sensibility we must consider the nature and significance of that grass-roots entertainment and recordkeeping process called folklore. The unwritten customs and traditions of a people as manifested in their magic, ritual, native song, storytelling, and other oral forms— folklore remains (even in a modern mass communications society) a reliable chronicle of a people, and it is indispensable to the study of any community which, like the Mexican-American, experienced a traumatic break of its social continuity. In the late 1800s and early 1900s, *raza*—that is, the "folk" of this study—generated a great deal of lore that was disseminated orally as well as in such ephemeral published forms as newspapers, chapbooks, and posters. Comprising *corridos*, legends, myths, *chistes*, superstitions, *remedios*, and so on, this folklore captured the spirit, attitudes, and experiences of Mexican-Americans in the face of the radical changes which Guadalupe Hidalgo forced on them. Chief among the folkloric forms was the *corrido* which flourished in the United States in this period.

*Corrido*, the Mexicans call their narrative folk songs, especially those of epic themes, taking the name from *correr*, which means "to run" or "to flow," for the *corrido* tells a story simply and swiftly. . . .

The Mexican ballad form known as the *corrido* dates no farther back than the middle of the nineteenth century. . . .

The period from 1836 to the late 1930s embraces the life span of the *corrido* of the Lower Border [of south Texas; also called the Lower Rio Grande Border].[8]

These narrative folk songs deal with a wide range of cultural experience including quotidian events and habits, incidents of rebellion, anti-Yankee heroisms, and the many sacrifices forced on *Méxicanos* as they adjusted to U.S. American life. *Corridos* are significant both as literary and as historical documents chronicling the evolution of the community and oftentimes serving as the only record of a particular way of life and the occurrence of certain events.

Exemplifying the form is the *corrido* telling of Gregorio Cortez, an actual *Méxicano* of the Lower Rio Grande Border, who, despite a relatively average childhood and young adulthood, became a folk hero of major proportions during his lifetime. The ballad of Gregorio Cortez underwent a history as remarkable as its heroic subject and has recently even been adapted into a feature-length film.[9] Cortez personifies the typical folk hero caught in iniquitous circumstances outside his control. He challenged authority and won, if not literally, then symbolically in the eyes of the people who supported his championing of the side of truth. At one time, he was hunted by sheriff posses, the Texas Rangers, federal marshals, as well as by local and out-of-state newspaper reporters seeking to be the first to publicize his capture. The importance of the Cortez *corrido* also stems from its scholarly analysis by eminent folklorist Américo Paredes whose book, *"With His Pistol in His Hand,"* demonstrates the rich viability of Chicano lore as both historical and literary material.

The *corridos* and other *raza* folklore flourished in the Southwest in the early decades of this century and in many ways offered more authentic mirrors to the culture than did the belletristic writing of the period which were most often written by Mexican-Americans of privileged backgrounds. One way to gauge the importance of Mexican-American folklore is to note that between 1934 and 1974 over fifteen major collections of it were published along with a number of shorter treatments,[10] whereas in that same time frame fewer than ten Chicano novels appeared in print. The extensiveness of these collections reflects the vastness of the available material which, in turn, documents the fact that it had a central place in the daily lives of most Mexican-Americans. One may conjecture, however, that the ready publication of *raza* folklore by established publishing houses, especially prior to 1970, reflected the publishers' perception of the group as a quaint and simple people without the native resources to produce high art and *belles lettres*.

That belletristic literature was in fact being written and published is attested to by the scrupulous research recently produced by a handful of revisionist Chicano scholars. For example, the *El Grito* bibliographies compiled by Padilla and Clark Moreno and containing over 500 titles of Mexican-American works from the 1800s to the 1960s typify that revisionism and its exposure of the fallacy of the non-literary Mexican.[11] Furthermore, although few novels or plays were published or produced before World War II, a large volume of Spanish-language poetry and short fiction appeared in scores of Southwestern newspapers and periodicals. As Tino Villanueva points out,

> Quiero dejar apuntado que es mucha la literatura chicano que no se ha publicado en forma de libro. Aparte de tanta poesía popular, inclusive los corridos, hay un abundante cuerpo de poesía que ha salido a la luz en los centenares de diarios que han existido desde 1848 en nuestros barrios. Las revistas literarias han sido todavía otro órgano de difusión literaria a lo largo de nuestra história.[12]
>
> [I should note that a great deal of Chicano literature has not been published in book form. Apart from much popular poetry, including *corridos*, there is an abundance of poetry that appeared in the hundreds of newspapers which have existed in our *barrios* since 1848. Still another outlet of literary dissemination have been the literary reviews which span our history.] (My translation.)

One popular regional writer whose work appeared in such publications was New Mexican Felipe Maximiliano Chacón. His poetry and stories covered topical subjects like the issue of New Mexico's statehood and details of *raza* life in the Southwest. Another prolific poet was Servando Cárdenas, born in Mexico but resettled permanently in Texas. He also founded a number of *raza* little magazines in South Texas in the twenties and thirties.[13]

Not until World War II did Mexican-American fiction of a serious quality begin to offer a genuine literary perspective at once stylistically rich, aesthetically crafted, and complex in rendering *raza* experience. U.S. writers like Fray Angélico Chávez (also a poet), Mario Suárez, and José Antonio Villareal, and Latin American-born writers like Josephina Niggli, José Revueltas, and Luis Spota began producing fiction about Chicanos in the United States incorporating the personal and social themes that yet persist in today's Chicano literature. To name Niggli's *Mexican Village*, Suárez's "Señor Garza," and Villareal's *Pocho* is to identify some of the most significant creative literature by Chicanos prior to its revitalization in the late 1960s. Suárez, in particular, reveals a fine literary sensibility as he transmutes the tumult of postwar life in the *barrio*, including aspects of *pachuquísmo*, into fiction that transcends its local color dimension. His frequently cited story "Señor Garza" and his other *Arizona Quarterly* fiction published in the 1940s combine fictional realism with philosophical irony to capture the peculiar spirit of the urban Chicano, one that looks ahead to the fiction of Ron Arias and the poetry of José Montoya and Alurista.

With the momentum that began after the war, then, *raza* literary expression surged in the 1960s. The convergence of the civil rights movement and its *Movimiento Chicano* offshoot led to a renewal of creative inspiration among the cultural descendants of Cervantes and García Lorca. Chicano presses appeared and began to publish a steady stream of fiction and poetry primarily, but drama and criticism as well. Because of its vitality this period has even been described as the "Chicano (literary) Renaissance," a rebirth in literature comparable to that in the United States in the middle of the last century and to the Harlem Renaissance of the 1920s. Coined by scholar Philip Ortego, the "Chicano Renaissance" subsumes all the literature and artistic activity directly spawned by the Chicano Movement as well as that produced by less engagé artists and writers addressing the *raza* heritage and experience in their work.[14] One of the most crucial participants in and seminal influences on the Chicano Renaissance was Luis Valdez and El Teatro Campesino.

The original farmworkers theatre, El Teatro Campesino (ETC) was founded in 1965 by Valdez, a farmworker actively engaged in supporting the United Farm Workers Union and its organizing efforts. To further that work as well as to boost morale for striking *campesinos*, Valdez adapted agitprop theatrical techniques to his needs and in doing so invented the *acto*-based *teatro*, one of this country's few, truly indigenous art forms developed in the modern era. The *acto* is "a short dramatic form . . . created collectively, through improvisation . . . [whose] major emphasis . . . is the social vision" it presents.[15] Characterized by a tightly focused plot centering on a specific sociopolitical topic, the *actos* typically employ humor, symbolism, mime, melodrama, music, and other dramatic tools making them ideal for enactment by a varied, multitalented repertory group. Indeed, ETC spawned a numberless host of *teatros* around the country in the 1960s and 1970s, and some (for example, El Teatro de la Esperanza and El Teatro del Barrio) are still performing. Both during its UFW days and its later period when it branched out beyond the Union's concerns, ETC's influence on Chicano literary expression cannot be underestimated. From A to Z—*actos* to *Zoot Suit*— ETC broke new ground in its manifold stage, screen, and concert hall activities. Its successful meshing of bilingualism, *raza* folklore, and sociohistory within a traditional aesthetic form had revolutionary impact on other Chicano artists, notably writers who had been struggling for years to capture the multiplicity of Mexican America in conventional unitary forms.

The last ten years have witnessed great productivity among these writers. Outstanding prose fiction works of the period include Tomás Rivera's " . . . *y no se lo tragó la tierra*" (1971), a serial narrative about migrant workers that is reminiscent of Sherwood Anderson's *Winesburg, Ohio*; Rudolfo Anaya's *Bless Me, Ultima* (1972), a novel of a boy's rite of passage to self-identity set in rural New Mexico; Rolando Hinojosa's sketches of life in South Texas—for example, *Estampas del Valle* (1973) and *Generaciónes y Semblanzas* (1977)—which have a robust, earthy quality that never loses sight of the imperfections inherent in human nature; and Ron Arias' *Road to Tamazunchale* (1978), a surrealistic novel about an old man's dying that turns the familiar quest theme on its head in García Márquez-like fashion.

In addition to these and other Chicano writers, one could mention a number of non-*raza* authors who over the years have published fictional treatments of the Chicano world and its heritage. Writers like Hanial Long, Charles Seltzer (aka Amado Muro), Edison Marshall, and Margaret Shedd have contributed to the Chicano literary *monde* by the very existence of their *raza*-related works labeled *literatura chicanesca* by critics.[16] More recent years have produced other significant writers like Daniel Peters, John Nichols, and Gary Jennings who have evoked and helped illuminate aspects of Mexican America, much as novelist B. Traven (aka Berick Torsvan) evoked and illuminated his adoptive Mexico. With his northern New Mexico series containing the critically acclaimed *The Milagro Beanfield War* (1974), the first novel in the series, Nichols is perhaps foremost among the writers of *literatura chicanesca* in capturing the complexities and the spirit of *raza* life.

Overall, then, contemporary Chicano literature represents the culmination of a solid literary past. Although rooted in the formal Spanish literature of its original *patria*, Mexico, as well as in the English-language literature of its later national homeland, the United States, Chicano literature grew directly out of *raza* oral traditions and their evocative reflections of the culture. What allowed this folklore to find its way into literature was the forceful social matrix of the Chicano Movement—the ideological yeast that activated the literary creativity. Chief evidence of that creativity is the subject of this book: "dating back to the 1840's, *poetry* has dominated the Chicano literary scene."[17]

## MODERN POETRY OF THE AMERICAS

Poets, especially those who also publish literary criticism (e.g., Poe, Whitman, Pound, Neruda, Borges, Paz) frequently write within a theoretical framework and recognizable poetics which operate either consciously or intuitively within the poet's fictionmaking process. This is not to say that such poetry springs formulaically from its creator's mind and experience, but, rather, that it emerges from a personally felt and reasoned logic motivating the poet's aesthetics. Often that *logic of aesthetics* may not be an overt part of the writer's original creative effort—as the example of Walt Whitman demonstrates. He wrote spontaneously in a variety of modes for several years before he seemed to discover his revolutionary raison d'être as a U.S. American poet. Once apprehended, he devoted his entire life to promoting his new aesthetics: the democratization of both prosody and subject matter to recreate traditional themes in New World terms. Sometimes—as with Neruda—the logic of aesthetics derives from an ideology that becomes a central force in the poet's life and letters. Nobel prize-winning Neruda consciously employed "elemental language" to capture the attention of "the folk," and in doing this he partly realized the socialist objective of furthering the cause of revolution against fascism. Thus his poetics was shaped by his ideology and both contributed to the logic of aesthetics apparent in his work.

A summary of the progress of American verse in the modern era further confirms the premise that distinct theoretical frameworks gird the work of major poets and significant schools of poetry. Accordingly, before introducing and explaining the critical method employed in this book, let us first briefly review the major poets and schools of modern poetry of the Americas. This literary historical sketch establishes a fertile context for interpretation of the contemporary Chicano poetry which constitutes the heart of this study. Our review begins with four major poets—Whitman, Dickinson, Martí, and Darío—who may be seen as the most significant American precursors of modern poetry, and it concludes with a constellation of U.S. poets and movements including the Beat Generation, the San Francisco Renaissance, and the Deep Image poets. The reader is reminded here of the caveat mentioned in the Prologue regarding the artificial neatness of historical sketches and, therefore, of the desirability of stressing context over causality and ambience over objectivity in order to achieve a fuller rendering of the past.

When Chicano poets like Ricardo Sánchez, Lalo Delgado, and Reyes Cárdenas hark back (consciously or not) to Walt Whitman and when Gary Soto and Inéz Tovar emulate (consciously or not) Emily Dickinson's poetic technique, they resemble countless other contemporary poets who through their work pay homage to these two nineteenth-century contributors to world literature. Whitman's and Dickinson's originality in revivifying conventional themes, their boldness in abandoning conventions, and their prescience in delineating aspects of the modern forms which form the fabric of our own literary age, all combine to solidify their positions as unparalleled literary figures. That they made their seminal contribution to literature during the bland orthodoxy of what Mark Twain called the United States' "Gilded Age" underscores their artistic brilliance even more.

Walt Whitman (1819–1892) is central to modern poetry because his deliberate refusal to conform to expected notions of literary subject, theme, technique, and taste has become the hallmark of twentieth-century literature. He revolutionized American poetry by persistently arguing for democratic comprehensiveness in it and by cavalierly practicing his theory without restraint. As a result, he produced verse that contained treatments of such taboo subjects as explicit sexuality and exhaustive catalogs of everyday life, including its squalor, and he did this in a technical form that was as unrestrained and unconventional as its creator in a free and open verse of uneven line, untraditional meter, and absence of rhyme. For these and other reasons, Whitman's important reputation abroad, like Edgar Allan Poe's, has been long established, but, unlike Poe, his star has also long shone in Latin America where he is generally acknowledged to be "one of the most important influences on modern Latin American poets from Darío to Neruda."[18]

The influence of Emily Dickinson (1830–1886) has also been considerable, although it had a late start because her work was not published until after 1890 and because the vast bulk of it did not appear in print as she had written it until 1955.[19] Despite the slowness and lateness of her emergence as a writer not to be denied, "there is very little dispute regarding [her] claim to a very high place among America's poets."[20] She is now understood as a poet whose striking prosodic inventiveness was matched by a profound intellect capable of apprehending in mundane experience both the tragic and the sublime, the ironic and the comedic. Dickinson's achievement swells with each new generation that encounters her work. Together, Dickinson and Whitman, despite the obvious differences in their styles, themes, and oeuvres, left their literary progeny a legacy of democratic zeal in allowing every experience, regardless of how routine or trivial, a place in poetry. They also bequeathed to our century a legacy of iconoclasm both regarding poetic technique and the use of form for figurative meaning. By rejecting "small coin . . . so-called literature" that "strikes the mean flat average," as Whitman put it in *Specimen Days*, and by freely indulging "a liquor never brewed" as well as the "divinest Sense" of "Much Madness," as Dickinson described the unspeakable richness of the poet's imagination, they not only opened doors to this century's literary temperament, but they also remodeled some archaic portals (like traditional meter and rhyme), salvaging them for the future.

Like their Yankee counterparts, Jose Martí and Rubén Darío are widely lauded for their lyrical eloquence and artistic innovation, and like Whitman and Dickinson their influence has extended far beyond their native lands. Contributing to the richness and complexity that comprises modern Latin American literature, a literature as diverse as the hemisphere that produced it and as consumed by contradictions as its peoples, Martí and Darío capture in their own work the complex contradictions and rich diversity of the continent. But they do this in quite different fashion.

A native of Cuba, José Martí (1853–1895) lived in the last half of the nineteenth century. His life was characterized by poverty, by active rebellion against Spanish hegemony over Cuba, and by poetry which he consistently wrote throughout his short life, which ended during a hard-fought Cuban expedition against the Spanish Army. Just as his life was characterized by political activism and dedication to a cause larger than himself, so too was his poetry marked by a keen populist spirit and by linguistic innovation. That spirit reflected both his nationalistic ideology and his dismissal of romanticism, the prevailing philosophical and aesthetic movement, which he found unsuitable for his creative energy. The logic of aesthetics manifested in his poetry is therefore democratic in subject and theme and simple and unadorned in form. The titles of two of his most significant works exhibit these qualities nicely: *Versos libres (Free Verses)* and *Versos sencillos (Simple Verses)*. By relying on straightforward, plain language with familiar images, Martí, the rebel as poet, achieved a realism that is striking for its simplicity and metaphorical resonance.

> Dos patrias tengo yo: Cuba y la noche.
> ¿O son una las dos? No bien retira
> su majestad el Sol, con largos velos
> y un clavel en la mano, silenciosa

Cuba cual viuda triste me aparece.
[I have two motherlands: Cuba and the night.
Or are they both one? No sooner has the sun
withdrawn in its grandeur than Cuba appears
beside me in silence, a mournful widow
who clasps a carnation in funeral robes.][21]

After his death Martí became a national hero in his country, and during the
1960s he developed a following among members of the Student Movement
in this country. Parts of his *Versos sencillos* were adapted to music in the song
"Guantanamera" which was popular in the United States and was often
heard at Chicano Movement gatherings.

Rubén Darío (1867–1916), well established as a central innovator in
nineteenth-century Spanish poetry, is credited with promulgating *modernismo* throughout the world of Spanish belles lettres. An indigenous reaction
against Spanish influences in literature, *modernismo* asserted the artistic
validity of "New" World idioms, subjects, and themes, and in this revolt
against Old World aesthetic values it cleared the way for radical changes in
poetic technique. Darío's canon discloses a logic of aesthetics that boldly
insists that "change [is] the only basis of tradition,"[22] a theoretical
framework that enabled him to experiment as dramatically as had his
maestro Whitman, whose resounding style is alluded to in "A Roosevelt":

¡Es con voz de la Biblia, o verso de Walt Whitman,
que habría que llegar hasta ti, Cazador! . . .
Eres los Estados Unidos,
eres el futuro invasor
de la América ingenua que tiene sangre indígena,
que aún reza a Jesucristo y aún habla en español . `. .
Mas la América nuestra, que tenía poetas
desde los viejos tiempos de Nezahualcóyotl . . .
Tened cuidado; Viva la América Española!
Hay mil cachorros sueltos del León Español.
[Big-Game Hunter, to reach your ear
One must cry in the Bible's voice or Walt
Whitman's verse! . . .
You are the great United States,
you are the future aggressor
of naïve America of native blood
which still speaks Spanish and still prays to
Jesus . . . .

But our America cradled poets
from Nezahualcóyotl's distant reign . . .
So watch your step! Long live Spanish America!
The Latino Lion has unleashed a thousand cubs . . . ]²³

Considered a prodigy, Darío began publishing at the age of thirteen in his native Nicaragua where he died in 1916 at the age of forty-nine. Darío was acclaimed in his lifetime for his contributions to modern Spanish poetry and the quality of his verse. His importance to modern literature remains secure.

These four important precursors of modern American poetry have helped shape and define nearly all the significant poetic accomplishments of the present century. Their voices, their idioms, their symbols, their very freedoms, all facilitated the poetic achievements that succeeded them, even the ones that rejected either their work or the features of their styles, for their progressive gift to their heirs contained in its very progressiveness the expectation that they—Whitman, Dickinson, Martí, and Darío—would surely be superseded if their experiments took hold. And they worked singlemindedly to make them hold fast. Nevertheless, their experiments seeded exciting thought and poetry which blossomed vigorously in the twentieth century. Vigorous among the blooms were the philosophy of T. E. Hulme, the preachings and poetry of Ezra Pound, and the mestizo-oriented poetry of Ramón López Velarde. All three exerted powerful influence on the new century's poetry in the Americas, and each had measurable influence on their contemporaries, both through their work and through their ideas about poetry.

In his brief lifetime, British philosopher and critic Hulme (1883–1917) held forth in a number of intellectual circles that helped define the reaction against romanticism that is now known as modernism. (It must, of course, be acknowledged that modernism is also viewed as the culmination of romanticism.) Hulme argued forcefully against "the excesses of romanticism," especially against its emphasis on such abstractions as infinity, the sublime, and a generic nature. His essay " 'Romanticism and Classicism' is one of the central documents in modern British and American poetry," and it, along with his theories of poetry, led directly to Imagism, the school of poetry founded by his preeminent disciple, Ezra Pound (1885–1972).²⁴ So much has been written about Pound and Imagism that we will avoid superfluity by simply pointing to the term "image" as Pound defined it, for it is a cornerstone of modern poetry. "An 'Image' is that which presents an intellectual and emotional complex in an instant of time," Pound wrote, in one sentence capturing a wonderful tension between opposites (intellect/ emotion) and fitting them to the magic temporality of "an instant." Despite Imagism's short life as an active school of poetry with devotees and practitioners, it nonetheless had lasting effect on modern poetry because it aptly reflected the shifts that were occurring in the collective literary temperament, shifts inspired by hope in the start of a new century with the concomitant rejection of the old one's values and also caused by the quick extinction of that hope resulting from the planet's first war of worldwide proportions. Imagism thus held an important place in the turn-of-the-century ferment which first enunciated modernism.

In Latin America, too, modernism reflected a felt spiritual crisis that some believe was perceived more acutely because "it was compressed into a short time-span . . . within twenty years, the impact of historicism and materialism, of the new *fin-de-siècle* spiritualism with its exploration of the occult, of aestheticism; all these were felt at once."[25] (A brief word distinguishing *modernism* from Latin American *modernismo*: Euro-U.S. modernism was essentially an avant-garde movement that challenged earlier conventions in art to produce cubism, surrealism, stream-of-consciousness, and similar breaks with the past; *modernismo* was more concerned with diminishing European influence, especially Spanish, and with instead emphasizing American indigenous traits, especially the Indian and African elements.) Manifesting the Latino modernist spiritual crisis especially well and also disclosing its nativist dimension is the work of Ramón López Velarde (1888–1921). Combining an idiom of homely directness with a tone of existential irony, Velarde took "[m]odernism into a wholly new direction when he rooted the conflicts in a Mexican provincial setting, and he did so without indulging . . . in regionalism."[26] His insistence on realistically depicting the mestizo heritage and character of Mexico in his poems and his often startling juxtaposition of vulgar details of life with elements of refinement exemplify the modern sensibility that made him an acknowledged forerunner of contemporary Spanish-language poets.

If the prewar years brought the emergence of modernism, the postwar 1920s and 1930s saw its confirmation as the principal logic of aesthetics governing artistic expression. These years also witnessed the brachiation of literary modernism—which from its inception exhibited many forms and faces—into a bramble of modes. In the United States William Carlos Williams' poetry and his theory of Objectivism developed as a striking contrast and alternative to the "textbook" poetry of T. S. Eliot and Pound whose imprint on twentieth-century literature was undeniably the major one before World War II. Concentrating on "the thing itself," Williams employed spare, elemental language to project a direct apprehension of the subject "thing" in his verse. He also furthered the innovative idea suggested by Pound, Eliot, and other modernists that poetry is not an escape from or evocation of reality but is a reality of its own. Like Pound's "image," this perception of a poem as a world complete in itself was extremely influential; indeed, an entire school of (New) Criticism was built around it.

In Latin America the key figures taking modernism to its limits and beyond to post-modernism included Gabriela Mistral, Nicholas Guillén, and Pablo Neruda. The Chilean Mistral (1889-1957), the first Latin American to receive the Nobel Prize for Literature, is known for the plainness of her poetic language, which she combined with archetypal themes to achieve a new way of seeing such commonnesses as motherhood, seed planting, and even schoolteaching. Despite her use of conventional meters, she broke tradition by writing of untypical subjects (e.g., issues usually reserved for women only). Like Mistral, Cuban Nicolas Guillén (1902– ) introduced new subjects into poetry and in doing so brought forth new themes and techniques. Concerned mainly with the African dimension of both his personal past and that of his country, Guillén was part of the vanguard Afro-Cubanist movement of the 1920s and 1930s which, for the first time, gave literary legitimacy to Afro-Cuban music, myth, folklore, dialects, and experience. Moreover, like so many Latin American literary luminaries, Guillén was actively committed to a life of leftist political *engagement*, a commitment that intensified after Francisco Franco's takeover of Spain when many intellectuals around the world including Guillén, joined the Communist party. Pablo Neruda (1904–1973), Chilean Nobel prizewinner, also became a Communist after the Spanish Civil War, but it was not politics that formed the beauty of his poetry or that accounted for its popularity when it gained a public audience with the publication of *Veinte poemas de amor*. It was his experience of *"la naturaleza"* that suffused his style "with pioneer energy and freshness"[27] and that gave his creativity a basic framework within which he experimented with elemental language, surrealism, and a personal system of symbolism. This background readied him for his magnum opus, the epic poem *Canto general*, a lyrical narrative about America that "traces the growth of the [poet's] political historical consciousness . . . from an empty individualism to assumption of his role as the voice of the oppressed."[28] *Canto general* shares with Whitman's *Leaves of Grass*, Pound's *Cantos*, and Williams' *Paterson* an ambitiousness of scope and vision that appears peculiarly American—the adamic urge to chronicle from a personal perspective the development of this hemisphere's special character—and perhaps this quality in Neruda's poetry accounts for its especially strong influence in the United States after World War II.[29]

By World War II, then, modernism and *modernismo* in America had developed into an array of distinct styles and philosophies sharing little more than a firm rejection of romanticism. There was also a general tendency to experiment radically with language, meter, and line and verse forms. The central and seminal innovators named here—from Whitman and Darío to Williams and Neruda—were not, of course, writing in isolation. Many other poets of merit and fame wrote and influenced others, just as many literary schools and movements appeared, swelled to prominence, and either vanished or disappeared into other schools and movements. Two of the most significant of these were Wallace Stevens (1879–1955), a U.S. poet whose emphasis on the imagination as the medium for apprehending reality brought the poem as metapoetry into prominence, and Jorge Luis Borges (1899– ), the Argentinian writer whose remarkable achievement in fiction first brought international recognition to the brilliant originality of Latin American writers. Although both wrote extensively for over five decades (Borges in poetry, fiction, and criticism), the unique, unparalleled originality of their styles and of their contribution to literature places them, to a large extent, outside the trends discussed here. In Stevens' verse, marked by a linguistic luxuriance that occasionally exceeds sensuousness and becomes baroque, we find several of the century's most memorable ideas and images: the supreme fiction, Sunday morning as a concept, ideas of order *as* being, and so on. Likewise, Borges' influence has been so profound and extensive that his style is often used as a signpost to demarcate periods in comtemporary literature, as in "pre- and post-Borgesian writing." In a word, the recipient of every major literary prize (except the Nobel) in the world and the acknowledged *maestro* of fantastic fiction (aka surfiction and metafiction) and post-modernist criticism, Borges was an originator of the avant-garde literature that became the post-World War II "norm."

The 1940s and 1950s witnessed the solidifying of the careers of a number of these postwar poets—Theodore Roethke, Robert Lowell, Nicanor Parra, and Octavio Paz—and the appearance of a number of significant literary movements. For example, the poets of the Beat Generation broadened Whitman's concept of democratic inclusiveness and unorthodoxy to include use of an unexpurgated vernacular and a more intense Eastern mysticism than that introduced into American literature by the transcendentalists. Appropriately enough, in keeping with the iconoclasm of the Beats, as soon as they gained fame and popular interest (primarily through Allen Ginsberg's *Howl*), their identification merged with the San Francisco Renaissance, a movement predicated on the Projectivist principles articulated by Charles Olson and the Black Mountain poets.[30] Projectivism—"antiacademic, antirationalist, embracing open rather than closed forms," relying on biological rhythms like breathing to determine the shape of the poem—got its name from Olson's belief that to truly experience reality, one must *project* outward, away from ego and intellect.[31] Accordingly, one way of assessing and interpreting contemporary poetry is to review the approaches to ego found in it.

Contemporary [U.S.] American poetry can be understood as a series of attempts to reinterpret the relation of [one's] inner world to the perceptual universe: the effort to expunge the subjective ego and concentrate on the object perceived, which led from Imagism to Objectivism to Projective verse; the . . . quite complementary . . . attempt of Confessional poetry to establish the legitimacy of not only private but often unconscious alogical experience, as an expression of communal consciousness; the mystic search for the oneness of being that cuts across most allegiances; and the seemingly endless variations on these basic themes.

The writers who constitute these "movements" are . . . different from one another; but they hold in common, for the most part, an important characteristic: they have little use for the self in the Western world. Norman O.Brown, Marshall McLuhan, and Frantz Fanon have told us . . . that the domination of one area of experience over another . . . or of one people over another, has had its day; they apocalyptically foresee the end of the Western, humanistic conception of individuality, in short the death of the ego. [These] poets, without . . . talking about the cataclysm, seem most decisively to be experiencing it.[32]

Although the above passage was written specifically about U.S. American poetry, it is relevant to post-modern poetry generally and pan-American poetry particularly.

Much of the important poetry of the 1960s and 1970s reflects the kind of ego-lessness or, at least, the diminution of the unitary, individualistic ego described above. Furthermore, this contemporary poetry insists upon an experiential seamlessness that would deny domination of any parts over any whole, that would reject the separation of poetry from the poet's politics much as it would reject the fragmentation or distancing of any aspect of the poet's consciousness from her/his poetry. It is, as Donald Hall notes, "subjective but not autobiographical. It reveals through images not

particular pain, but general subjective life."[33] Outstanding examples in the
United States include, for instance, the work of (1) the Confessional Poets,
like John Berryman, Sylvia Plath, and Anne Sexton who brought naked
personal experience, stripped of public conventions of sanity, to literature;
(2) the Deep Image poets typified by the movement's most prominent
voices—Robert Bly, James Dickey, and Jerome Rothenberger—who find
the central energy of a poem in images from the unconscious (as opposed
to images from external reality) seeking to express a unified, synthesized view
of reality; and (3) the poets emerging from a variety of ideological
movements—like Black poets Imamu Baraka and Sonia Sanchéz and feminist
poets Maxine Kumin and Mona Van Duyn and, of course, Chicano/a poets—
all determined to add to the writing of our times the historically dispensable
voice of the powerless articulated in a variety of styles, shapes, and subjects
that, paradoxically, proves wondrously powerful.

In Latin America the novel has flourished grandly; indeed, its singular
vitality energizes the very genre itself as the Nobel Committee recognized
when it awarded Gabriel García Márquez the 1982 Literature Prize.
Although contemporary poetry in Latin America exists in the novel's
shadow, the eclipse is not total as the number of active poetic forms (like
neo-surrealism, concrete poetry, and a reactionary *post-modernismo*) evidence.

Overall, then, twentieth-century poetry of the Americas comprises a
striking array of modes and methods characterized by a strong reaction to
both nineteenth-century romanticism and turn-of-the-century realism.
Modern American poetry is thus modernist, post-modernist, anti-modernist,
and sometimes neo-traditional, but it is nearly always enlivened by a nativist
(i.e., non-European) spirit and the technical freedoms derived from use of
open (non-conventional) forms. Furthermore, the tendency of this poetry has
been to move to an all-inclusive logic of aesthetics that holds that all-reality
and all-consciousness are fit subjects of poetry and that the poet's total
experience and consciousness can provide both the means to and the substance
of the art. From here the shift is easy to concrete poetry, to poetry as
multimedia product, to poetry as ritual event, to anti-poetry. All of these
varieties of American verse forms are represented in the multifold subject
of this book, Chicano poetry.

## SUMMARY OF CRITICAL THEORY AND METHOD

Surely the preceding skeletal summary of modern poetry of the Americas
is so neat and so implicitly "inevitable" in its hindsight as to be reductive—

reductive obviously in scale, spanning well over one hundred years of literature in under fifteen pages, and also in suggesting that the course of twentieth-century poetry can be adequately described by referring to but a few names and terms. Although this summary lacks the inclusiveness and the nuanced fullness of its manifold subject, it is hoped that its reductiveness does not negate its utility as a brief preface, a bare-bones backgrounding of the macro literary context from which contemporary Chicano poetry partly emerged, even though, as the first part of the chapter explains, the social and cultural milieu provided the primary seedbed for this poetic activity. Accordingly, the summary in this section has a twofold purpose: to provide a broad historical context for the analyses to follow and, more immediately, to serve as a guide to the introduction of the analytical approach of this book.

Because Chicano literature in general and poetry specifically partake of such a multiplicity of forms, idioms, and personal worlds, its interpretive analysis demands flexibility. The approach here is thus eclectic in selecting from an array of methodologies the critical praxis best suited to the text which, as explained below, is perceived within a total field. A synthesis of various critical methodologies, then, this approach can perhaps best be discussed by explaining its praxis, its linguistic orientation, and its underlying theory.

*Praxis,* of course, refers to applied critical analysis—the actual interpretation of a given text. Throughout this work, an attempt is made to let each poet's work determine the practical approach best suited to the text's particular description, definition, and interpretation. Historical and biographical analysis appears in this study just as comparative analysis, New Criticism, and other critical modes do. Nevertheless, the basic approach throughout is guided by a distinct linguistic orientation. Hence, the reader will discover descriptions of the text's structure—its phonology, morphology, and syntax—descriptions that enhance appreciation of the poem's surface features which, in turn, promote discovery of its deep structure and thematic possibilities. The linguistic orientation permits us to consider any literary text as an autonomous language construct (a speech act, for example) amenable to exhaustive descriptive analysis.

Still, this eclectic praxis and linguistic orientation do not in themselves explain or account for the mundane fact that each text is written by a person in a particular sociocultural context about finite aspects of experience whether lived or imagined. Nor do these practical assumptions in themselves acknowledge and explain the intertextual factors that exist within, between, and among a set of texts or even the entire universe of Chicano poetry—itself existing within the multitudinous non-aesthetic (i.e., "real") world. To take these disparate and complicated aspects into account in such a manner that their differences, even their contradictions, can be comprehended *along with* their samenesses requires an underlying theory as flexible and expandable as a *sarape*. A serviceable article of clothing that retains its shape and structure while it covers and wraps *other* objects according to *their* shapes and structures, *sarapes* are as basic to Latino society as sunshine is to summer. To achieve these manifold desiderata a modification of Walter A. Davis' "radical pluralism" theory of criticism has been chosen. In certain respects, Davis' model resembles both French structuralism and phenomenological discourse theory, but its rootedness within more traditional modes along with its insistence on a unified theory that accepts the viability of alternate interpretations prevents its easy placement within any one particular school. Moreover, since my own theoretical foundation is a modification of Davis' method, we will simply identify it as *an attempt at a unified field theory*.[34]

The Davis model of radical pluralism requires several indispensable steps which, when followed conscientiously, lift the reader/critic toward a greater consciousness and understanding of the text, culminating in *Aufhebung*— literally, "progressive uplifting," used to refer to the consciousness one has of knowledge that has been built on a careful progression of information.[35] These steps may be seen as a series of tasks.

1. Establish confident *familiarity* with the text.

2. Develop an *inventory* of key elements in the text. This is not to be confused with the act of criticism itself; rather, this is a listing of all the text's central parts— for example, narrator, major symbols, characters, linguistic features—to produce an inventory of textual items that must be explained and accounted for by the ultimate, overarching interpretation.

3. Review the critical analyses of the text provided by others to determine a set of significant *alternate readings*.

4. Consider alternate readings within the context of one's own familiarity with the text and determine *negative applications*. In other words, assess where the other readers' interpretations do *not* apply (e.g., by overlooking key elements in the inventory or by leaving serious questions about the text unanswered) and isolate these negative applications.

5. Identify *supra- and extra-textual elements* which must be understood in order to comprehend the work. This requires recognition and understanding of both

social and literary contexts, biographical features, allusionary framework, and so forth. At this stage, it is helpful to describe the text and its total context as constituting a *field*—a locus of information and literary energy containing discrete features that interact with one another.

6. Allow the process of *radical pluralism* to proceed according to its own momentum. At this point we find that our direct experience of the total field coupled with our movement through steps one through five has left us with questions, contradictions, and hypotheses about the work's meaning and purpose. As a consequence, we come to a recognition that "all problems and questions [about the text] are necessarily interrelated."[36] Out of this knowledge comes self-movement toward a discovery "that uplifts (*Aufhebung*) the entire process by establishing a single order of thought" through which a cogent interpretation of the text is assured.[37]

7. Reflect on our changed awareness of the text *in silence*. The text is no longer the same language unit it was when first encountered. Instead, the text *has become our full apprehension of it* within our heightened consciousness. In silent contemplation of the text, the process, and its effect on us, we discover ourselves and our perception of the world anew. Silence serves here as our medium of enlightenment.

Clearly, these tasks require concentration and discipline if the ideal *Aufhebung* is to be attained. On the other hand, poetry lovers by definition are usually sensitive, intelligent readers with advanced critical skills. Accordingly, the overarching heuristic exercises implicit in tasks 1 through 3 are very likely matters of habit which are automatically, if not intuitively, accomplished when encountering any text. Similarly, the hermeneutic exercises implicit in tasks 4 though 6 are steps often taken in literary analysis, though not in the precise and systematic manner expected here. The meditation implied in the seventh task is known to many readers as a private experience, mental and subliminal and, if lucky, mystical. The difference within this unified field criticism is that silent reflection is required as an obligatory concluding step.

Like the attempt by scientists to unify all the basic laws of physics within one general theory, Davis' radical pluralism and the adaptation of it here would seek to synthesize criticism into an eclectic but coordinated model of effective analysis. To test the internal logic of this approach, its validity and viability in answering questions generated by Chicano poetry must be considered. Does it address the manifold desiderata described earlier? Is it, in short, as serviceable as a *sarape*? It is hoped that succeeding chapters of *Chicano Poetry; A Critical Introduction* offer a satisfactory affirmative response to these questions.

Finally, several apt analogies may be pointed out between the holistic
approach just discussed and certain Chicano concepts prominent in Mexican-American culture and lore. As explained in the Prologue, *mestizaje*, a
fundamental concept of *raza* identity which originally described the new
racial mixture resulting from Indian/European interbreeding, today also
refers to the blending of Indian and European traits which defines the
Chicano heritage and/or experience. In its synthesis of vastly opposite elements—Old/New Worlds, Christian monotheism/Mesoamerican poly-
theism, and advanced technology/advanced astronomy, for example—*mestizaje* parallels the theoretical synthesis of the critical approach used here.
Similarly, the importance and centrality of *la familia* as a social unit and
as a matrix of personal and cultural identity among Chicanos correspond
with the exercises delineated in the fifth and sixth steps presented above.
Every *familia* is a collection of different individuals, habits, and interests
which—despite the differences and even contradictions—are nevertheless
bound together as one unit sharing aspects of a common identity. So,
too, is Chicano poetry in its multiplicity and concomitant unity. So, too,
is the critical methodology employed in this book. The last analogy to
note is that between this holistic critical approach and the Chicano literary concept of *flor y canto*. Literally translated as "flower and song," the
phrase *flor y canto* has become synonymous with Chicano poetry itself.
Playwright and founder of El Teatro Campesino, Luis Valdez, along
with the poet, Alurista, were the first major promulgators of this idea
borrowed from the ancient Aztec lexicon, and it deserves careful
explanation.

To the Aztecs, or more precisely, the Nahuas of ancient Mexico, poetry
was inextricably bound to prayer, to incantation in rituals designed for the
gods.[38] The Nahuatl expression for this prayer-poetry was *in xochitl in
cuicatl* which translates literally as "flower and song" (to the Spanish, "flor
y canto"). Such a literal rendering, however, robs the phrase and the
concept it represents of its profound mystical essence, an essence traceable
to the Nahua term for "communion with the divine Giver of Life,
Ométéotl," a godhead representing male/female duality and the origin of
all life. To achieve immortality, humans sought mystical union with
Ométéotl through their prayer-poetry *in xochitl in cuicatl*, and this resulted
in the communion of earthly with divine forms. Linguistically, then, *flor y
canto* joins images which, in conjunction, mean something else, and the
meaning derives from *both the images and the conjunction*. By yoking the
flowers of the earth in their aromatic, colorful, natural beauty to the human

created song of the air, the Nahuas demonstrated their recognition of the transcendent quality of poetry.

| flor | y | canto |
|---|---|---|
| the seen | + | the heard |
| the natural | + | the stylized |
| the earthbound | + | the ethereal |
| the literal | + | the imagined |
| in xochitl |  | in cuicatl |

The very term, its disparities brought together in wonderful communion, embodies the holistic, synthetic power of poetry to transform mundane experience into mystical insight. Analogously, the critical approach, taken in this book, particularly in its insistence on the seventh task of silent reflection, seeks to achieve the same kind of insight through the act of interpretation.

## NOTES

1. A variation of the chronological outline first appeared in Julian Samora and Patricia Simon, *A History of the Mexican American People*, (Notre Dame, Ind.: The University of Notre Dame Press, 1977) in chapter 20 which I wrote.

2. It is generally conceded, though without undisputed proof, that the earliest inhabitants of the Western Hemisphere migrated from Asia thousands of years before the outline's starting date of 1000 B.C. Given the ancientness of that migration, however, it is appropriate to describe these prehistoric peoples of the Americas as "native tribes."

3. Rudolfo Acuña, *Occupied America: A History of Chicanos*, 2nd ed. (New York: Harper & Row, 1981), chapters 2–5; and Frances L. Swadesh, *Los Primeros Pobladores: Hispanic Americans of the Ute Frontier* (Notre Dame, Ind.: University of Notre Dame Press, 1974), chapters 1, 7–8.

4. Jean Franco, *A Literary History of Spain, Spanish American Literature Since Independence* (London: Ernest Benn Ltd., 1973), 19.

5. The basic assumption undergirding MELUS, both the society and its literary journal, is contained in the following comment by Katharine Newman, the founding spirit behind MELUS: "For four hundred years and more there has been a steady pouring together of cultures [in the United States]. . . . Today, as ever, American literature is both interactional at home and international in its ties with the original homelands of our people. . . . The cosmopolitan nature of our literature was spotlighted when the Nobel Prize was awarded [in 1979] to an American citizen [Isaac Bashevis Singer] who writes in a dying language for an audience of ghosts." *MELUS*, 5:4 (Winter, 1978), 1.

6. José González, "A ella," in Tino Villanueva, ed., *Chicanos; Antología histórica y literaria* (México, D.F.: Fondo de Cultura Economica, 1980), 213.

7. *El Clamor Público, El Nuevo Mundo, La Gaceta*, and so on; see *El Grito*

bibliographies, in note 11 below, for additional examples of nineteenth-century pre-Chicano periodicals.

8. Américo Paredes, *"With His Pistol in his Hand": A Border Ballad and Its Hero* (Austin: University of Texas Press, 1958 [paper, 1971]), xi, 129, 132.

9. Ibid., chapters V-VII. The film, "The Ballad of Gregorio Cortez," was co-produced by the National Council of La Raza and Moctezuma Esparza Productions in 1982; I served on the NCLR SOMOS Committee which planned, helped fund, and script-edited the film.

10. Tréjo, *Bibliografía Chicana: A Guide to Information Sources* (Detroit: Gale Research Co., 1975), 24–41 and 79–83; and Luis Nogales, *The Mexican American: A Selected and Annotated Bibliography* (Stanford, Calif: Stanford University Press, 1971), passim.

11. Joseph A. Clarke Moreno, "A Bibliography of Bibliographies Relating to Studies of Mexican Americans," *El Grito*, 5 (Winter, 1971–72), 47–49; and Ray Padilla, "Apuntes para la documentación de la cultura Chicano," *El Grito* 5 (Winter, 1971–72), 3–46.

12. Villanueva, *Chicanos*, 50.

13. Chacón, *Obras de Felipe Maximiliano Chacón, El Cantor Neomexicano: Poesía y Prosa* (Albuquerque, N. Mex.: [self-published], 1924).

14. Ortego, "The Chicano Renaissance," in Livie I. Duran and H. Russell Bernard, *Introduction to Chicano Studies*, 2nd ed. (New York: Macmillan, 1982 [essay first published 1971].

15. Luis Valdez, *Actos* (San Juan Bautista, Calif.: Cucaracha Press, 1971), 5–6.

16. Francisco Lomelí and Donaldo Urioste, *Chicano Perspectives in Literature: A Critical and Annotated Bibliography* (Albuquerque, N. Mex.: Pajarito Publications, 1976), 107–10.

17. Rolando Hinojosa, "Mexican American Literature," in Francisco Jiménez, ed., *The Identification and Analysis of Chicano Literature* (New York: Bilingual Press/Editorial Bilingue, 1979), 13.

18. Cheli Duran, ed., *The Yellow Canary Whose Eye Is So Black* (New York: Macmillan, 1977), xxii.

19. Thomas H. Johnson, ed., *Final Harvest, Emily Dickinson's Poems* (Boston: Little, Brown & Co., 1961), v.

20. Ronald Gottesman et al., eds., *The Norton Anthology of American Literature*, Vol. 1 (New York: W. W. Norton, 1979), 2350.

21. Jose Martí, "Dos patrias" in Duran, *The Yellow Canary*, 68–69; translation by Duran.

22. Duran, *The Yellow Canary*, xxii.

23. Ruben Darío, "A Roosevelt" in Duran, *The Yellow Canary*, 80–85; translation by Duran.

24. Karl Malkoff, "Introduction," *Crowell's Handbook of Contemporary American Poetry* (New York: Thomas Y. Crowell, 1973), 5.

25. Franco, *A Literary History of Spain*, 99.

26. Ibid., 131.

27. Ibid., 193.

28. Ibid., 197.

29. Donald Hall, "Introduction" and "Preface to the Second Edition," *Contemporary American Poetry* (Baltimore: Penguin Books, 1962 rev. 1971), 32 and 36.

30. Most of the remaining luminaries of the Beat Generation (Allen Ginsberg, Lawrence Ferlinghetti, Robert Creeley, William Burroughs, et al.) commemorated the twenty-fifth anniversary of the publication of Kerouac's *On the Road* in July 1982 in Boulder, Colorado.

31. Malkoff, "Introduction," 252–53 and 9–14.

32. Ibid., 3–4.

33. Hall, "Introduction," 33.

34. Obviously, I am immensely indebted to Davis and his provocative *The Act of Interpretation: A Critique of Literary Reason* (Chicago: University of Chicago Press, 1978), but I do not wish to saddle his theory and methodology with my interpretations of it nor with my improvisations on it, for my interpretation is perhaps idiosyncratic and my improvisations are many. Nevertheless, I gratefully credit Davis for his stimulating ideas about criticism and literature.

35. Davis, *The Act of Interpretation*, 51. Davis bases his approach on the Hegelian process of *Aufhebung* in which various impressions and interpretations of a subject (a literary text, for example) evolve progressively to a greater refinement and deeper understanding. This dialectical progression depends on the canceling and preserving of initial interpretations until an uplifting to greater understanding occurs. As Davis explains, "the interpretations appear to enact a process of Hegelian *Aufhebung*: the first interpretation is preserved and deepened in the second, and both, implied throughout the third, achieve in it their true significance. In an order of increasing complexity, the . . . interpretations thus appear to progressively approximate the substance of the work" (51).

36. Davis, *The Act of Interpretation*, 95.

37. Ibid., 97.

38. See, for example, Miguel León-Portilla, *Pre-Columbian Literature of Mexico* (Norman: University of Oklahoma Press, 1969) and Jacques Soustelle, *Daily Life of the Aztecs on the Eve of the Spanish Conquest*, trans. Patrick O'Brian (Stanford, Calif.: Stanford University Press, 1961) for extended discussions of Aztec beliefs and rituals.

# 2

# Chicano Poetry, Phase I:
# Movement Poetry

In this era of post-structuralism, we know that all aspects of experience are interrelated and interdependent and that only conceptual convenience justifies isolation or emphasis of one aspect over another. We know, for example, that political revolution does not occur in a vacuum visited only by politicians, generals, and subversives. Rather, a permeable membrane of influence exists between political revolution and the arts (or any other cluster of common purpose). The Mexican Revolution of 1910 and the Irish Civil War of the 1920s—to give two illustrations—yielded not only political upheaval and modest governmental reform; they also begat the revolutionary art of Mexicans Siqueiros, Orozco, Rivera, and Azuela, and that of the Irish Yeats and Synge. Their art reverberated well beyond the boundaries of aesthetic encounter because they kept the revolutionary stimulus permanently alive in their work. These general points hold true for the contemporary Chicano Movement and the art forms that emerged simultaneously with Movement activities. Accordingly, this chapter examines Phase I of Chicano poetry: Movement poetry.

As explained in the Prologue, the Chicano Movement—*El Movimiento*—encompasses a congeries of sociopolitical activities taking place in U.S. society since World War II. The principal energy of the Movement has been directed to the political and economic empowerment of Mexican-Americans, as well as to their social and spiritual betterment. Historically, Phase I Chicano poetry is tightly linked to the energy and force *del Movimiento* so that its dominant character partakes of the Movement's political core. Later phases, on the other hand, evidence a shifting away from direct political statement. Temporally, Phase I poetry appeared roughly between 1967 and 1974, although "protest poetry" of this kind is seldom confined to only one time period and, in fact, is still being written.

What, then, are the characteristics of Phase I Chicano poetry? Thematically, it evinces a number of striking polarities that are usually undisguised by metaphor. The thematic polarities often center the structure and import of the poem in language that makes explicit the side of the equation the poet favors. The primary thematic oppositions are the following:

| | | |
|---|---|---|
| *Raza* nationalism | vs. | universalism |
| México and Aztlán | vs. | the United States |
| Equity and justice | vs. | racism |
| Tradition and communalism | vs. | capitalism |
| Holism and pre-Americanism | vs. | Euro-Western worldview |

The first three oppositions signify the vast chasm which many Chicano writers perceive as separating most of the Chicano population from Yankee ideals of democracy. Similarly, the emphasis on *raza* nationalism over a universalist philosophy reflects a view held by many U.S. minorities and Third World people that universalism is often used as an intellectual euphemism for First World hegemony, one that does not adequately recognize the importance and compelling power of ethnic and cultural distinctions. Likewise, the promotion of México over the United States reflects the Movement's realism in assessing the impoverished socioeconomic status of most Chicanos. By embracing México, and more especially Aztlán, over U.S. materialism and racism, the Movement (and much of the early protest poetry) expressed solidarity with another universe of people similarly oppressed first by unrestrained imperialism and now by unrestricted capitalism. It also represents the compatibility of Chicano history with the formidable cultural heritage of Mesoamerica, one that reflects the commonalities between north and south Americans.

More theoretical than the first three, the last two polarities relate to several philosophical assumptions underlying the Movement's political framework. Both represent a rejection of the Western world's basic ethos out of which have evolved such excesses as laissez-faire capitalism, unbridled industrialism, and a labor feudalism that has included slavery.[1] *Raza* epistemology finds these isms in need of change because they have produced various forms of elitism and materialism, as well as both a narrow humanism indifferent to the earth's ecology and a high technology reductive of humane values. Oppositely, the keen recognition of the planet's organic interdependence—for example, communalism and holism—leads to an equally keen regard for the inherent sanctity of nature which is fundamental to Chicano philosophy. Part of this regard is a concern for the well-being of non-industrialized human communities which, in their relatively pristine forms, are particularly vulnerable to disturbance and even destruction by technologically mightier societies. In addition to these polarities, Phase I themes are also characterized by an intense concern for the nature of Chicano identity. Indeed, the theme of Chicano identity is a natural outgrowth of literary and philosophical interest in the thematic polarities just described. By rejecting the principles listed on the right-hand side of the opposition, Chicanos give a definition of self and culture based on negation—that is, we are *not* defined by U.S. American values. Conversely, by fostering the principles on the left-hand side, a positive definition of self and culture emerges, one evolving out of both actual and imagined worlds. Because identity is a central theme in Chicano poetry (some might even argue that it is the only theme), it is enough here to introduce it, for it will subsequently be discussed at length.

As these comments about theme make clear, this poetry is quintessentially *moral* in its sense and essence. That is to say that its primary impetus is to teach—in Chaucer's terms, it emphasizes "sentence" (propriety) over "solas" (delight)—to instruct the world about *raza* experience and the Chicano worldview. Its fundamentally moral purpose thus connects it directly to other political literature—propaganda—that underscores the work's politics over its poetics, its activism over its aesthetics, and its literalness over any lyricism.

With regard to formal (or structural) characteristics, Phase I poetry discloses four important features. To begin with, of all the phases of Chicano verse this group is the most given to use of traditional forms—that is, to the employment of such conventions as strict meter and rhyme. This is not to suggest that free verse forms never appear in this phase, but only to point out that the conventional patterns appear more frequently here than in subsequent types. A second characteristic of form is the high incidence of poems built around imperative verb constructions. Grammatically, the imperative mood (second person) is used to express command, strong wish, or desire; accordingly, the imperative modality conforms nicely with the basically moral purpose of Phase I protest poetry. Third, both the formal and semantic elements of this poetry are frequently declamatory, thereby evincing the stylistic extravagance so often associated with political propaganda of any sort. Related to this is the fourth formal feature prominent in this group: its essential prosiness. The symbolism and prosody of Movement verse more closely resemble the prolixity of prose than they do the economy of poetry. Despite the prominence of the thematic and formal traits enumerated on these pages, Phase I Chicano poetry exhibits certain other particular stylistic features which will be addressed in the individual interpretations.

## *I AM JOAQUÍN*

In several important ways *I Am Joaquín* by Rodolfo "Corky" Gonzales differs markedly from other Movement poetry. For one thing, this work—subtitled "An Epic Poem"—is the most famous of all Chicano poems, equaling the novels *Pocho* and *Bless Me, Ultima*, in distribution and recognition both within and without the *raza* community. Prior to its publication by Bantam Books, *I Am Joaquín* was distributed by its original publisher, the Denver Crusade for Justice which Gonzales founded, in mimeograph, xerox, and chapbook versions totaling upwards of 100,000 copies.[2] Subsequently, Bantam Books released three printings of its paperback edition and thus extended the poem's readership well beyond the alternative press audience. Indeed, the fact of the Bantam edition itself contributed to the work's uniqueness within Chicano poetry, for Bantam's editors added to the original composition extensive accoutrements like footnotes, illustrations, and a narrative chronology of *raza* history. With the editorial appendages, the approximately twenty-page poem could now fill a 122-page book in convenient, marketable size. Also unique to *Joaquín* was its adaptation into a movie produced by El Teatro Campesino in 1967.[3] A 16mm color production, the filmed version of the poem enjoyed wide circulation in the early years of the Movement. Among its many screenings were those sponsored by various grass-roots groups in Colorado in 1970, in Indiana in 1973, and in Idaho in 1976. *Joaquín* also differs from its literary siblings in that it is its creator's only work of any renown. Although Gonzales has written other literary pieces, neither his principal vocation nor his principal contribution to *El Movimiento* has been in literature. Like Harriet Beecher Stowe's *Uncle Tom's Cabin*, Kate Chopin's *The Awakening*, and Ralph Ellison's *Invisible Man, Joaquín* appears to be the product of a one-oeuvre author, a trait unrepresentative of Chicano poets in general.

Regardless of these important contrasts, however, *Joaquín* shares a number of significant features with other Movement poems. Like the preponderance of Phase I poetry, *Joaquín* presents a strongly affirmative, nationalistic view of Chicanos and *raza* society. This view, along with the declamatory tone, were employed both to arouse cultural pride among Mexican-Americans and to rouse the group to united action against what the poet calls "the muck of exploitation" (86) caused by the dominant society. Even though later phases of Chicano poetry endorse the positive value of *chicanismo*, they nonetheless move away from such one-dimensional approbation of all things Chicano and strive instead for more complex rendering of *raza* experience in all its variety and fullness. Similarly, *Joaquín* and its counterparts share a staunch androcentric perspective. From its title's masculine name through its scores of examples of "great men" in *his*tory to its closing lines alluding to "Aztec prince and Christian Christ," *Joaquín* presents a male, often chauvinistically macho, view of the Chicano world. Indeed, out of the poem's approximately 475 lines, under forty acknowledge the presence of women within the Mexican-American heritage and contemporary experience. Moreover, these lines, unlike the numerous others referring to specific men in history, make, with one exception, only anonymous references to *la mujer*. The exception is the poet's allusion to the Virgin of Guadalupe and the Aztec goddess Tonantzin—that is, to mythical as opposed to historical figures of idealized femininity. Chicano poetry, like American poetry in general, thus reflects the basic sexism of modern cultures formed according to patriarchal values. Finally, *Joaquín*, in keeping with a major characteristic of Phase I verse, contains the thematic polarities and structural features discussed in this chapter's introduction.

As explained in the Introduction, a structural feature of Movement poetry is its adherence to and employment of literary conventions. A good example of this is Gonzales' conception of his work as "an epic poem," a type of poetry characterized by the following traits.

1. The hero is a figure of imposing stature, of national or international importance, and of great historical or legendary significance.

2. The setting is vast in scope, covering great nations, the world, or the universe.

3. The action consists of deeds of great courage. Supernatural forces—gods, angels, and demons—interest themselves in the action and intervene from time to time.

4. A style of sustained elevation and grand simplicity is used.

5. The epic poet recounts the deeds of his heroes with objectivity.[4]

Famous epics in literary history include *The Iliad*, *El Cid*, *Paradise Lost*, and *John Brown's Body*. All of these are "long narrative poem[s]" centered around a major character, usually of high social position, involved in "a series of adventures which form an organic whole through their relation" to the hero and also through their importance "to [the hero's] nation or race."[5] Epics traditionally begin *in medias res* (in mid action, in the middle of things) with the poet stating the work's theme and invoking a muse.

*I Am Joaquín* exemplifies most of these epical characteristics, and where it does not it most often adapts them effectively. The poem begins *in medias res* with the title hero "lost in a world of confusion/caught up in the whirl of a/gringo society" and forced to choose between a self-defined "victory of the spirit" or "a full stomach" that results from acquiescence to "gringo" demands (9).[6] Gonzales' source of inspiration is implicit in the poem's opening lines and explicitly invoked right before the fictional Joaquín's adventures are catalogued; his muse is nothing less than the entire social matrix of Chicano society: "I withdraw to the safety within the/circle of life—/ MY OWN PEOPLE . . . MI RAZA" (12–13). The rest of the poem appeals to his muse in a variety of ways that explain why Gonzales equates "the circle of life" with his *raza*.

Applying each of the six epical traits, we find that Gonzales modifies the epic heroic model by exchanging the "figure of . . . national or international importance" for a composite figure embracing a wide field of characters—from the historical Cuauhtémoc and Cortéz to the legendary Juan Diego and his Virgin to the nameless *campesinos* and *coyotes* of daily experience. But *Joaquín* is not a vague embodiment of the everyman figure, for his *tocallo* (i.e., namesake) "is almost certainly . . . Joaquín Murieta, the famous bandit-hero of California gold-rush days" who sought to avenge the brutalities committed against the native Californios by the hordes of incoming Americans from the United States. "Joaquín's identity was mysterious . . . [and] in the search for the bandit, other Mexicans were hunted down and put to death."[7] By modeling his epic hero after a particular legend, Gonzales enlivens his character with specific heroic traits in spite of Joaquín's representation of all Chicanos throughout time. In addition, both the setting and the action of the poem conform to the conventional epic formula (points 2 and 3 above), for the stage on which the poem is performed is the complete panorama of Mexican and Chicano history, and its action is replete with "deeds of great valor [and] . . . courage." For example,

> I have been the bloody revolution,
> the victor,

the vanquished.
I have killed
   and been killed.
      I am the despots Díaz
      and Huerta
and the apostle of democracy,
         Francisco Madero. (40)

The setting encompasses five and one half centuries of history taking place on the Western Hemisphere, and as the passage indicates the speaker embodies all aspects of his heritage and ancestral geography.

Although Gonzales makes reference to gods and religious authority in the poem, he pointedly adapts the fourth characteristic—the intervention of supernatural forces in the hero's adventures. Instead of including deities, demons, and angels in his narrative, he describes the special forces of injustice and oppression that have plagued *el pueblo* for centuries in non-human, one might say "supernatural," terms. Hence, he indicts the "monstrous, technical,/ industrial giant called/ Progress" (10); "the mines of social snobbery" and the "fierce heat of racial hatred" (86), thereby drawing a comparison between their destructive powers and that of the omnipotent gods in traditional epics. Also conforming to the epical model is *Joaquín's* style and tone (point 5). It is at once elevated and grand (e.g., 69–70) and simple and folkloric (e.g., 96–98); the following passage captures both aspects aptly.

Here I stand
   before the court of justice,
      guilty
for all the glory of my Raza
   to be sentenced to despair.
Here I stand,
   poor in money,
   arrogant with pride,
      bold with machismo,
      rich in courage
         and
      wealthy in spirit and faith. (64)

Although Gonzales adheres for the most part to the traditional epical pattern, he emphatically rejects the last-mentioned trait, the requirement of an objective point of view (point 6). Instead, his narrative voice is intensely biased in its nationalistic idealizing of Chicano culture and its denigration of Anglo society. In support of this bias, it can be argued that, inasmuch as *raza* experience has historically been overlooked or distorted by racism in the literature of the dominant society, *Joaquín* contributes to objectivity simply by presenting the *raza* experience from a *raza* perspective and thus helping to balance the literary record. Moreover, the very notion of epical objectivity refers more to the presentation of facts and document-able material than to the rendering of attitude and point of view. In regard to the epic poem's form, it is quite enough to recognize *I Am Joaquín's* intended epic scale and purpose as well as its achieved congruence with many of the form's defining characteristics.

Still another way to analyze the poem is to consider its four distinct thematic units. Although Gonzales does not formally divide the work, it contains four isolable parts united organically around a central theme. The first comprises the poem's opening thirty-seven lines (pp. 6–13 in the Bantam edition) and may be seen as the poet's exposition of his subject and theme and his invocation of the muse. This first section introduces Joaquín and his socially schizoid position between two inimical forces, "gringo society" and *"mi raza."* As such it presents the basic polarity of Movement poetry: Us versus Them. Part of the hero's social schizophrenia derives from his characterization by Gonzales as the composite Chicano everyman, the mestizo who is quintessentially a blending of opposites, "both tyrant and slave" (19), a condition conducive to feelings of unresolved polarity. In other words, Joaquín's dilemma is caused by both internal and external factors: the internal relate to the genetic fact of *mestizaje* and its cultural implications, and the external relate to *la raza mestiza* living in the margins of U.S. American society, especially on the periphery of the Anglo "mainstream." Joaquín thus embodies the socially fractured experience of the minority citizen as victim of bicultural marginality. Eventually, however, the poem's first unit ends on a positive note of self-identity—the last line declaimed in bold upper-case letters: "I withdraw to the safety within the/ circle of life—/ MY OWN PEOPLE." Gonzales underscores this withdrawal through the poem's mirror symbol which, as Juan Rodriguez points out, is a physical emblem of the hero's search for self, a classic use of the mirror as mimetic device. The withdrawal to his "own people" parallels the conventional literary act of peering into the looking glass to discover the identity of the self.[8]

The second and third units of the poem are about equal in length, each approximately 200 lines, and each focuses on Mexican-American history and lore. Syntactically, these two sections comprise an extended phrase in apposition relative to the noun that ends the first section, for these units define and explain more fully (i.e., appositively) the subject, "MI RAZA," that precedes them. In the second section (16–48) we find a capsule summary of Chicano history from the Conquest of Mexico to the contemporary, mid-twentieth-century period. It mentions most of the famous names and events contributing to the heritage of *el pueblo*, and it also includes references to the countless individuals who were part of that history anonymously. In this section the reader detects a quality of rising action, of an episodic momentum moving toward a specific dramatic conflict. That momentum peaks in the third unit (51–86) where the poet moves away from the specifics of past history to the general realities of the present. Here, Gonzales points to the new "indignity" suffered by Chicanos: "Inferiority/ is the new load" (51)—the brutal "rewards/ this society has/ for sons of chiefs/ and kings" (69). The poet thus lays out the specific dramatic conflict as a polarity—the noble, formidable *raza* past pitted against the hostile dominant society's perception of *raza* as ignoble and without value. Adopting a reflective, quiet tone, Gonzales suggests resolution of this conflict (in literary terms, the falling action) by becoming increasingly lyrical.

> I shed the tears of anguish
> as I see my children disappear
> behind the shroud of mediocrity . . .
>
> > I must fight
> > > and win this struggle
> > > for my sons, and they
> > > must know from me
> > > who I am. (82)

In this passage we apprehend the nature of the poet's response to the heritage that produced him, a response that does not allow the centuries of subjection and agony to overcome the human will to act as an agent of self-determination.

The will to act is mobilized in the last unit which, like the first is brief—approximately forty lines (pp. 93–100). It contains the logical climax—resolution—to all the facts, opinions, impressions, and ideas catalogued in the preceding sections. It is a resolution profound in its simplicity: "we [*raza*] start to *move*" (96). That is, we rebel against the dominant culture's negation of Mexican America, and we reclaim the source of our future power which lies in the legitimation of our identity. With Joaquín "we refuse to be absorbed" by the larger society because our "spirit is strong" and our "faith unbreakable" (100). The famous closing lines assert themselves in a form resembling a "performative utterance,"[9] a statement that, by its very utterance, is intended to assure the actual implementation of appropriate action: "I shall endure!/ I will endure!" The saying is integral to the doing.

As indicated earlier, *I Am Joaquín* was a remarkably successful literary flag in the late 1960s and early 1970s, a nationally known banner capturing much of the passion and hope *del Movimiento*. Described as "one of the most significant pieces of creative Chicano poetry" and as "still the best-known Chicano poem,"[10] *Joaquín* partakes of the ideological formula in political fiction enunciated by novelist Carlos Fuentes. Like such fiction, *Joaquín* is "caught in the net of the reality close at hand and can only reflect it. That surrounding reality demands a struggle in order to be changed, and that struggle demands an epic simplification: the exploited man, because he is exploited, is good; the exploiter, also intrinsically, is evil."[11] Although the ideological formula may not actually be required by political art or propaganda, it has been repeated throughout history at the start of popular movements of liberation and self-determination. The pattern is so distinct as to nearly qualify as a recipe for a people's politicization. For that reason I disagree with novelist José Villareal's position regarding early Movement writings.

. . . there was a proliferation of writing called Chicano literature and, as long as a work fit the mold created by the activists, it was not only considered good but was exorbitantly lauded. This led to statements by people who knew better such as . . . [the] favorable comparisons of *I Am Joaquín* to *Martín Fiérro*. . . . In this way, we performed a great disservice to the Movement as well as to the idea of literature. It came about because we refused or could not understand that we could be didactic without sacrificing our artistic qualities, that even though the primary aim or intent of our work might be to propound an ideology . . . we need not rule out an aesthetic presence.[12]

Villareal appears unwilling to accept the eventual literary value of certain kinds of literature that in some ways lack stylized artistry and conventional craftsmanship. He also seems indifferent to Fuentes' point about protest writing being especially "close" (or engagé) to "the reality" it captures. For instance, Villareal would deny the dormant but real aesthetic vigor and, more important, the literary potentiality of works (like *Joaquín*) that abound in any modern society containing grass-roots movements. While such works may not be masterpieces, they contain themes, images, symbols, and other elements that future artists will employ with artistic grace. Villareal is correct in stressing aesthetic quality as a *sine qua non* of literature, but he is wrong to fault early Movement writing for its transparent politics. Wrong, because that early political fervor was both an important thematic ingredient and a necessary conceptual catalyst for the literary accomplishment of later Chicano writers.

Assuredly, *Joaquín* can be faulted and not only for aesthetic lapses. Like other Phase I poems it is weak in its prosy prolixity (e.g., 44 and 56) which makes it sound, as others have pointed out, like "an effective political speech."[13] Stylistically, it is also weak in its chaotic line arrangement (e.g., 70) and its use of cliché (e.g., 93). Furthermore, the poem is seriously flawed by its blatant sexism, previously discussed, and by its less overt racism. Despite its rousing call for equity and social justice for Chicanos, the poem exhibits racial chauvinism when it offers, without explanation, glib statements like "I am the mountain Indian,/ *superior over all*" and "my blood runs *pure*" (39 and 62, my italics). The implicit racism even leads to some errors of fact and to questionable poetic judgment, as in the following lines:

> Part of the blood that runs deep in me
> could not be vanquished by the Moors.
> I defeated them after five hundred years,
> and I endured.
>> Part of the blood that is mine
>> has labored endlessly four hundred
>> years under the heel of lustful
>>> Europeans. (82)

Gonzales apparently does not accept the obvious truth that the *mestizaje* that he acknowledges with pride is by definition *not* "pure" as he asserts. It is, rather, mixed blood within a blended gene pool. He futilely rejects the African blood and culture transmitted to Spain during the Moorish takeover between 700 and 1200 A.D., even though after centuries of Moorish occupation, Spain's people, culture, and language were visibly altered by the intermingling of peoples. Questionable poetic judgment is also evident in the confusing personification of "blood" and in the boastful "I defeated them *after five hundred years.*" Some defeat!

Nevertheless, as the overall tenor of this discussion makes clear, these shortcomings do not diminish the vast significance of *I Am Joaquín* as a Movement landmark of great ideological and literary influence. It proved that the possibilities of a Chicano literature were there to define, and because of its remarkably large audience, that proof was a stimulus that blended into the general atmosphere of the Movement and became part of the very air of the sixties. As poet Bernice Zamora has commented, *I Am Joaquín* "was the first important milestone in Chicano literature because it gave to Chicanos a significant place in the world, politically, sociologically, historically, and literarily. It united us as a people unlike any other piece of Chicano literature before or since its appearance."[14]

## ABELARDO DELGADO AND RICARDO SÁNCHEZ

If the dissemination of *Joaquín* was a rousing and unifying epic call in the early days of the Movement, it took the persistent activism of specific individuals to promote Chicano poetry as a viable and legitimate form of belletristic expression. Among the most committed and engagé of these individuals were Abelardo Delgado and Ricardo Sánchez, whose faith, optimism, and will to write within a largely unreceptive literary climate would not be denied. Like Rodolfo Gonzales these two writers initially distributed their work in mimeograph and xerox form and then published it themselves in small, usually non-literary, presses. Eventually their work was published professionally, largely in the Chicano publications that constituted the first wave of the *raza* alternative press movement. Moreover, these writers were actively involved in Movement activities, combining non-literary occupations with sociopolitical protest and advocacy for Chicano causes. But although they formed part of the mostly nameless Movement troops of the late sixties, Delgado and Sánchez strove, even then, to stimulate a literary wing within the *Movimiento*, to generate interest in Chicano artistic creativity, and to encourage *raza* artists to unfetter their muses from imitation of the dominant culture's literary touchstones and conventions.

One of the most dedicated of these writers is Abelardo "Lalo" Barrientos Delgado, who at fifty-one is the grand old "Don" of Chicano poetry and certainly one of the most widely known of *raza* poets. He publishes his work under Abelardo Delgado or, simply, Abelardo; his voluminous productivity and his enthusiasm as a reader have given him a vast grass-roots following, just as his sincerity and tirelessness in encouraging other writers and in promoting Chicano literature have earned him respect even among some whose critical assessment of his work is not unvaryingly favorable. Accordingly, it is a commonplace in Chicano literary circles that Abelardo could use an editor, that his prolific effusions need rigorous expurgation, and that his natural talent, real and original as it is, demands considerable surgical restraint. Abelardo himself admits this.

I tend to be prolific and turn out great quantities of stuff. In doing this I sacrifice quality and turn out a lot of junk. . . . I know I will never be a good writer because I am basically too lazy to polish what I do. . . . [15]

I write a piece and put it away, turn it out as is. This is an act of arrogance. . . . This is wrong and I know it. If only I had someone to push me for perfection, to edit my work. [16]

Even without that "someone to push" him Abelardo has produced some extremely memorable poems, and his canon as a whole cannot be over-looked. Like *I Am Joaquín*, his early poetry has considerable historical significance, and some of his later work is thematically powerful. Characterized by the features of Phase I Chicano poetry enumerated earlier in this chapter, Abelardo's protest poetry was a staple of many Chicano rallies and demonstrations throughout the Southwest, particularly in Colorado and Denver where he lives. The most effective examples from this period are "stupid america" and "el imigrante," while "To the Minority Health Providers of Tomorrow" is more representative of his style. However, these three poems are but a fraction of his vast output during this time.

Included in *Chicano: 25 Pieces of a Chicano Mind*, "stupid america" and "el imigrante" contain some of the poet's finest images concentrated in cleanly crafted verses devoid of most of Abelardo's characteristic weaknesses. Widely anthologized, "stupid america" is the only one out of the collection's twenty-five poems that is written entirely in free verse. This is significant because Abelardo's devotion to conventional meters and rhyme in this early period too often forced him to stylistic contortions that grossly damaged his verse (e.g., "el macho" and "poema"). In this poem, instead, the poet develops a powerful conceit—the United States personified as an individual insensitively witnessing and contributing to the destruction of the Chicano artist.

Developed within a second person verb construction, the poem establishes a tone of immediacy between the speaker and the listener, "stupid america," but it is an angry immediacy that intensifies the speaker's estrangement from the listener. The poem is built around a framework of three images—Chicano as sculptor, as poet, and as painter. These images thematically integrate the present "chicano with a big knife" who is an immediate threat, with the more distant "chicano" you only "hear . . . shouting curses," to the remote as memory "chicanito/ flunking math and english" in past school days.[17] In other words, Delgado opens in the present and shifts to the past, a chronology he reverses later in the poem. When the poet presents specific artist types he starts in the distant past with the sculptor of "christ figures" which recalls the archaic woodcarving *santero* tradition in the Southwest. He then refers to Spanish artist Picasso, who typifies modern art, and places us in the contemporary present. The result of this subtle reversal of time and space is the emphasis upon the revolutionary power of poetry to change the oppressed status of *raza* in "stupid america."[18] Similarly, one of the most effective features of the poem is its juxtaposition of images of constructiveness with images of destruction as in the manifold meanings of "knife" in lines 2, 4, and 6 and also in the image of the poet frustrated to explosiveness. The last three lines constitute one of the finest subtleties in Abelardo's corpus. The word "hanging" is appropriately denotative in referring to an artist's masterpieces which deserve to be hung in galleries and museums, but it is simultaneously connotative in evoking the artist's persecution and even death by hanging—the punishment of a harsh society. Similarly, the refrain "stupid america," which is repeated only four times but nonetheless persists as an echo in one's consciousness, has subliminal effect in suggesting—by its very repetition—the constricting pain and anger felt by the artist in a hostile homeland.

The homeland's hostility is also part of the thematic Us versus Them polarity in "el imigrante,"[19] a poem published entirely in Spanish in *25 Pieces.* Abelardo translated the poem for inclusion in *It's Cold: 52 Cold-Thought Poems* where it appears entirely in English. Opening and closing with rhymed couplets, a favorite Abelardo device for this period, "el imigrante" is held together by a muted irony which is not typical of the poet's normally more declamatory style. To be sure, the poem contains some obvious lapses (e.g., lines 8, 26, 27), but its overall tone is of gentle irony. For once, the political protest poet does not have all the answers about "his people"; he does not know, for example, why they migrate. Perhaps, he speculates, like the "golondrinas" or "salmones" the migratory urge is natural, or, perhaps, it is "the love of soil" or, even, the need for "a rest from texas," their home state, that motivates them. The poem ends on this note of speculation and uncertainty: "the truth is they themselves don't even know," for they are the victims of an arbitrary God (1.25). Likewise, just as the poem opened with the incongruity of "swallows cutting beets," a poetic yoking of air and earth, so the poem ends with the incongruous yoking of "lettuce" and "justice," a tangible agricultural product and an intangible abstraction. Comparable to the poet's use of the word "hanging" in "stupid america," the term "lettuce" here has multiple meanings: it is at once the product of the migrant farmworkers' harvest, a symbol of the food that is central to their survival, and also a colloquial term for the money which is a primary concern of their impoverished lives. By juxtaposing "lechuga" with "justicia," a lofty Yankee ideal, Abelardo achieves an effective final irony by calling attention to the *in*justice of an affluent nation's indifference to the plight of the *campesinos*.

In "To the Minority Health Providers of Tomorrow," first published in *It's Cold*, Abelardo iterates his concern with "poverty and oppression" in a poem that typifies the early protest poetry of the period. Explicitly stating its central message, the poem seems intended for a *raza* audience well acquainted with the problems associated with health delivery services for poor people: "we desperately need chicanos. . . to come back/to the rural communities/. . . how pleasing it is to be co-writers of a new american history."[20] Delgado worked as a community health coordinator in the 1970s, and it is evident that this piece derived from that experience and, possibly, was written as an occasional verse for a particular event. The Us/Them polarities of Phase I poetry are implied here in a number of ways. The title, for example, is dedicated to the "minority health providers of *tomorrow*" because there are few of them *today*, revealing a clear dichotomy between social classes. Similarly, the colors—dark/brown/*morenas*/black—included in the poem obviously contrast with the color associated in leftist rhetoric with power and affluence—white. Also symbolizing the chasm between Chicanos and the majority group that controls the health care system is the poem's bilingualism, a technique seldom used by Abelardo in his early work which was usually written either entirely in Spanish or entirely in English. Here, the poem's opening lines resemble a *dicho*, and they establish a tone of *raza* solidarity, hope, and love that is intended to carry through as an inspiration warmed by *"manos morenas"* and the comfort of *"todo está bien."*

Not as poetically effective as "stupid america" and "imigrante," "To the Minority Health Providers of Tomorrow" more closely approximates the kind of poetry that dominated in the early years of the Movement. Thematically explicit, stylistically prosaic, and sentimental, the early protest poetry by and large sought to promote Movement ideals and objectives by sheer force of statement and an insistence on the rightness of the cause. Most of Abelardo's work from this period shares those weaknesses. Whether in "To the Traffic Fatalities 52 and 53" where the poet's sentiments appear without stylistic restraint, or in "Los Sembradores" where the convoluted rhetoric diminishes the images and turns them into clichés, or in "El 16 de Septiembre" where the forced rhymes undercut the flow of ideas and theme—Abelardo's early poems seemed to shout themselves into being. As with any voice that is too loud, the message was often not heard.

Like Abelardo Delgado, Ricardo Sánchez was one of the earliest distinctly Chicano poets heard in the late 1960s, and like Abelardo, he is identified with loud, hortatory protest poetry. Indeed, his first collection is titled *Canto y Grito Mi Liberación* ("I Sing and Shout My Freedom"). Committed to the political goals of *El Movimiento*, Sánchez was in certain ways a direct beneficiary of the Movement's pressure politics. While in prison he was profoundly, if indirectly, influenced by the support and encouragement he received from learning of the work of a number of Chicano activists, including Tijerina and Chávez. In the early months of his life as an ex-convict, his family and the efforts of Abelardo Delgado and Tomás Atencio, one of the founders of the Academia[21] in New Mexico, helped smooth out many of the difficulties normally encountered by *pintos* (a vernacular term for convicts) seeking to adjust to society outside prison.

Sánchez is one of a handful of names associated with Chicano *pinto* poetry, a considerable quantity of verse produced by Chicanos in prisons in the first stage of the Movement. Because the two key elements uniting *pinto* poetry as a body were the facts of incarceration and of ethnicity, it is a mistake to consider it a distinct stylistic school identifiable by a unique poetics. The shared ethnicity and circumstances clearly spawned a common cluster of subjects—for example, confinement, social isolation, unmitigated loneliness—and images—such as the uniformity of the walls, fences, steel bars, uniforms—and these commonalities gave *pinto* poetry a strong topical unity, occasionally reinforced by use of terms from the *pintos'* patois. Despite these shared circumstantial features, in style and theme *pinto* poetry was like other political protest poetry. Its evocation of *raza* consciousness, its condemnation of capitalist institutions of oppression, its insistence on radical social change, and its promotion of a new political order and of *chicanismo*—all of these identified it thematically with Phase I Chicano poetry. Stylistically, too, *pinto* poetry resembled other Phase I work even though Sánchez and Raúl Salinas, the two best known figures, were more inclined to experiment with form (language and line especially) than were most Phase I writers.

All of Sánchez's *pinto* poetry is concerned with the physical condition and mental state of the convict, the miserable creature caught in the merciless tentacles of unfortunate circumstances and whose every experience of life is defined and controlled by those circumstances. "Soledad" (1961) discloses the poet's concern by opening with a focus on the convict's mental state— "solitude," "loneliness," "tears,"—and then by subtly shifting to a focus on details of his physical condition—"the steel," "grayness," "barbed wires."[22] The shift becomes complete as the speaker's despair ("my identity's lost") carries his thoughts to "my other life/ . . . of my peasant origin" (28). But the escape is brutally brief as "soledad"—referring to aloneness, to loneliness, to a common Spanish feminine name, to the name of a California mountain range as well as to the U.S. federal prison—intrudes on the speaker's reverie: "your keys clang at midnight/ your phantoms stalk, search,/ and/ haunt" (29).

Similarly, "Reo Eterno" (Eternal Prisoner; undated but probably composed between 1961 and 1963) captures the horror of monotony which *pintos* experience and which, if they are to survive, they must transcend. Opening with a chant-like repetition that foreshadows the poem's tone and theme, the speaker describes the dehumanization that results from total immersion in "leaden labyrinths" where "love is a four letter word/. . . and playboy fold-outs" (*Canto*, 43). Part of the horror arises from the speaker's realization that the prison's "chingaderismo" and its "same thematic desmadre" extend beyond the walls, "out in the streets" where "all humanity/ [is] but an external convict/ suffering the binding of the soul" (43–44). "Reo Eterno" holds no hope or cheer to sustain the guilty *pinto*; such affirmation must come from knowing that the very existence of the poem—its creation and design—constitutes affirmation. Interestingly, in this context, the poem contains allusions to art, in the form of *I Am Joaquín* and the film *Z*—for art offers almost the only human form of redemption that contrasts with the monotony and brutality of prison.

Both "Soledad" and "Reo Eterno" share characteristics of Phase I poetry. For example, besides dealing with the polarity embodied in the contrast between prison and barrio, Sánchez writes "Soledad" primarily in the second person verb form, just as "Reo Eterno," written bilingually, deals with the discrepancy between the sentences of "hard nosed justices" and the

extreme punishments of "prison garbed demons." Other poems from this
stage of Sánchez's writing also reflect Phase I characteristics even while they
evince all the trapped agony of the *pinto*'s consciousness and experience. In
"[pinta/slammer/joint]"* we find a striking contrast between the sounds
and meaning of the English words and those of the Spanish, a contrast that
reinforces the thematic polarity pitting "prison systems," whether in the
penitentiary or in life, against "vida, chicanismo, y movimiento.²³ The
poet addresses his peers, a group of "carnales" *pinto* poets, and he frames
some sharp questions for them in a format that moves from the hideous
coldness of the first line to greater and greater personalization and human
warmth. The poem moves from the phonological hardness of "pinta,"
"joint," "bamming," "gouging," "tearing," and "enraging" to a quite
dissimilar catalog listing his carnales' names and nicknames, whose sounds
are both euphonious and funny. It continues to the end on this affirmative
note of gentleness and generosity.

> i hope you understood
> and offered coffee and cigarros
> y un abrazo por un bato
> que se enfrento armado    (41)

Sánchez foreshadows the phonological change at the end through a political
statement, presented midway in the poem. That statement regarding the
hypocrisy of penal rehabilitation methods spurs the speaker to ask about
Reies Lopez Tijerina, the Chicano activist who was himself imprisoned for
his political activities on behalf of the *raza* land rights organization he
founded. In completing this shift to lyricism the poet reveals that genuine
"rehabilitation" occurs only through the selfless efforts and courageous
examples of leaders like Tijerina.

Also reflecting Phase I features are "[la crucigrama vita]" and "[sun
blazing]" which describe prison cruelties as representative of a more general
"oppression" both "in la pinta as [well as] in la libre" (*Hechizospells*, 43–44).
Both poems employ bilingualism to make explicit statements about the
"social order" and the "camino de la liberación" (*Hechizospells*, 44), and both
assert—insist on—the essential humanness and dignity of the *pinto* despite
the institutional dehumanization endured: "sweat and tears/ assert the
hungers/ that live in soul" (35). In this way, these and, in fact, most of

---

*Following standard literary practice, untitled poems, like this one, are referred to by their
first line.

Sánchez's other *pinto* poems disclose the theme of self-identity. Despite the lived horrors of "whip/lash/slap/bang" and forced obsequiousness to the guards and tougher convicts (35–36), Sánchez suggests that the *pinto* poet does not allow the experience to reach his inner being and destroy his selfhood. Thus, through fantasies of life at home, through a switch from English to Spanish, through imagined conversations with his "carnales" or his family, the *pinto* poet, *through his poetry*, asserts himself, and his *self*, to himself and, eventually, to the world.

The *pinto* poems in *Canto y Grito* and *Hechizospells* were written in the 1960s, and although Sánchez continued to refer to his prison experience in some of his later work, using it to symbolize other subjects and themes, *la pinta* ceased being his primary focus in the early 1970s. Overall, his *pinto* poetry exhibits such notable strengths as emotional intensity, intellectual vitality, and a striking poetic idiom and imagery. Conversely, this body of writing contains many stylistic problems that reappear throughout Sánchez's *oeuvre* (like, for example, overt didacticism, gratuitous prosiness, and an abundance of solecisms). Employing the free-flowing openness associated with the Whitman tradition in North American poetry, Sánchez is most effective in poems like "Reo Eterno" where the form, though open and loose, matches the theme precisely without overstatement and prolixity, without preachiness and polysyllabic solecisms.

Abelardo Delgado and Ricardo Sánchez compiled one of the first anthologies of Chicano poetry to be published in this country, *Los Cuatro*, which appeared in 1970, a year designated by some *raza* activists as "the year of the Chicano."[24] The year was certainly one of widespread Chicano consciousness- raising and emerging Brown Power, of introduction to OEO (Office of Economic Opportunity) programs and to grass-roots political organizing, of the planting and sowing of a genuine *chicanismo* in literature and other art forms. *Los Cuatro* was part of that planting, but time has clearly faded the flower of the book's verses, and the anthology falls within the stage of Chicano literature that poet José Montoya once described as *"bien terrible."*

Once we were allowed [to publish] everybody started singing, and we wrote some *bad* songs. . . . Just like a bird who has always been kept caged and suddenly they open the gate. That bird isn't going to fly right away. The first couple of times he'll stumble around, bump into a few barns, but eventually he'll hit a current and learn what to do with his wings and soar. That happened to Chicano poetry. At first, in . . . early underground newspapers, there was some poetry que era bien terrible. . . . Everybody was writing.[25]

Accordingly, some of Abelardo's worst rhymed couplets appear in *Los Cuatro*:

> my lord, the gut inflates with disgust
> in a minute my breakfast out will gust
> my integration consists
> (my, how the thought persists)
>
> let the lettuce wait at center, colorado
> until every worker agrees he's bien pagado
>                                 (*Los Cuatro*, 5, 7, 13)

Likewise, the anthology contains some of Sánchez's worst bombast:

> AMERIKA,
>                     irrelevant malcreance,
>                     screwed-up money grubber
> the streets puke out
>           the morbid resin of your perversity,
>           and you sit smugly at washington desk
>           pavlovianly expecting
>                     grovelling, muted responses
>                     from those that you oppress.
>                                 (*Los Cuatro*, 41)

Shortcomings like these pervade the book, which also suffers the textual errata so often seen in the publications of non-literary, amateur printshops. Nevertheless, despite its deficiencies, *Los Cuatro* can still be viewed as a significant document in *raza* literary history, for it is a partial record of the dynamic energy of the Movement's first wave of contemporary poets, and it contains the early work of two Chicano poets who honed their craft as the Movement developed. Indeed, as José Montoya also remarked, "some of the same terrible poets have trained themselves and learned."[26]

## OTHER PROTEST POETS

The first wave of Chicano poetry was exactly that—a wave, not a trickle or a stream. As such it comprised a crowd of voices from every *rincón y barrio de Aztlán*. The dominant character of this writing was related to the ideological core of the Chicano Movement with its concern for the political and economic empowerment of *raza* and for the freedom to be *raza* without assimilation of the majority society's values and norms. As stated earlier,

Phase I poetry is quintessentially moral in its sense and essence; it seeks primarily to arouse its hearers to pragmatic action much as politicians and preachers do through their words. Because poetry qua poetry is ultimately neither solely speech nor sermon, however, the vast majority of this early Chicano verse suffered fatal injury, when, to use José Montoya's metaphor, like a caged bird suddenly free, it stumbled and bumped around in its first flight. Still, some survived. Besides Gonzales, Delgado, and Sánchez, a few other survivors deserve mention here, for their work also contributed to the creation of distinctly Chicano literary themes and forms and thus helped broaden Mexican America in the public mind.

The important literary theme of social polarity in Chicano protest poetry is well represented by a number of still active writers. Angela de Hoyos, a Mexican-born writer and artist whose bi-cultural worldview was nurtured in San Antonio where she grew up, has been writing since the late 1960s. Her poem "Arise, Chicano!" (from the early 1970s) succinctly presents the central thematic tension so frequently seen in Phase I poetry of Chicano misery in stark contrast to the world around it. Whether it be the "migrant's world . . . of never-ending fields" or the "festering barrios of poverty," the predominant Chicano experience, suggests de Hoyos, is always "bitterness" because "wherever you turn for solace/ there is an embargo."[27] Although her answer to this inequity is conveyed in traditional religious terms, it is meant to signify an untraditional message, the rejection of Catholic notions of salvation through piety.

> Arise, Chicano!—that divine spark within you
> surely says—Wash your wounds
> and swathe your agonies.
> There is no one to succor you.
> You must be your own messiah. (14)

As the citation discloses, de Hoyos writes in the imperative voice typical of Phase I verse. Similar in theme to the previous poem, her "The Final Laugh" (1972) juxtaposes the "gluttonous omnipotent alien white world" with the very basic physical reality of "an empty stomach," a persistent "grumbling belly" that does not understand "the necessity of being white" (32). As these two examples disclose, de Hoyos' work captured the cultural nationalism of Phase I Chicano poetry without regard for feminism or for the specific concerns of women. Chicano/a neglect in literature of issues of gender equity reflected the general neglect within the Movement which in turn reflected the dominant patriarchy which defines human society.

Like de Hoyos, Raymundo "Tigre" Perez, another early Movement
protest poet from Texas, repeatedly returns to the Us/Them polarity in his
work. Indeed, the entire body of his work seems to divide naturally into
two groups, poems dealing with Phase I thematic polarities and poems
dealing with self-identity. Less lyrical than de Hoyos, Perez's poetry is
nonetheless memorable for its emotional intensity and effect. Borrowing
Ralph Ellison's archetypal symbol of invisibility to express the situation of
migrant farmworkers in U.S. society, Perez penetrates through layers of
social cant in "Invisible People" to point to one crucial fact: "I pick the food
on your table."[28] The families "hidden from your view" wearing "worn out
shoes" and "oversized clothes" keep "you" fed (2). In the closing lines
presented in the voice of "Them," the poet further sharpens the gap
between the two worlds.

> . . . "I wonder what they are up to now?"
> Pay them no mind, John, it's only migrants. (2)

By shifting voices and perspectives to those of the insensitive majority, the
poet dramatically underscores the social schism and the magnitude of the
breach between the haves and have-nots.

Perez employs the same approach to the same polarity in "Hunger
Strike," one of many poems written to mark the fasting that César Chávez
and other advocates of the farmworkers engaged in as non-violent protest
in the early 1970s. The nature of the dichotomy changes, however, in
"What Have You Done?" even though the two opposing sides remain the
same. In this piece, Perez challenges conventional notions of "Experience,
history and patriotism," concepts usually perceived as being determined by
"great men." In reality, he says, their "experience" was "got by others" and
their "[h]istory is a string of lies" and "[p]atriotism" is only a euphemism
for the abuse of "power" permitted by "a law badge."[29] On the other side
are both the benevolent forces of the "[b]eautiful people marching" as well
as the more sinister force of the speaker whose "anger in my blood" impels
him to state, simply, "I am here to kill you" (Los Cuatro, 20). The cold
directness of that statement signifies the ultimate form of resistance
possible against oppression.

A similar progression from calm description to expressions of frustration,
rage, and violence occurs in "Under a Never Changing Sun" (1971), a poem
by Jesus Maldonado "El Flaco," a less well-known poet of that period. The
poem opens with a pastoral depiction of dawn when even "the fresh
morning/ still sleeps" and then offers a bucolic picture of the speaker, a
farmworker, walking alone to work, his feet "slowly kiss[ing] the dirt."[30]

The same quiet tone continues to the middle of the poem where the gentle pastoral note begins to strike a jarring chord as the scene fills with the image of the speaker's "burning back" under the "Azteca sun," whose intense heat seems to "reflect. . . grains of sand" falling through the "hour- glass of history" (33). The poet's irony suddenly becomes clear when he recalls that "yesterday/ my father also left to work/ alone," a thought that leads him to remember that "day before yesterday/ my grandfather" (34) also worked like a slave. The last four lines punctuate the irony and make complete the progression away from the opening pastoral tone.

> La pinche vida
>       que a tirones la vivimos
>             under a never changing sun
> nos sigue jodiendo. (34)

Maldonado thus parodies conventional pastoral verse by transforming the opening rustic serenity to angry bitterness about the truth of the *campesinos'* harsh life. The images in Maldonado's poem of the *campesino*, the sun, the clock, and other generations of farmworkers provide the framework of another poem about farmworkers, "Day-Long Day" (1972), written by Tino Villanueva, a south Texas poet and college professor whose sole book of poetry in this period, *Hay Otro Voz Poems*, received critical praise. But Villanueva's poem contains an additional element from the *campesino* milieu: the hardship of forced migration which turns people into

> a family of sinews, and backs,
> row-trapped,
> zig-zagging through Summer-long rows
> of cotton: Lubbock by way of Wharton.[31]

In lyrical emphasis of the poem's sun/sweat/time theme, Villanueva writes, "[b]ronzed and blurry-eyed by/the blast of degrees,/ we blend into earth's rotation" (30).

Defiance of the seeming natural law which states that the downtrodden must "blend into earth's rotation" is the theme of Villanueva's poem "Aquellos Vatos" (1972). It addresses the question of *raza* self-identity which figures prominently as subject, theme, and emblem in Chicano poetry. By rejecting the side of the polarity defined by the empowered majority ethnic group, Chicano poets define themselves and their culture in terms antithetical to U.S. American values. By fostering, on the other hand, the principles associated with pluralistic *raza* values, the poets give a positive rendering of self-identity, one integrally based on the *mestizaje* of their heritage, history, and quotidian experience. Villanueva's poem expresses the identity theme through its subject, *pachucos*, and through the complex nature of its bilingualism. Pioneer educator George Sánchez was one of the first to publicly recognize (and as many revisionist scholars of Mexican-American history have since agreed) that the *pachuco* phenomenon of the 1940s and 1950s may be considered a precursor to the strong Chicano nationalism of the 1960s.[32] With their distinctive dress and hairstyles which made them conspicuous even in a crowd and with their well-developed private language which blended Spanish, English, and totally new coinages to produce *caló*, a hybrid dialect, *pachucos* identified themselves as distinct from both the hostile white world and the social inferiority of Chicanos within that world.[33] "Aquellos Vatos" (i.e., "Those Cats" or "Those Dudes") captures these qualities perfectly.

A reminiscence about adolescence, "Aquellos Vatos" opens with a one-word line, "Simón," which refers both to a masculine name and to the word "yes" in *caló*, the latter meaning establishing an affirmative tone for the next three stanzas. The speaker is recalling his *carnales*, friends and acquaintances from the past, and in doing so, he effectively conveys the exciting dynamics of the *pachuco* ambience.

> Simón,
> we knew him as la Zorra—uncouth but
> squared away;
> messed around unpaved streets. No different
> from el Caballo de Littlefield, or from
> la Chiva de McAllen who never let himself down;
> always had a movida chueca somewhere up town.
> Then there was el Pollo de San Anto—
>
> (*Hay Otro Voz Poems*, 42)

All the friends are recalled by their nicknames, all of which happen to be names of animals: Fox, Horse, Goat, Chicken, and so on. Each person is imaged by a characteristic activity or interest that, along with the descriptive nickname, evokes him in a strikingly particular way: "el Gorrion," for example, was "un carnal a todo dar—/ never said much, but his tattoos were sure a/ conversation piece" (42–43). It is this personalizing particularity, which the *pachuco* movement actively promoted, that Villanueva fastens onto to present his theme of defiant self-identification and autonomous self-identity. The last stanza underscores this point with a subtlety unusual for Phase I poetry.

> They're probably married by now,
> those cats,
> and their kids try to comprehend culture and
> identity by reading "See Spot. See Spot run,"
> and by going to the zoo on a Greyhound bus with
> Miss Foxx." (43)

The references to Spot, zoo, Greyhound bus, and Miss Foxx, significations of animals from the dominant society, contrast sharply with the *pachuco* "animals" of the previous stanzas. "See Spot run" represents the educational system which historically has failed most Mexican-Americans, while the "Greyhound bus" symbolizes the American business ethos and its exploitative labor and advertising practices. Unlike the menagerie of free-spirited and creative *pachucos* in the poem, the "zoo" reference calls to mind images of caged animals lacking natural freedom, and the closing line of "Miss Foxx" returns us to the opening line and Simón's nickname "La Zorra." With fine economy, the Zorra/Foxx contrast culminates the last stanza's metaphoric reversal from focus on the *raza* subculture to focus on the Anglo majority culture, and the contrast effectively reduces the dominant society's power to an unappealing set of abuses and oppressions. Here again, Chicano poetry demonstrates the compelling force of the Us/Them polarity and its centrality as both a social and literary theme of *raza* identity.

Other variations on the Chicano identity theme appear in the poetry of Juan Valdez (pseudonym of Magdaleno Avila), an El Paso poet discovered and encouraged by Abelardo Delgado. In spare, elemental language reminiscent of postwar minimalism, Valdez in "Poem II" (1970) asserts the principle of self-determination in a quiet restatement of Shakespeare's "to thine own self be true."

> I am to be what I am
> I will be no one's flower
> I will not be put in a window
> I am what I look like. . .
> I am not what you think I am

> (*Los Cuatro*, 47)

The poem suggests that self-definition establishes one's identity and that that very fact determines the nature of being: "I will not be a mirror/ I will not be an echo/. . . I can't change my ways" (47).

Employing similarly spare diction and an equally quiet, even subdued,

tone Valdez embeds the theme of identity within an antiwar message in
"My Uncle Sam," another poem from this period. "Yesterday my Uncle
Sam wrote./ . . . He says he wants me" (*Los Cuatro*, 53)—and thus simply,
directly, the speaker introduces the subject of his draft notice. The prospect
of service to an "Uncle" who "is a funny man/ . . . I never loved his ways"
alarms the speaker into repeating what he has already mentioned once
before:

> He says he wants me.
> He didn't say much else
> He never does. (53)

The closing three words, "He never does," underscore the problem for the
speaker—that the demanding "Uncle" never justifies or even explains his
demands ("He doesn't write much")—and this explains the narrator's fear
and dismay. The real problem, of course, is that the speaker's life, like
millions of others, is jeopardized by Uncle Sam's orders and, thus, "his
letters/ Send my heart a jumping" (53). Embedded within this antiwar
message is a portrait of the "I," who emerges as a mildly ironic man who,
like his Uncle, also "doesn't say much." But, though he doesn't, he says
enough to indicate his opinions unequivocally, and it is that clarity and
firmness of thought, coupled with the speaker's quiet stoicism, which
disclose the basic dignity undergirding his self-identity.

Still another way of evoking identity found in early Chicano poetry is one
that relied on detailed descriptions of mundane activities to project the
literal reality of *chicanismo*. By extending the boundaries of poetry to include
*raza* subjects and idioms, Chicano poets offered another perspective on the
nature of Chicano identity. "La Jefita" (1972) by José Montoya, a New
Mexican poet/artist/college teacher and founder of the parodic Royal
Chicano Air Force,[34] is one such poem. It begins as a reminiscence of early
childhood—"[w]hen I remember the campos"—but it quickly becomes a
portrait of the speaker's mother, *la jefita (caló* for "mama") of the title.
Through the poet's recollection of the nocturnal sounds that used to lullaby
him to sleep at night, the picture of a woman of indefatigable energies
emerges. She would ceaselessly work at night after a day of work in the
fields; her bustling activity was the last thing he would hear at night and
the first thing he heard in the dark of dawn when her preparations for the
day awoke him. Although the piece opens in the present with the speaker
recalling past time, its conclusion remains in the past evoked in the
speaker's mind: "Mi jefe. . . decía/ That woman—she only complains/ in

her sleep" (21). Indeed, the development of the poem suggests that it is patterned after the nocturnal ritual of his youth, presenting the speaker as he was drifting off to sleep and ending with "sleep," the poem's last word. The many references to quotidian sense impressions (like the sounds and smells of the tortilla making, the beans boiling, the dogs barking and so on) without reference to any other world outside his own, along with the natural rhythms and words of colloquial speech, assert a *raza* identity, unique and indissoluble in his mind and, through the poem, in ours.

Important to the effectiveness of "La Jefita" is its easy-going humor about some of the unavoidable crudenesses and silliness of daily life. Humor is crucial, however, to the import and purpose of "Oda al Molcajete" ("Ode to the Mortar and Pestle") by Jesus Maldonado "El Flaco" whose "Under a Never Changing Sun" was discussed earlier. Although he uses the mock heroic tradition as a stylistic framework, Maldonado does not follow the convention and satirize his subject, for his acknowledgment of the *molcajete's* singular importance to mestizo cuisine is genuine. The subject of the poet's satire is the Chicano protest poet who blithely substitutes exhortation and bombast for lyricism and style and calls the substitution "poetry."

> Magic rock of three squat little legs
> > you sit on baggy culottes
> > > Majestically
> In your bespattered womb
> > you grind your daily magic
> casting spells
> > on humble foods
> > > Mmmmixxxeer!

(*Literatura Chicana*, 119; my translation)

By employing an excessively elegant style to memorialize the lowly *molcajete* and by engaging in rhapsodies of emotion to describe the object's grand effect on the Chicanos' daily lives, Maldonado burlesques those treatments of Chicano culture that overstate the obvious and, in doing so, trivialize the very subject meant to be celebrated. The poem's arbitrary line arrangement also serves a parodic purpose, recalling much of the (in José Montoya's phrase) "*bien terrible*" free verse of Phase I work. Despite the humor and the parody, Maldonado's careful attention to details from *raza* life, his emphatic use of dialectal Spanish, and his confidence in using the mock heroic form when Chicano nationalistic fervor ran high, all contribute to the poem's ultimate, overall effect of asserting a genuine Chicano identity.

Numerous other writers offered their verses to (largely approving)
Chicano audiences in the late 1960s and early 1970s, including Alurista,
whose work will be discussed at length in subsequent chapters. Some of
these poets continue to write, give public readings, and publish, sometimes
infrequently and almost always in small presses. For example, Luis Omar
Salinas, whose *Crazy Gypsy* (1970) enjoyed great popularity within the
student wing of the Chicano Movement, waited nine years to publish
another book of poetry, while Nephtalí de León, whose writing includes
stories for children, has had his work published almost annually (albeit
mostly by his own Trucha Publications). Between these two extremes is
Sergio Elizondo who has published consistently, though not prolifically,
over the years. On the other hand, a good many of the early protest poets
followed the path taken by Rodolfo "Corky" Gonzales, whose *I Am Joaquín*
stands alone in his poetic oeuvre, and virtually ceased publishing after one
or two works. Among these were José Angel Gutiérrez, Guadalupe Saav-
edra, Marcela Trujillo, and Evangelina Vigil. Nevertheless, by their very
presence in the national *raza* literary landscape, all of these writers joined
those others discussed in this chapter to help forge a new American poetic
metal, *de bronce*, of course, one traceable to Homer and to Nezahualcóyotl,
to Cervantes and to Shakespeare, to Sor Juana and to Whitman, and
especially to the America that is Aztlán and México as well as the United
States. Ricardo Sánchez recently wrote that three of these early poets
(Abelardo Delgado, Nephtalí de León, and Raúl R. Salinas) "gave voice and
shape to Chicano history. . . [and] created a poetic existential statement
based on. . . a love which goes beyond the self."[35] Surely Sánchez's
summation applies to all the writers, himself included, mentioned in this
chapter.

Accordingly, the protest poetry characterized as Phase I Chicano poetry
(not all of which, of course, could be addressed in these pages) holds many
features in common. Thematically, polar oppositions figure prominently in
this work, in particular the Us/Them polarity which serves as an abbreviation for the concept of "internal colonialism" to explain the politically
disadvantaged status of Chicanos in the United States.[36] The other central
Phase I theme concerns *raza* identity—its nature, its recovery from under
layers of colonialist wrappings, its definition, and its redefinition. Formally, Phase I poetry departs radically from any linguistic norm north or
south of the Mexican border in its assertive use of Spanish, English,
bilingual dialects, and widely varying combinations of these. However,
despite the radical approach to language, this work is by far the most

conventional of Chicano poetry in the appearance of rhyme, strict meter, and regular stanza patterns. Also common to Phase I form is the frequency of appearance of the second person imperative verb form which is especially compatible with the loud stridency so often found in the verse. And this loudness is compatible, too, with the raw ebullience that still invigorates many of these poems, some nearly two decades old. In sum, the protest poetry addressed in this chapter is generally strongest in its literal statement of meaning and weakest in its overall aesthetic composition. By contrast, later phases of Chicano poetry offer a poetic lyricism that cannot be easily be dissected into categories of meaning and aesthetic craftsmanship, into theme and form; in other words, structure and content intertwine, often seamlessly, in the later poetry.

## NOTES

1. Others have traced these excesses and social abuses to the post-Baconian, post-Cartesian world with its insatiable need for vast reserves of labor. See, for example, the Friedrich Engels classic *The Origin of the Family*; John K. Galbraith, *Economics and the Public Purpose* (Boston: Houghton Mifflin, 1973), and Raymond Williams, *Marxism and Literature* (Oxford, England: Oxford University Press, 1977).

2. This figure is taken from Gonzales, *I Am Joaqín* (New York: Bantam Books, 1972 [1967 first copyright]), 2. Subsequent references to the poem will appear parenthetically within the text.

3. Another poet, Ricardo Sánchez, helped write the script for the 1978 film, *Entelequía*, produced by Juan Salazar, but although some of Sánchez's poetry is heard in the film, it is not based entirely on his verse.

4. C. Hugh Holman, *A Handbook to Literature*, 3rd ed. (Indianapolis,: Ind. Bobbs-Merrill, 1972), 194.

5. Ibid., 194.

6. Following standard literary practice in quoting poetry within a prose text, a verse line is indicated here by a slash, /, immediately following the last word in the line.

7. Carlota Cárdenas de Dwyer, *Chicano Voices: Instructor's Guide* (Boston: Houghton Mifflin, 1975), 16.

8. Juan Rodriguez, "La Busqueda de Identidad y sus motivos en la literatura chicana," in Francisco Jimenez, ed., *The Identification and Analysis of Chicano Literature* (New York: Bilingual Press/Editorial Bilingue, 1979), 170–78.

9. The term "performative utterance" is used by linguist John L. Austin to identify those speech acts that in themselves denote (or achieve) specific acts or changed states—for example, "I will" in the marriage ceremony.

10. Respectively, Arnulfo D. Tréjo, *Bibliografía Chicana; A Guide to Information Sources* (Detroit: Gale Research Co., 1975), 33, and Juan Bruce-Novoa, *Chicano Authors: Inquiry by Interview* (Austin: University of Texas Press, 1980), 16.

11. Fuentes quoted by Luis Leal, "Identifying Chicano Literature," *Modern Chicano Writers* (Englewood Cliffs, N.J.: Prentice- Hall), 4.

12. José Antonio Villarreal R., "Chicano Literature: Art and Politics from the Perspective of the Artist," in Jiménez, ed., *Identification and Analysis of Chicano Literature*, 165.

13. Cárdenas de Dwyer, *Chicano Voices*, 16.

14. Zamora in Bruce-Novoa, *Chicano Authors*, 217.

15. Delgado in Bruce-Novoa, *Chicano Authors*, 100.

16. Delgado, "Abelardo on Abelardo," unpublished xerox pamphlet (Denver, Colo. n.d.), n.p.

17. Delgado, *Chicano: 25 Pieces of a Chicano Mind* (Denver, Colo.: Barrio Publications, 1969), 32.

18. Bruce-Novoa, *Chicano Authors*, 12.

19. Delgado, *25 Pieces*, 14.

20. Delgado, "To the Minority Health. . . , "It's Cold* (Salt Lake City, Utah Barrio Publications, 1974), 85: subsequent references to this edition will be made in the text.

21. The Academia de la Nueva Raza, originally "Academia de Aztlán," was founded in New Mexico in 1969 to promote *raza* culture.

22. Sánchez, "Soledad," *Canto y Grito Mi Liberación* (New York: Anchor Books, 1973), 27–30 [first published in El Paso, Tex. Mictla, 1971]; subsequent references to this collection will be made in the text.

23. Sánchez, "[pinto/slammer/joint]," *Hechizospells* (Los Angeles: UCLA Chicano Studies Center Publications, 1976), 41–42; subsequent references to this collection will be made in the text.

24. Delgado even published a chapbook titled *1970—The Year of the Chicano* (Denver, Colo.: Barrio Publications, 1970). Also see Sánchez's "We Have" in *Los Cuatro*, 38; and Raymundo Perez, "Rebirth 1970," *Free, Free at Last* (n.p., n.d.), 28.

25. Montoya interview in Bruce-Novoa, *Chicano Authors*, 134.

26. Ibid.

27. de Hoyos, "Arise, Chicano!" *Arise, Chicano! and Other Poems* (San Antonio, Tex.: M & A Editions, 1975), 12; subsequent references to this editiòn will be made in the text.

28. Perez, "Invisible People," *Phases* (n.p., n.d.), 2: subsequent references to this edition will be made in the text.

29. Perez, *Los Cuatro*, 20.

30. Maldonado, "Under a Never Changing Sun," in Antonia C. Shular et al., ed., *Literatura Chicano, Texto y Contexto* (Englewood Cliffs, N.J., Prentice Hall, 1972), 33; my translations into English. Subsequent references to this edition will be made in the text.

31. Tino Villanueva, *Hay Otro Voz Poems* (New York: Editoria Mensaje, 1972), 38; subsequent references to this edition will be made in the text.

32. George I. Sánchez, "Pachucos, in the Making," *Common Ground* 4:1 (Autumn 1943), 13–20. Carey McWilliams in *North From Mexico* (1948) and Octavio Paz in *Labyrinth of Solitude* (1950) also offered enlightened views on *pachuquísmo* in an era when it was equated with "gangsterism" in the public mind.

33. "There is nothing esoteric about these 'sharp' sartorial get-ups in under-privileged groups, quite apart from their functional aspect. They are often used as a badge of defiance by the rejected against the outside world and, at the same time, as a symbol of belonging to the inner group. It is at once a sign of rebellion and a mark of belonging. It carries prestige." McWilliams, *North from Mexico*, 243.

34. Montoya, "La Jefita," in Toni Empringham, ed., *Fiesta in Aztlán, Anthology of Chicano Poetry*, (Santa Barbara, Calif.: Capra Press, 1982), 20 [first published in 1972].

35. Sánchez, "A Literature by Chicanos: Recapturing a Lost Voice," *Texas Circuit Newsletter* (February/March 1982), 9.

36. "Internal colonialism". . . argues that American political and economic structures hold Chicanos, as they do Third World peoples, in permanent subser-vien[ce]. . . . They are a colonized people, permanent second-class citizens. It also says that conflicts between Chicanos, [B]lacks, and other minority groups are more the result of competition for scarce resources than reflective of cultural differences." See Matt S. Meier and Feliciano Rivera, eds., *Dictionary of Mexican American History* (Westport, Conn.: Greenwood Press, 1981), 175.

# 3

# Chicano Poetry, Phase II: Toward a Chicano Poetics

The indifference to Chicano poetry of the vast majority of the dominant culture's literati has already been noted elsewhere.[1] Despite the beginning of the Chicano Renaissance over sixteen years ago and despite the international recognition (in Europe and South America in particular) of Chicano poetry in the last five years or so, the literary establishment is for the most part still as ignorant of *raza* writing as it was in 1960. A few years ago Felipe de Ortego y Gasca observed that none of the recent books purporting to deal with contemporary American poetry which he had surveyed contained any mention of any Chicano writers. The most recent volume Ortego y Gasca listed was Poulin's widely used *Contemporary American Poetry* published in 1975.[2] Unfortunately, the situation has not changed appreciably. My survey of books of or about allegedly "contemporary American" verse reveals the same ignorance and neglect,[3] a condition especially ironic in view of the literary establishment's instant acclaim of the memoirs of the self-described "scholarship boy Rich-heard Rodree-guess," the Phyllis Schlafly/Jerry Falwell of the Chicano intelligentsia.[4] Accordingly, an observation by influential U.S. critic Donald Hall about Black poetry is salient in this context.

A world of [B]lack poetry exists in America alongside the world of [W]hite poetry, exactly alike in structure—with its own publishers, bookstores, magazines, editors, anthologists, conferences, poetry readings—and *almost entirely invisible to the {W}hite world*. Like the rest of the [B]lack world. . . .

The world of [B]lack poetry seems to be thriving. I find it hard to judge these poems, as if I were trying to exercise my taste in a foreign language, which I am. . . . [This poetry] is a poetry of character, attending to qualities like courage, defiance and tenderness. I suspect that a great deal of the best American poetry of the last third of our century will be written by [B]lack Americans.[5]

If one were to substitute *"raza"* or "Hispanic" wherever Hall refers to
Blacks, the citation's description would still be accurate. Although Chicano
poets are not forced to disseminate their work through a *samizdat* underground, they are by and large required to rely on a network of alternative
presses, which means that the quality of the final product is uneven at best
and that the audience is patchy and small—never the national readership
the work deserves, just like the *samizdat* audience. (It must be pointed out,
however, that Iron Curtain writers have often even fared better—in terms
of U.S. publication and distribution—than Chicanos native to the so-called
free world.)

Still there is cause for joy: the Establishment's neglect did not abort the
birth of the Chicano Renaissance. Indeed, as this and subsequent chapters
attest, despite its fairly recent onset, one arm of the Renaissance, Chicano
poetry, has persisted and flourished. In fact, some poets—notably Alurista—who were part of the genesis of Chicano poetry demonstrated back in
the 1960s the amazing talents and possibilities within the new literary
movement. That the work of these writers transcended political protest
poetry in a narrow sense explains the exclusion of most of them from the
previous chapter. Yet it should be stressed that most of them were writing
contemporaneously with the Phase I poets, though it is the work of these
Phase II poets which led directly and forcefully to a genuine Chicano
poetics.

In determining the nature of that poetics—that is, the aesthetic principles that set Chicano poetry off from other schools or movements—it is
useful to return to an idea referred to in Chapter One, the "logic of
aesthetics" discernible in a given poet's work. In the strongest writers this
creative logic is always distinctive and usually internally consistent. The
poetry of William Carlos Williams, for example, discloses an unwavering
concern for concreteness and precision in both idiom and image, a concern
matched by a conscientious effort to avoid any trace of abstraction and
literariness. The example of Pablo Neruda's work reveals a similar consistency of both technique (spare, quiet diction in natural speech-like
rhythms) and theme (the recovery of a subrational, preconscious memory of
"what we were" before we were born).[6] In both cases, these distinctive
characteristics give each poet's work its special definitive character, and *how*
these characteristics determine that character forms what I am calling the
poet's logic of aesthetics. Accordingly, to understand Chicano poetics we
must understand the logic of aesthetics informing the poetry of Alurista,
who, along with Abelardo Delgado and Ricardo Sánchez, has written and

published uninterruptedly since the first appearance of *I Am Joaquín* in the late 1960s. Although other poets have influenced the evolution of Chicano poetry and, thus, the shape and substance of its poetics, Alurista's work is fundamental in providing the very terms used to define the field. Consequently, this chapter is to a great degree devoted to the analysis of Alurista's first two books, for they helped establish the basic elements of Chicano poetics. For convenience, these elements may be divided into three categories—language, symbolism, and ritual—which will be discussed in generic terms before specifically addressing Alurista's *Floricanto en Aztlán* and *Nationchild Plumaroja*. It should be underscored that most often in the poetry itself these three dimensions cohere indivisibly.

The first category, language, is distinguished by its most apparent feature—its bilingualism, Spanish/English and English/Spanish. But that is only if one is not looking or listening very hard, for if one is attentive, what is most readily apparent is its *multi*lingualism, its polyphonic codes of sound and sense, its complex use of at least six different language systems:

1. Standard edited American English.

2. English slang (regional vernaculars including Black English).

3. Standard Spanish.

4. Dialectal Spanish (regional vernaculars including *caló*).

5. English/Spanish or Spanish/English bilingualism.

6. An amalgam of pre-American indigenous languages, mostly noun forms in Nahua and Mayan.

Moreover, Chicano poetry manifests a variety of combinations of these six systems so that a given poem could very likely be written in a seventh combination form language, while another poem could be written in yet another combination form and so on. The point is that the phonological, morphological, syntactic, and semantic possibilities of Chicano poetry are astonishingly flexible and extensive.

The linguistic elements of Chicano poetics comprise more than just lexicons of words employed to give the poetry cultural authenticity or a flavor of a particular region or community. Rather, for Alurista and most other Chicano poets, *as for a great many native bilinguals*, the first five -lects above are an absorbed aspect of their total repertoire of knowledge, which means that their multilingualism is an externalization of their consciousness. On the other hand, acquired more formally, the sixth form is an adopted lexicon of Indian terms, concepts, and names that Chicano poets adapt more self-consciously into a poetic vocabulary much as Pound integrated Orientalist elements into his work as a result of his translations of, primarily, the poetry of Li Po. Unlike the other five language systems, the pre-Columbian vocabulary is not one generally shared by most *raza*— a circumstance which, in fact, explains why Alurista (and also Luis Valdez of El Teatro Campesino) used it: they sought to recover sources of the Chicano *mestizaje* in origins untouched by Anglo, Northern European influence.[7] It was a nativist, or more precisely, an indigenist ideological awakening during the *Movimiento's* earliest signs of national momentum. As Guadalupe Valdés Fallis has pointed out, Chicano poets employ bilingual forms for a number of reasons, but one of the most important is the *foregrounding*—"the use of . . . language in such a way that its use itself attracts attention"—that is achieved.[8] This is particularly true of Chicano poetry's incorporation of the pre-American amalgam into its literary idiom.

Language is the only skin we share. We each have our very own epidermis just as we each have our very individual idiolect. But language is the only universally shared system that can cover every facet of human experience, just as our skin covers us throughout a lifetime of multitudinous experience. Language is the only skin large enough for us to share, but when we try to objectify it for empirical analysis the result is much like Don Fausto's experience in *The Road to Tamazunchale* when he peeled off his skin at the beginning of his *viaje* to self- discovery and found that its mass was so small he could place it in the palm of his hand.[9] The narrow objectivist study of language sometimes yields about as much as Don Fausto's skin: a palmful of alphabet representing a taxonomy of phonemes. Language is the only skin we share, but it is vastly, complexly more than the skin itself, past and present, actual and imagined. Hence, to comprehend the nature of that experience as captured in Chicano poetry requires that the linguistic analysis of the poetry be supplemented by consideration of its two other important categories, its *symbolism* and its *ritual*.

The category of symbolism in Chicano poetry falls into four broad areas: (1) the pre-American, (2) *mestizaje*, (3) *el Movimiento*, and (4) the non-*raza* Other (especially the Establishment). Taken from historical and anthropological sources dealing with indigenous life in what is now known as Mesoamerica, pre-American symbols on one level convey specific information about life in the Western hemisphere before European influences became pervasive. On other levels, however, these symbols convey more abstract meaning. They communicate a sense of the uninterrupted continuum of human experience from the earliest legends about Aztlán to the Chicano adaptations of the meaning of Aztlán for contemporary purposes— a millennium's span in time, a continent's span in space. They also convey a dissatisfaction with and, often, a rejection of the post-Baconian Western European worldview that gave rise to the Industrial Revolution and to post-Industrial mass culture and middle-class conformity. On this level, the symbolism evinces a political cast that goes beyond the ideological protestations of Phase I poetry. In addition, pre-American symbolism has philosophical import, conveying meanings and qualities derived from pre-Columbian mythology and cosmology. Because their full meaning obtains solely from the total poem context, it is slightly misleading to cull a list of symbols from the poetry and label them "pre-American symbols." Nevertheless, such enumeration can serve a helpful analytic function. Accordingly, the main symbols of this category are Aztlán, *bronce*, cactus, eagle, *flor y canto*, pyramids, el Quinto Sol, and serpents—all of which may be represented in several of the six language codes discussed earlier.

A second group of symbols found in Chicano poetry arise out of *el pueblo* as it exists today, and these relate to the culture's *mestizaje*, the genetic blending of Indian with Spanish racial features and the bi-culturalism that results from that blending. As indicated earlier, Chicanos have increasingly come to use the term more comprehensively than its original meaning to refer to the syncretion of all the manifold cultural elements present within the culture, including not only the Indian and Spanish but also the Moorish influences in Spain from the eighth to thirteenth centuries and the Anglo-American from the modern period.[10] Rudolfo Anaya's fiction and El Teatro Campesino's drama, for example, exemplify this new *mestizaje* through the multiply hybrid nature of their subjects, themes, and styles.[11] Chicano poets use mestizo features to evoke (and sometimes to arouse) *raza* nationalism, to obtain realism, and to abbreviate figuratively as in synecdoche. *Mestizaje* in the poetry appears in a number of forms, the most central being use of a bilingual or multilingual idiom and reference to *raza* food and folkways, to customs, religion, and to history which evidences a recognizable synthesis of the many cultures out of which Chicanos emerged.

The two remaining areas of symbolism in Chicano poetry both stem directly from the ideological bases of the Chicano Movement. One set of symbols is taken directly from the rhetoric and history of *el Movimiento* itself. Terms like *huelga*, *¡sí se puede!*, UFW, *El Plan de Aztlán*, the Courthouse Raid, Crystal City, and the RUP, for example, immediately call to mind events and people that formed the very heart and life of the

Movement, and these appear, usually synecdochically, to suggest those dynamics. Related to these symbols is the second set referring to "the Establishment." Most often these symbols are formulaic and stereotypic as in Them, the Man, the Machine, *la Gaba*, Coca-Cola, and ameriKa. The effect is to reduce the value of the dominant culture in a way that exposes its weaknesses and simultaneously transforms its power over the ethnic poor into a more manageable reality. Oftentimes, symbols from these two patterns appear together to convey the thematic polarities that figure so strongly in Phase I poetry.

The third category of elements which help define Chicano poetics concerns ritual, understood both in its usual lexical sense as "a set form or system of rites, religious or otherwise"[12] and in its ethnopoetic sense as the intersection of primitive, communal, and shamanistic impulses. This ethnopoetic dimension conforms with the post-modern rejection of the Eliotic emphasis on the poem-qua-text. Thus comprehended, ritual in Chicano poetry comprises an array of tendencies congruent with those found in the post-Projectivist poetry of Allen Ginsberg, Gary Snyder, Jerome Rothenberger, and others.[13] One of these tendencies perceives the poem as a total field consisting of the performance or reading of the work, the engagement of the poet with the audience during performance, and, of course, the prepared verse. Important to this perception is the relevance of features traditionally* seen as "non-poetic" but which, here, are deemed crucial to the total field. Features like the physical setting of the reading/performance, the arrangement of space between poet/performer and audi-ence/performers, and the use of such non-verbal aids as music, dance, and stage props—all emphasize the poem as existing solely in relation to the Other (the non-poem) and, thus, in relation to the larger universe.[14] Just as preprint communal societies viewed art only in relation to something else—religious rite or tribal unity, for instance, which are integrated within the entire tribal community—Chicano poets with affinities for this ritual dimension consider their poetry as bound to (if not inseparable from)

---

*Ethnopoetics rejects the Eliotic view of poetic tradition which sees the poem almost exclusively as a text (on paper) amenable to exhaustive critical analysis (on paper). "[W]e can't restrict [tradition] to a monolineal inheritance, but have to use it in a new sense as 'discovery' or 'map': a mapping of those times & places, simply those works in which envisioning occurred. These can include the 'Western' classics as presumably familiar ground, but should in no sense be taken as culminating in them. And the beginnings would be as far back as we can see them . . . to Lascaux . . . to 'Siberian and American Indian traditions' [which] bring us back to something universal maybe: the last truly intercontinental culture. . . . This is the source of that '*mainstream* of poetry that goes back to the old tribes & has been carried forward by the great subterranean culture'—*the* tradition if I were finally to name it."[15]

the performance context. Furthermore, like their primitive counterparts, shamans, priests, and medicine men, these Chicano poets recognize that the poetic vocation perceived in terms of ritual confers other than aesthetic responsibilities upon them, responsibilities having to do with visionary, healing, unifying, and related purposes vis-à-vis the "tribe," in this case *la raza en Aztlán*.

From this discussion of the language, symbolism, and ritual of Chicano poetry we can isolate the following characteristics of Chicano poetics. *It is multilingual*. This characteristic promotes both social verisimilitude and literary foregrounding in the poetry. *It is symbolic in an identifiably Chicano way*. Its symbols stem, for the most part, from the culture's pre-American heritage, from contemporary *mestizaje*, from Movement history and values, and from the culture's experience of the dominant society defined largely in colonialist terms. *It is grounded in ritual*. Both in its overt replication of a communal rite through the poem/performance and in its recognition of an ethnopoetic tradition extending from the present to the primitive past, Chicano poetry is most fully comprehensible within a context of ritual. These characteristics of Chicano poetics derive directly out of the poetry, and although not every poet or poem exhibits every one of these features, in general we find aspects of them (singly and combined) throughout the work, including much of Phase I poetry where it appears in rudimentary form.

By 1970, three years after the first publication of *I Am Joaquín*, Chicano poets were finding the limitations of American literary orthodoxy unsuitable for effective representations of Chicano experience. At first, most poets tried to fit their subjects to the requirements of the monolingual, monocultural expectations of the dominant literary perspective, whether of the United States or of Mexico and Latin America, but the deficiencies of that approach quickly rendered it inadequate. Out of these initial frustrations and also out of the energy and promise of the Movement emerged the qualities and principles just described as constituting a Chicano poetics, a description possible only from the erudite vantage point of hindsight. Hence, the title of this chapter is *"Toward* a Chicano Poetics"—(the preposition indicating incipience, tentativeness, and, most importantly, process, for during this phase writers were actively seeking the forms and terms most appropriate to their craft. They were seeking to go beyond the bald political assertions and emotions characteristic of Phase I verse, aiming instead to capture most fully the multidimensionality of *chicanismo* and its complex life in the contemporary world. Looking back we can see that the progress of Chicano poetics was indeed forward, an advancement, but only because of the willingness of the poets to move both backwards in time and sensibility as well as to move diffusively as artists, eclectically picking up techniques from all quarters as long as they could be brought to bear on Mexican America.[16] In sum, Phase II poetry reveals a clearcut tropism toward a Chicano poetics.

## ALURISTA

More and more one finds references calling Alurista "the poet laureate" of *la raza*,[17] a tribute meant to honor him by bestowal of the highest accolade available to him: the title of the preeminent poet of his entire people. Although this praise and the motivations behind it are understandable and, even, perhaps, laudable, they are nonetheless somewhat inappropriate, for the label itself, *poet laureate*, comes out of the Western European heritage and tradition that Alurista has been rebelling against throughout his professional life.[18] Moreover, in recent times poet laureates have not often been the most creative, most exciting poets of their eras—think of laureates Alfred Austin and Robert Bridges who wrote contemporaneously with William Butler Yeats, the greater writer.[19] Alurista is closer to a *tlamatinime* or *curandero*, to a trickster or *tortillero*, or, simply, to a *poetamaestro*, all enviable, respected figures of great talent and estimable power and, importantly, all rooted in *el mestizaje*.

Born Alberto Baltazar Urista Heredia in Mexico City in 1947, Alurista discovered his vocation as a poet and established his *nom de plume* in his early twenties. Nothing is known about the relation of his pen name to his poetry, but it is strikingly congruent with his basic style. In its blending of forms—"Alurista" from his first and third names—and in its abbreviated compactness—eight letters out of an original twenty-eight and four syllables out of thirteen—the pen name reflects the same linguistic and cultural blendedness and compact brevity found in his poetry. The adopted name also underscores the poet's perception of his self-identity in terms related to the stylizations of his craft. Names and naming are clearly important to Alurista as a glance at the names of his children—Tizoc, Maoxiim, Zamna, and Zahi—and the titles of his books—*Floricanto*, *Nationchild Plumaroja*, *Timespace Huracan*, *Spik in glyph?*, and *Dawn's Eye*—attest. No "José" or "María" or *Poems* or *Obras* for him. His life and his art are extensions and interweavings of each other, and he is particularly conscious of the value of personal myth to the artist.

*I was born* in the womb of my mother. *I emerged from the belly of my mother.* As to when, it was after nine months, like everybody else. I don't like to get into date and place of birth; *it identifies one in a manner which to me seems unreal.* What really counts is the experience and the creativity that one is able to derive from it, *don't you think?* . . . where I was born . . . *has no real importance, though* . . . *I was born in the Lake of Texcoco in* what is known today as Mexico City . . . [Italics in the original indicate translations from Spanish.][20]

Like, say, Whitman, Ginsberg, and even Borges, Alurista's personal story cannot be separated from his work as can the private and literary lives of, say, Eliot, Williams, and Paz. This connectedness, this cultivated unity of private and public, has implications for the poet's style, and it was apparent in Alurista's first significant publication, *El Ombligo de Aztlán* (1971).

An anthology of student writing co-edited with Jorgé Gonzalez, *Ombligo* was designed as a forum for "non-degreed people" in a credentials-conscious society.[21] Although *Ombligo* cannot be viewed as a major part of the Alurista canon, it and Alurista's work in it exhibit certain distinguishable features that, with later refinements, ramify into a distinct poetics. First, the book's textual format highlights the poetry and minimizes individual authorship in a way that suggests that the thematic unity of the messages is more important than their particular individuality. This democratic leveling establishes a creative connectedness among the writers and work that parallels the fraternity theme, *carnalismo*, on which the book is centered. Second, although about half of Alurista's eleven poems are written somewhat conventionally in either Spanish or English, the other half are bilingual Spanish/English, not a formally accepted literary idiom in 1971. Moreover, the last of Alurista's pieces appearing in the volume, "me retiro con mis sueños" (*Ombligo*, 76), foreshadows the poet's later multilingualism and pre-Columbian symbolism. Another poem, "day and fire," also contains allusions to the Amerindian past. An additional stylistic foreshadowing in *Ombligo* relates to Alurista's use of chant-like repetition (as in "el carnalismo nos une" [viii] and "got to be on time" [40]), a device that is especially effective in a reading and one that looks ahead to his later concern with ritual and with poem as performance. These features, then, while rudimentary and undeveloped, nevertheless point to the poet's later direction.[22]

That direction is more clearly charted in *Floricanto en Aztlán* (1971), the first collection of Alurista's poetry to be published. To permit a thorough discussion of this seminal work, the ordering principle followed here repeats that used earlier in the generic analysis of Chicano poetics. That is, the explications and general discussions of the poems are organized according to the three broad groupings—language, symbolism, and ritual—mentioned earlier and, of course, within each part of this trinity occur the other subcategories also discussed above. Before doing this, however, let us examine the inscription to *Floricanto* which is taken from Carlos Castañeda's *The Teachings of Don Juan*, a source that appears a number of times in Alurista's corpus and that partially indicates the range of his reading, acknowledged to be vast and voracious.[23]

Fear! A terrible enemy—treacherous, and difficult to overcome. It remains concealed at every turn of the way, prowling, waiting. And if the man, terrified in its presence, runs away, his enemy will have put an end to his quest.

Don Juan, from his teachings.

The choice of this inscription is interesting, for although it does not illuminate the poetry itself, it does suggest that spirit in which many of the poems were written and in which they are dedicated to his audience. It is a spirit of fraternal lore and guidance—*carnalismo*—directed, as he says in "el carnalismo nos une," to his "raza, raza, raza, raza," the "pueblo ascendiente" of the future (*Ombligo* xi) which he addresses throughout *Floricanto*. In addition, the Castañeda epigraph here (and also in *Nationchild Plumaroja*) bears witness to the poet's personal struggle with fear, and "Castañeda has, obviously, had a profound influence upon . . . this Chicano poet. Knowledge is power in Alurista's scheme of things, and Castañeda's *Yaqui Way of Knowledge* has helped him name his way and his enemies: Fear, Clarity, Power, and Old Age."[24] *Floricanto* is a testament to the efficacy of the poet's rite of passage.

## Language

"Although it is impossible to be sure that Alurista is the first contemporary Chicano poet to compose poems from selective mixtures of Spanish, English, and 'Chicanismos,' he is certainly one of the pioneers."[25] And he was also a "pioneer" and a seminal innovator (with Luis Valdez) in the use of pre-American words, names, and concepts, a practice that greatly expanded the possibilities of Chicano poetic language. As Gary Keller points out, "[o]f all our poets perhaps Alurista has been the most deliberately mindful of multilingualism."[26] To be sure, in *Floricanto* we find examples of five of the six linguistic modes described in this chapter's introduction.

The monolingual pieces* in the book share a few similarities, most strikingly their surrealistic imagery. Two of the monolingual Spanish poems, *"the pores of my skin"* and *"i shun {others} like the owl,"** contain dreamlike images and bizarre word combinations, and all present their subjects in the free flowing associational manner that denies conventional logic. The same techniques appear in the monolingual English poem, "sacred robe," where the speaker's perception of the sun, "crimson/blown by the wind—rimmed with gold," merges with his apprehension of his shadow "walking down with me/ to light my path." This moment of solitude in nature, "—out the sacred cove/ four worlds, four ways, four winds" so awes him that he weeps "of joy" (57). Likewise in *"songs of the old frogs"* Alurista achieves a surreal effect of heightened illusion by presenting his subject, sorrow at the passing of primitive traditions, through a series of surreal associations like *"lakes of bitterness"*; *"slimey tombs"*/ *"ancient thrones"*; *"emerald tears"*/ *"frogsong."* Although the surrealism of these poems derives mostly from their subjects and symbolism, it is also reinforced by the monolingual idiom itself. Reliance on one language uninterrupted by codeswitching when other poetic choices are available represents a linguistic evenness and consistency that allows the poet to engage in the fullest freedom in his choices of imagery. In other words, the comparative simplicity of monolingualism within a polyglot context balances off the semantic complexities of Alurista'a surrealistic images.

Oppositely, in a number of poems, Alurista employs a bilingual code combined with dialectical forms to achieve a broken, disrupted idiom compatible with the themes in those poems. For instance, in "cat walked in" the subject of hunger and deprivation within an affluent society is underscored by the English/Spanish/Black English diction. Suggesting the callous insensitivity of U.S. institutions is the standard English of the "chick" behind "the desk," and representing human need and desperation are the Spanish and Black English of the two unemployed "brothers" (66).

---

*The poems are "sacred robe" (*Floricanto*, 57); "Once, I wrote a letter to Emiliano" (58); "cantos de ranas viejas" (73); "los poros de mi piel" (74); "lanchas carnes" (81); and "me rehuzo como el buho" (82). In discussing the Spanish-language pieces here and subsequently, I use my own English translations when referring to or quoting from them, and the italics signal the translation.

**For the convenience of the reader, throughout this book I have translated most of the Spanish in the poetry into English. However, in acknowledgment of the original Spanish and also to give the reader a sense of the original text, the translated passages are italicized. Spanish is retained when the meaning can be gleaned from the context or when an English translation would greatly distort the meaning.

> cat walked in. said. . . .
> jig i need. i's here. to do. a jig to get. . . .
>> *my legs hurt*
>> *—i didn't sleep last night*
>> *empty pockets*
>> *—without change*
>> a jig i need.
> a chick. a desk. with glasses i see. . . .
> she. sitting stared. sit, an order from her
> mouth. "sit. and take a number. wait." to wait? . . .
>>>>                             (*Floricanto*, 66)

As the passage indicates, the trilingual codeswitching emphasizes the class separation between the bureaucrat behind the desk and the destitute clients in front of it. But it also heightens the *carnalismo* between the two men which surfaces at the end of the poem when the "other brother" says " 'brother, you hungry? want jig? have bread.' sin centavos he ate" (66). Similarly in "allá ajüera" ("outside, over there"), the slang magnifies the vulnerability of the barrio mother and son in the face of the overwhelming social odds against them. "why am i here/ . . . wanna go play/ (no mijo, tene que trabajar)/ porque mama/ yo tambien/ . . . quero jugar/ quero vivir/ allá . . . " (83). Use of the vernacular instead of a more formal, conventional idiom represents the estrangement of the speaker's family from the conventional bourgeois comforts of U.S. society. The diminutive form "diocito" used later in the poem also underscores the natural bond between the mother and son and their innocent trust in God, as if they shared a private code.

Two of the most successful bilingual poems in *Floricanto* are "when raza?" and "address," both widely known and anthologized. The poems are written in a very simple, elemental bilingual form lacking the metaphorical richness and occasional obscurity characteristic of Alurista's more typical style. Built around the stereotype of the lazy, procrastinating Mexican whose middle name is reputedly "mañana," "when raza?" addresses the theme of time with Alurista urging on "la gente" a Marvellian message: "now, ahorita define tu mañana hoy" (1). Here, the simplicity of the bilingual code, which includes repetitions and immediate translations, suggests a strong concern for clarity of communication. The poet seemed to seek contact with every possible segment of "la Raza" in order to heighten awareness of the need for political activism on behalf of Chicano causes. In this, "when raza?" contains most of the features of Phase I political protest poetry.

Linguistic simplicity, even to the point of formulaic minimalism, also occurs in "address" where the entire English-language section is composed solely of nouns, without verbs, articles, or any trace of normal syntax. The Spanish section, on the other hand, is written with grammatical completeness, contributing to an even stronger bilingual contrast.

    address
    occupation
    age
    marital status
    —perdone . . .
            yo me llamo pedro
    telephone
    height
    hobbies
    previous employers . . .
    —perdone mi padre era
            el señor ortega
            (a veces don josé)
    race

Through the dramatic bilingual contrast, Alurista emphasizes the striking disparity between Pedro Ortega and the dominant society's perceptions, experiences, and cultures. Like "cat walked in" and "allá ajüera" the poem deals with the insensitivity of a bureaucracy which has become as impersonal as the machine-produced forms it uses as a substitute for a genuine dialogue with the people it is supposed to serve. Especially effective is the poem's ending with its careful placement of "race" in isolation as the last line to draw attention to the fundamental significance of race and racism in American society. By isolating "race" this way, Alurista confirms what the rest of the poem implicitly suggests—that, despite the strengths and richnesses of his culture, Señor Ortega is precluded from socioeconomic opportunities because of one thing, his race, the same thing that separates him from the bureaucracy and the dominant culture that produced it.

The sixth linguistic mode in Chicano poetry is that derived from some of the strengths and richnesses of Señor Ortega's culture, the Amerindian sources which Alurista pioneered during the first stirrings of the *raza* literary renaissance. In their subjects, allusions, and imagery, most of the work in *Floricanto* is directly affected by the Amerindian sources, but consideration of two titles will suffice to illustrate here the effect of Amerindia on Alurista's poetic diction: "a cualquier hora" ("at any hour")

and "grietas paredes" ("cracked walls"). The Amerindian amalgam in these
poems consists primarily of names and words from Nahuatl—like, in the
first instance, Teotihuacan, Tlaloc, Ométéotl, Quetzalcóatl, and in the
second, feathers/plumas, sacrificial heart, and bronce/bronze. However,
this combination idiom also contains certain more complex pre-American
concepts that are expressed in Spanish and/or in English—for example, the
*guerreros*, the sacrifices to Tlaloc, and an array of myths associated with the
designated deities.

Accordingly, in *"at any hour"* Alurista alludes to the ancient Mesoamerican city of Teotihuacan, to the Aztec rain god Tlaloc, and to the
Aztec goddess of motherhood Tonantzin. These allusions serve to establish
an uninterrupted continuum of time and habit from the primordial past of
Teotihuacan when "la cucaracha pray[ed]/ for bread" to the dawn of modern
history and the 1517 miracle of "juan diego/ *and the* virgen de guadalupe"
(34). To underscore the fundamental nature of metaphyscal meanings
within universal human experience, the poet links the ancient "sacrificial"
offerings "to tlaloc/ [of] *the hearts of maidens"* with the Virgin Mary's
miraculous gift of "red roses/ to juan diego" (34). Through this linkage,
Alurista shows the hearts of human sacrifice and the Virgin of Guadalupe's
roses as originating in the same primal mythic urge. In addition, *"at any
hour"* manifests the Amerindian idiom through its references to such
customs and concepts as the "feather shielded warriors" who call to mind
the Flower Wars of pre-Cortesian Anahuac.[27] This allusion also brings into
relief the destructive extremes of religious faith and blind devotion to
religious custom.

The same stylized linguistic code appears in *"cracked walls"* where
Alurista refers to Éhecatl, the wind spirit manifestation of Quetzalcóatl; to
Ométéotl, the supreme creator representing male/female duality; to Tonat-
iuh, our present epoch of El Quinto Sol (Fifth Sun); and to Quetzalcóatl,
the most revered Aztec deity credited with the origin of love, art,
agriculture, astronomy, and crafts.[28] Through these allusions Alurista
illustrates the continuing presence of the autochthonous heritage. He
challenges today's *raza*, addressed in the personal second person verb form
"tu" to discover their native classic roots: "*(have you forgotten)* . . . *do you
remember?* . . . *God's breath/—the aquarian éhecatl"* (71). Whether or not
Chicanos "remember," the poet nonetheless asserts that

— Ométéotl molded you . . .
in your veins grow [quetzal] feathers

—and quetzalcóatl adorns himself
your children play marbles . . .
—you were born
    you were born and you are
mud
    bronze mud in your profile
and in your cracked walls [skulls] (71; original entirely Spanish)

In sum, both poems convey the central thought that mythical archetypes remain within the racial memory forever and that vestiges of them surface throughout time "at any hour," even in the contemporary "urbanity" of "asphalt" and "cracked walls." The shaman-poet's goal is to pry loose these mythic archetypes from underneath the layers of Euro-American values that have buried the Amerindian aspects of the mestizo for centuries.

As this discussion of literary multilingualism in *Floricanto* indicates, Alurista's "use of language is another way of being revolutionary [and his] linguistic expansionism itself . . . [is] a poetic alternative to common communication."[29] He perceives language not as a mere medium (except in the McLuhanesque sense that equates it with meaningful content) or instrument of communication, but as a system of possibilities—structural, metaphorical, philosophical, political, and so on—possibilities that mirror *raza* culture and heritage even as they transcend them. In poet Robert Creeley's phrase, "form is nothing more than the extension of theme."[30] And language to Alurista is a dynamic, almost self-generating, self-directed exemplification of form.

## Symbolism

The four broad areas of symbolism in Chicano poetry are well represented in Alurista's work, and, in fact, he originated several of them. For example, although some pre-American allusions appear in *I Am Joaquín*, they do not substantively affect Gonzales' basic style. And whereas *Ombligo de Aztlán* does contain some references to pre-America, they do not significantly affect the fundamental quality of Alurista's contribution to that anthology. Not until Alurista's *Floricanto* is Amerindian indigenism introduced as a pervasive, integral stylistic quality in U.S. American literature. In a sense (and as Gustavo Segade has observed), Alurista's indigenist philosophy was his "answer to the *problemática* of the Chicano['s]" colonized status.[31] Alurista "attack[ed] Anglo-American values by reaffirming those of the Amerindian cultures. Nature, as Alurista viewed it through Amerindian eyes, included humankind. To 'conquer' nature, as Western man had done, was to destroy humanity itself."[32] Accordingly, pre-American symbolism functions in many *Floricanto* pieces sometimes as a minor stylistic feature of the poetry and sometimes as a central force within the entire body of a given poem. "Minor" indicates that the Amerindian references seldom define or shape the flow of the poem, nor do they usually constitute the artistic center of the piece. Rather, these allusions, like other patterns in them, fit within a thematic framework not directly related to pre-Columbian Mesoamerica.

In "what's happening," for instance, the poet focuses on the ignorance and indifference of the dominant society, personified as "mr. jones," in its relations with ethnic minorities, and he employs pre-American images to express his theme.

> you tell me you care
>     do you . . .
>          mr. jones?
> *the eagle of our pride*
>     is now settled on the cactus of your apathy
> devouring
>     the serpent of inhumanities
> that crawled viciously in your amérika (19)

By alluding to the archetypal Mexican symbols of the eagle, cactus, and serpent associated with the legend of the founding of Tenochtitlán/México City, Alurista simultaneously appeals to *raza "orgullo"* for its heritage and also underscores the longevity of that heritage in comparison with this hemisphere's Anglo antecedents whose cultural archetypes originated on the other side of the Atlantic in Europe. Similarly, in "flesh of your lips," a love poem addressed to the lover whose "bronze skin" and "fragrance" is like Tonantzin's "flowers," the pre-Columbian images form one figurative part of the love theme (41). Interestingly, in alluding to the flowers "on the lap of juan diego," the poet avoids mentioning the Catholic name of the deity in question, the Virgin of Guadalupe, using instead the name of the indigenous goddess, Tonantzin, the native counterpart of *La Virgen*. He thus suggests the primordial nature of his "love" and its affinity with the spiritual love *raza* have for the patron saint of México.[33] Again, in "tizoc left us his hair" the Amerindian emblems join other symbols to convey Alurista's belief that "my ancestry" is "a sacred host," that is, a sacrament (24). Along with the legacy of Tizoc, an early Aztec *tlatoani* (king), Chicanos are also enriched by "the legacy of Zapata/ foliage on our lip" and the Dionysian-like *"revelries of the Yucatecas,"* referring, respectively, to the ubiquitous Mexican moustaches and fiestas. Furthermore, Alurista compares this inheritance to "the mystery of matthew's/ and bach['s] and vivaldi's inventions" (24), thus signifying both the richness of Mexican-American roots and their legitimacy as part of an ancient classical heritage.

Unlike the three previous titles, "flowers in the lake" and "memory of my crickets" can be comprehended *only if* the pre-American symbolism is understood. In the latter poem Alurista presents a personal reminiscence in surrealistic language that taps the Amerindian past without the restraint of logic. The poet uses "crickets" to refer to the way certain private memories persist unnoticed in one's consciousness just as the sound of crickets in an "old marsh" lingers in one's mind on a "cool night" (68). And his recollection, described through free association in surrealistic imagery, takes him back first to the past of his callow youth during the "green moon" and then to the ancient past of "Tenochtitlán and the afternoon/ of hot reality" when the "lake" was "fresh" in the center of Anahuac, the pre-Cortesian name of the valley of central Mexico. Alurista's personal reminiscence thus gives way to a reverie about his people's past and the genesis myth of Tenochtitlán when "the eagle/ devour [ed] a snake/ staring at the sun/ perched on a cactus" (68). But the persistent "crickets of my solitude" return the poet to his youth and to himself recalling the "tender [cactus] fruit/ tropical breeze/ cool night" and, always, the "sad crickets" (68). That Alurista chose crickets instead of cockroaches, one of his (and other Chicano writers', notably Oscar Z. Acosta's) favorite symbols for *raza*, probably stems from the double meaning of the Spanish word *grillo*. It denotes a "cricket" as well as "seed" or "sprout," conveying the poet's concern with the origin—that is, the seed time—of Mexico's past. Likewise, the subject of "flowers in the lake" is the destruction of Tenochtitlán, and both its imagery and its theme reflect Amerindian symbols and history. Alurista links the violence of the city's origin with the violence of its destruction by the Spaniards. By juxtaposing images of tranquil beauty with images of violent carnage, the poet captures the paradox of the mestizo sensibility which was shaped out of both Mexico's natural beauty and indigenous artistic achievements as well as out of the "passion of the tiger," the wasting of human blood.

> flowers in the lake
> and swans

> *the birds and their trilling*
>> the woods and the jungle . . .
>> an eagle settled
> *—devouring a serpent*
> Tenochtitlán . . .
>> *from the ploughshares of* [cacique] *silence*
> *withered flowers*
>> in the lake
>> we bleed
> *torrentially*
>> *warm redness* (39)

In these two works, then, just as in later Aluristian creations, the Amerindian element defines the heart, soul, and flesh of the poem, demonstrating what Mexican literary scholar Salvador Rodríguez Del Pino describes as

un tono innovador y vanguardista a través de la forma poética, ya concientemente creada; . . . Con esta innovación estilística, Alurista crea un vivido mosaico de imágenes duales superimpuestas en varias dimensiones perceptibles solamente al iniciado en la experiencia chicana [an innovative and avant-garde tone through the poetic form, already consciously created; . . . With this stylistic innovation, Alurista creates a vivid mosaic of dual images superimposed upon a variety of dimensions perceptible only to one familiar with Chicano experience].[34]

The second important cluster of symbols in *Floricanto* also partakes of the stylistic innovation cited above. These symbols derive from the distinctive racial and cultural admixture that constitutes *mestizaje*. *Mestizaje* appears in Alurista's work as a dynamic field, a wide and diverse whole comprising a multitude of parts sometimes in compatible harmony and sometimes in conflictive tension. Perhaps it is simplest to state that because Alurista is a mestizo and a poet, his poetry must contain *mestizaje* within it. One poem that effectively conveys Alurista's use of mestizo symbolism is "el pan nuestro" ("our bread") which concerns the gnawing, all-consuming reality of "hunger." Through repetition and Spanish/English bilingualism, the poem's form itself parallels the constancy of "hunger pangs" and a "growling stomach" (52). In especially striking imagery, the poet introduces the family in the poem by referring to their eyes as "balls of cottonfire/ grapefire/ tomatofire/ pizcafire/—stare at beans" (52). The fire in their eyes reflects the fire under the "clay olla" in which the beans are cooking for supper, while the mention of cotton, grape, tomato, and *pizca* (harvest) refers to the crops picked by farmworkers to earn their "daily bread" (52).

In a poignant image the poet observes that the same eyes that reflect the crops all day in the hot sun's "fireharvest" are in the evening *"nailed/ on the beans."* *Mestizaje* informs the poem's diction in such original combinations as pizcafire/fuegopizca, balls of cottonfire/bolas de fuegopizca, and in the word for bread, *pan* (pronounced pAHn) which conjures up its English graphemic equivalent "pan" as in "pot," leading right back to the "clay pot" of "beans" with its hypnotic hold on the hungry family's *"black eyes."* Through these techniques the message communicated in "our bread" is, paradoxically, that lack of food is a common problem for the *campesino* harvesters of the nation's food.

Paradox is also at work in "the man say we making noise" which is built around a generic trait commonly associated with Chicanos, the love of music and dance. As a stereotype this characteristic assumes the form of a slur: Mexicans as lazy, fiesta-loving, irresponsible hedonists causing public disturbances that lead "the man [the police and/or Anglos in general]" to "say we making noise" (99). The paradox is, according to the poem, that "we quiet all the time/ calladitos sin hablar." The quietness is Alurista's way of connoting the lack of political voice, the absence of a listened-to power base, among Chicanos. In the middle third of the poem he also gives one suggestion for noisemaking:

> *make noise broken windows*
> *street fires gasoline in flames*
> *in asphalt* fired up
> *with mariachis*
> *sitting on the ground serenade* relieving *dreams*
> buñuelos *and* piñatas
> *fair* and fire crackers
> cracking skulls no more but running
> *dancing in the streets* (99)

With the line "dancing in the streets" the poet returns to the musical tradition characteristic of *mestizaje*, the "mariachi orquestra corrido," three terms that unite the folkloric with the cultured forms of music, an art form that is greatly valued by the poet. (Music as a subject, musical imagery, composers and musicians, and allusions to songs, all appear frequently in Alurista's work and is discussed below.) He concludes "man say we making noise" ironically: *"much noise/ much fiesta/ when we quiet all the time"* (99). In addition, the poem contains other images of *mestizaje* (e.g., "buñuelos" and "piñatas") to convey a hint of the culture's richness, though "the man" cannot understand, of course, for all "he" can perceive is "we making noise."

Symbols of *mestizaje* are used in "others in the quilt" to again dramatize the social conflict between Chicano and Anglo, but Alurista's approach differs from that in the previous poem in two ways. First, on a structural level, he employs verbals and metrical repetition to create an insistent, percussive quality.

> *the Chicano thinker*
>    *hoarse voice*
> *—exclamations of clay, steel, and bronze*
> *in the mountains*
> *—pearls*
> anglo
>    anglo
>       anglo!
>          anglo!
> to you
>    to say . . .
> the superiority
>    in me found
>    —to a degree
> the degree to which
>    my recognition sees
> that, man,
>    you
> —believe it or not—
>    are equal
>    —to me (61)

The technique of repetition leads directly to the second difference, a thematic one, and that is "to affirm" to the "man" that "he" is "equal" to "Raza" (61). Hence, Anglo society should forget its arrogance and accept the "others in the quilt" of life. That acceptance would in turn lead to the philosophical awareness that "any clay turns out bronze" (61). In other words, the poet finds an apt metonym for the entire species in the mestizo, the bronze synthesis of Old and New Worlds (Vasconcelos' *raza cosmica* again). Alurista bases this belief on the Mayan concept "*in lak'ech* which means 'you are my other self.' And this applies to everything. . . . All things are living . . . in motion. Even if something appears to be static, like this table, science tells us, *as the Mayans told us, no, this table is in full motion. Electrons moving around nuclei. . . . Everything is alive and is part of the whole.*"[35] This is essentially nineteenth-century U.S. transcendentalism in bronzetone, brought up to date by virtue of its drawing its images and ideas out of the autochthonous Occidental past instead of, as Emerson and Whitman did, out of the Orient. He also informally meshes those ideas with concepts from modern physics.

Particularly illustrative of this transcendental *mestizaje* is "el sarape de mi personalidad" ("sarape of my personality") in which the sarape, the universally known emblem of *mexicanidad* represents the "basic/ essentially *fundamental . . . essence of my Raza*" (10). Although Alurista addresses Anglo xenophobia in the poem, that is not his primary concern. Rather, his purpose here is to celebrate the "fantastic colors" and "the radiance of our quilted heritage" which is "life itself" (10). This "spectrum of wool" also constitutes his source of magic as a poet:

> *and with the warm breath of life*
>     *with the rough wool of my sarape*
>         *i activate the seen*
> *and my sun* shines on
>     to propagate
>     the joy of our people (10)

In the last six lines of the poem he introduces an explicitly transcendental metaphor, the "wheel," all inclusive in its circularity and primal in its representation of the "somatic source" of human creativity.

> nuestro sarape
> versatil
>     and masterful
> electrifying warmth of somatic source
> where the objects of form* come
>     la esencia de mi Raza es fundamental
> basic
>     to the chromatic wheel of humanity (10)

The citation exemplifies the poet's belief that, for the Chicano, creative energy and life itself begin within the social matrix of *la raza*. A similar example of transcendental circularity is the poem "las canicas y mis callos" ("marbles and calluses") where playing with the spherical "marbles" and

---

*In *Floricanto* the word "form" is misprinted as "from" which would not be meaningful in the poem's context.

eating the round "tortillas" helped make the speaker "free in the dust/ of/ our marble land/ land rolls/ on round/ round on" (8). Symbols like these signifying a syncretic New World transcendentalism, whole and interdependent, pervade the Aluristian canon.

## Ritual

As explained in this chapter's introduction, Chicano poetics is grounded in ritual, both in its overt replication of a communal rite through the poem/performance and in its ethnopoetic understanding of the primordial impulse still discoverable and attainable in contemporary poetry. *Alurista brought this element to Chicano poetry.* He did this, first, as the primary founder/organizer of the annual literary ritual he christened Festival Flor y Canto. For several years the Festivals were, as Bruce-Novoa has observed, "the major event on the Chicano literary calendar . . . [bringing together] writers—critical and creative, established and unknown—to share their work not only with each other, but also with the Chicano community."[36] Established in 1975 and taking place in various cities of Aztlán, the Festivals eventually even led to the publication of proceedings.[37] Although Alurista has not been active in organizing these annual rites since 1977, his influence was critical in the formative years, and it was motivated by an awareness of the importance of bringing Chicanos/as together regularly to share and celebrate their literature, their heritage, and themselves.

Furthermore and more importantly, Alurista brought the ritual element to Chicano poetics through his work itself. As Tomás Ybarra-Frausto has written,

Experimenting with an indigenous lifestyle, Alurista also experimented with poetry to be sung, chanted, and danced. . . . [A group he belonged to] "Servidores del Arbol de la Vida" (Guardians of the Tree of Life) . . . attempted to re-create Indian chant and ritual singing and dance forms in a modern context. While maintaining a reverent attitude toward the spiritual intent of their performance, they wove a secular sociopolitical commentary into their texts. . . . Playing the conch . . . Alurista developed a style of recitation which is a cross between Gregorian chant and monotone. The intent is to locate poetry not only in the mind but also in the viscera.[38]

Non-textual features like those cited by Ybarra-Frausto emphasize the poem in relation to the Other, the non-poem, and this emphasis unites Alurista's work with that of his primitive counterparts—priests, shamans, healers. This deliberate invoking of the sacred invests it with a social responsibility that extends beyond the aesthetic. Hence, we find abundant allusions to "my Raza," "mi pueblo," and "the people" in *Floricanto*.

Poems that seem especially designed to convey this social responsiblity, and, thus, to stress the ritual quality of his poetry are "fruto de bronce" ("bronze fruit") and "tú sabes" ("you know"). Developed within a series of birth images, "bronze fruit" depends on repetition and short broken lines to achieve its chantlike rhythm.

> i've seen
>> i've seen
> i've seen the bronze child
>> —on his little (round) head,
>> hair locks of black
>> *curled hair*
> *and his mother*
>> *—his mother*
>> *his mother guadalupe*
> i've seen her bronze skin
>> *guadalupe mother*
> *blessed womb*    (53)

With his mention of the *"blessed womb"* the poet immediately links the "bronze fruit" image to a line in the most common Catholic prayer to the Virgin Mary: "and blessed is the Fruit of thy womb, Jesus."[39] The "bronze fruit," now sanctified by this allusion, is none other than "ChicaNos," cleverly made concrete by the uppercase "N" which breaks the word in two to give us "small" (chica) as in "young" and "us" (Nos). Similarly, the second half of the poem recalls another birth "i've seen,"

> *the birth*
> *the birth of my pueblo*
> bronze child
> bronze skin
> bronze virgin
>> i have seen the bronze birth
>> *—the bronze guadalupe*
> *has been delivered to my pueblo . . .*
> i have seen la Raza
>> i have seen la Raza
> i have seen la Raza be born    (53)

Traditionally, the birth of a child is cause for celebration and prayer and
Alurista exploits that fact in this poem by comparing the advent of the
*Movimiento* to first the birth of a child, then to the birth of Jesus Christ, and
finally to the miracle appearance of the Virgin of Guadalupe. In performance, the prayerful language and repetitive meter evoke a visceral,
emotional response that affirms the blessedness of *el pueblo, el fruto de bronce*.

The poem "you know" opens with a similar traditional religious allusion,
but its tone quickly shifts from prayers to politics.

> *you know*
> > *yes*
> *you know well*
> and know
> you know your cheek is red
> and that jesus once said
> the other
> > the other cheek must turn
> to turn is not rejoice
> > in pain
> > do not rejoice but act
> and turn (13)

The cheek-turning must not be "masochistic," says the poet, but strong as
"the human conviction in the luster/ *of your bright eyes*" (13). Moreover, by
referring crossculturally to both the Greek "thanatos" (death) and "medusa
cabeza" (Medusan head) as well as to Christ, Alurista underscores the
powerfully persistent nature of "the hand of injustice/ that has slapped you
once" and will "slap you once again" (13). The repetitive "you know" in
both Spanish and English calls attention to the way suffering produces
knowledge. Despite the relentless injustice, the poet quietly insists that

> you know you have to turn
> > *your already inflamed cheek*
> *you know well that yes*
> > that only then
> today . . .
> > can you hope to have mañana
> graze in the lacerated pastures of your
> > inflamed cheek
> > tú sabes
> > > si
> > tú sabes bien (13)

Here again the poet stresses the power of time by fusing past, present, and future. Ultimately, through the verbal repetition, the Christian allusions, and through use of the familiar second person form "tú," the poet circumscribes a ritual space around himself and the you that is his audience.

That audience is served in a different way in "with liberty and justice for all," a poem that brings out the shamanistic quality of Alurista's verse. By invoking a phrase that represents a publicly revered U.S. principle that nonetheless remains outside the reality of most Chicanos' experience, Alurista, like a shaman with magical powers, seeks to transform the remote principle into a palpably *raza* form. He does this by offering the first ten lines in English and then abruptly codeswitching to Spanish and bilingualism in the last thirteen lines.

> with liberty and justice for all
>     who blind—do not see
> the massacre of our minds
>     in the nation under god . . .
> to police the earth
>     with big sticks
>     to crack skulls . . .
>         —*of those who see* . . .
> no liberty
>     or justice (29)

The shift from English excludes those who do not understand the Spanish and, logically, includes all who understand and "protest" against "the genocide/ of terrestrial creatures" (29). The verbal shifts culminate with the emphatic closing lines referring to the "hunger/ for LIBERTAD,/ MUERTE con 'JUSTICIA' " (29). The conclusion demonstrates the poet's magic in transforming the title phrase from an unrealized ideal to a more accessible *raza* refrain, one that derives from the group's own history and language. In this poem (and also in "oppressive chains," "what's happening . . . " and "chicano infante") the poet purges the hypocrisy of the dominant society from immediate consciousness and in the process unites his audience into a closer-knit *familia* of shared values stemming from shared experience and, importantly, shared language.

Another poem illustrating the ritual aspect in *Floricanto* is "los niños crecen" ("the children grow"), where Alurista takes on the mantle of healer. The poet addresses "Chicano brothers" and asks, in an intensely urgent tone, that they be alert "to the children." He is concerned that they be taught "all the time," a phrase that is repeated six times in English and twice in Spanish in the brief twenty-two line poem (56). Through its repetition alternating with images of "the children," Alurista implicitly offers two explanations for some of *el pueblo*'s social problems: its collective failure to "teach" the children "all the time" and its traditionally cavalier attitude toward time, a theme prominent throughout the collection beginning with "when raza?," the first poem in *Floricanto*. His appeal is personal and pressing in its charge to the group,

> to the children
> teach
>     —all the time
> y la Raza
>     *always*
>     *at all hours . . .*
> *the children grow*
>     all the time
> let their times be doing
>         (time *is* all the time) (56; Alurista's italics of "is")

Unlike the bulk of his *Floricanto* poetry, this ritual invocation is not overlaid with allusions to the past or to the dominant society's role as oppressor. Here the poet is simple and direct in giving a prescription for future social health: teach "los niños" without pause and "define tú mañana hoy" (from "when raza?" p. 1).

As the discussion of *Floricanto* has shown up to this point, Alurista's work exemplifies the three major characteristics of Chicano poetics—its multilingualism, its *raza* symbolism, and its use of ritual—and, indeed, this collection helped define and shape the contours of the entire field. Nevertheless, despite his important achievement within those boundaries, it is a mistake to perceive Alurista and his work as expressive only within this taxonomy. His creativity and originality extend well beyond these categories. Moreover, the catholicity of his taste and sensibility is indicated by the fact that his poetry contains both the array of features discussed in the previous section and knowledgeable references to Greek mythology, the Bible, and also to classical and rock music. The discussion of *Floricanto* therefore concludes with a consideration of representative titles from this other poetry, which stands in somewhat anomalous relation to the three-part organization followed above.

One of these anomalies is "i found the world outside of me," one of the collection's small number of personal poems revealing a private or interior consciousness instead of the usual portrait of the public persona addressing the concerns of the commonweal. Here, Alurista deals with the nature of cognition and the relationship of epistemology to reality. Comprising three major premises, the poem presents them in three parts that move from objective description to greater poetic lyricism. In the first five lines he describes how the mind perceives and processes external reality.

> i found the world outside of me
> to be inside my mind
> to recognize
>     and realize
>         to syncretize (43)

The first person intimacy here provides a welcome departure from the poet's customary public voice of teacher-priest. In the middle ten lines he adds a mystical element to the cognitive process in a Kierkegaardian assertion of faith that is carefully bound to the poet's sense impressions.

> *with the hand of god*
>     —on your head
> settled
>     soft
>         simmering
>             song
>                 salutes
>                     solidified
>                         sun (43)

The next two lines summarize the effect of this process, "outside you/ and inside your mind," and lead directly to the conclusion.

> *a dream*
>     but it has been always
> *in your imagination*
>     *and in mine* (43)

With tight logic and great economy, the poet has defined reality as essentially fictive and our appreciation of it as indispensable to its very being, and, importantly, he has done this by carefully leading his audience through a maze of private philosophical puzzles.

With similar economy and conceptual density, Alurista develops "la
musica en mis venas navega" ("the music in my veins travels"), a poem that
can serve as a gloss to the numerous others in his corpus treating musical
themes. This piece describes, in a synaesthetic diction and imagery recalling the French Symbolists, the centrality of music in the poet's life and also
how his experience of music relies on the integration of all the senses, not
just hearing. The poem asserts that through music the poet travels widely
in space (e.g., Carl Orff's antiquity in *Carmina Burana* and Heitor Villa-
Lobos' Brazilian jungles in *Uirapúrú*), and he also crosses the barriers of
time when the music takes him back to his "dancing grandparents" (22).
As audience, we, too, share the poet's experiences and sensory experiments.
Moreover, the musical allusions exhibit an eclecticism—from Orff to
Villa-Lobos to Beethoven[40]—that conveys a sense of the multitudinous
versatility of life itself. To Alurista music is "like the honey/ del maguey/
of the silent desert" for the "cálida melodía warms my heart" (22). Like
ancient Homer's lyre, then, music serves as lyrical muse for the modern
poet.

Other poems in *Floricanto* and later books bear out the centrality of music
to the poet's sensibility. For example, he builds "you know that i would
be untrue" and "take you down" around two songs popular during the
1960s Student's Movement—"Light My Fire" and "Strawberry Fields
Forever," respectively.[41] The poet not only alludes to the songs' lyrics, but
he also integrates their meaning into the very themes of the poems.
Similarly, the poem "jimi hendrix," a tribute to the musician/composer's
importance to contemporary popular music, yokes Hendrix's music of
"mythological multitudes" with Alurista's understanding of his own heritage "of inclán perhaps/*or of* cuitlahuac" (38). He suggests that his poet's
"veins" (22) circulate both blood and *the harvest of musical notes"* (38), and
his poetic temperament arises as much from this fact as from any other in
his biographical experience. He thus reifies the concept of poet qua singer
in a way that enriches his verse and our comprehension of the poet's role in
contemporary society. That Alurista ties his personal identity to music is
shown in yet another poem, "man thinks you just began it" where he
connects his *canto* to both Icarus and Ulysses.

> i am bright spotted in the sky [like Icarus]
> ulysses Chicano
> ciclope gringo i'll see you
> to hear me sing

> to fly, *to fly and to finish*
>> what's been started
> *ought be finished*
>> sitting with my guitar (98)

By associating his verse with the ancient Greeks (Ulysses, the voyager king; Cyclops, the one-eyed giant; and Icarus, the daring son who risked his life to reach the sun) as well as, elsewhere, with the ancient Hebrews and, of course, with the pre-American ancients, Alurista asserts the true universality of his poetic vision. And it is music, the *song* of *floricanto*, that coheres all the disparate cultural elements together.

*Nationchild Plumaroja* was first published in 1972 and has been called "a work of synthesis and ongoing dialectic in which [Alurista] continued to experiment with bilinguality and with the linking of indigenous themes to Chicano actuality."[42] A great many of Alurista's experiments advanced several stages in style to a level of polished craftsmanship and conceptual sophistication seen only intermittently in *Floricanto*. The best poems in this second volume, in fact, reflect the same themes and techniques found in the first book but with a striking difference: the overall quality is stronger, more controlled and mature. Nevertheless, Alurista does move in new directions in *Nationchild Plumaroja*, and some of these new avenues warrant mention. My discussion of *Nationchild* thus begins with a look at the poems reflective of *Floricanto* concerns and continues to a consideration of poems addressing two of the book's new directions.

In "A Child To Be Born" Alurista combines multilingual diction, Amerindian concepts, and mestizo symbolism to achieve a fusion of ideas which is mirrored in a fusion of words and phrases. The poem contains some of the poet's favorite images—*la raza* aborning, clay, crickets, frogs, Quetzalcóatl, and Aztlán—arranged to connect the theme of Chicano identity with Mayan autochthonous life on *"the redearthcontinent."*[43] Although Alurista uses the child motif, his treatment of identity does not portray Chicanos as either childlike or embryonic in development. He sees, instead, the American locus of *raza* experience, the geographic space itself, as "pregnant . . . the continente/ *the clay and the* raza" (32), that is, as fertile and teeming with possibility. And the space, repeatedly identified as "aztlán"—whether "on our forehead" or "aztlán of the continent" or "aztlán/ the seed planted by our father quetzalcóatl"—this locus of experience is *"already germinating"* (33). It has sprouted

> *in the womb of our*
> *earthmothercontinent*, amerindia
> nationchild de su padrecarnalismo kukulcán (33).

The reference at the end of the poem to Kukulcán, the Mayan rendering of
Aztec Quetzalcóatl, suggests that Alurista seeks to recover the Chicano's
bronze roots farther back temporally than the Nahua world which dominated *Floricanto*. The Mayan heritage is also more immediately attractive
because of its record of artistic achievement and generally humane social
order.[44] Moreover, the foregrounding achieved through use of blended
morphemes like "madretierraroja" and "nationchild" underscores the basic
cultural synthesis of *mestizaje*. These wordblends—not literally constituting
"neologisms"[45]—appear more extensively in this collection than in the
first, for the poet is more concerned here with transcendental harmony as
a basis for both a collective ideology and a personal ethos, and the
synthesized morphemes emphasize that concern. They also effectively
convey the poet's faith in the fundamental interconnectedness of life's
multeity.

The nature of that synthesis and faith is explained more fully in "Nuestra
Casa—Denver '69." The poem describes a Chicano Movement demonstration, presumably in 1969 in Denver, with *"the [UFW] flag/* razaroja praying
to the sun" and *"the Mexican flag* kiss[ing] the heights" (31–32). The event
is described as a "marcha-mestiza" that by its very being and from the energy
of the marchers builds "liberación." As the description of the march unfolds
(just as the actual march itself wound through its Denver route), so too does
the ideology of *carnalismo* unfold which, we are told, *"is born like the prickly
pear between thorns of sweetness"* (31); that is, Chicano confraternity emerges
out of the sharpest adversity ("espinas") of shared experience and is only
randomly punctuated by shared joy ("dulzura"). Alurista's prescription for
right conduct ramifies directly out of the *carnalismo*:

> *we must work together*
> *we must organize . . .*
> *we must build from* [our] *adobehearts*
>    a casacalor *of liberty fire . . .*
>    we gonna sleep with sarapes
> to dream our *dreams of fire*
> to wake *the spirit that vibrates*
>    *in the blood that our* razaroja
>      *already cries for,*
>      *already clamors for justice* (31–32)

Part of the prescription is a refusal to any longer make spiritual or social penance "*on our knees*," a refusal to offer "more apologies for being of flesh/ and of bone" or for "being hungry" (31). The poet thus adamantly rejects the servility and meekness which are expected of the poor by countering with an assertive "¡chale!"

"Nuestra Casa—Denver '69" may also be read as a gloss on the meaning of the term "nationchild," the same personification of *el pueblo* and its culture used in "A Child To Be Born" and, of course, in the title (discussed below). In "Nuestra Casa" Alurista describes the Chicano's racial origins and suggests that only by pridefully displaying this heritage openly—"con el frijol en la frente/ with cheekbones facing *the naked sun*"—will "*the brown truth*" silence the "tongues once forked" and babbling against us (32). The "nationchild" is at once that burning spirit within "el pueblo" that recognizes its heritage, accepts it, and sees within the heritage itself the basic source of *raza* unity out of which will come needed social solutions, and it is also the actual tangible *pueblo* occupying a physical, geographical space—"la casa" and "Denver" in this poem and "el continente" and "aztlán" in the previous one. Alurista attempts to meld space and consciousness together to make them one, and in that fusion time and identity are transformed and redefined. The "nation" occurs *where*ever the mestizo spirit has existed—in Aztlán, Amerindia, amerika, Denver—and the "child" is the youthful energy (or, in 1969, the new awareness) among *raza* that takes the collective Whole seriously as a political force to be reckoned with and as a spiritual source to invigorate the individual soul.

Elsewhere in *Nationchild* Alurista states that "*the nation is young*" in the "dust" and the "clouds" before dawn ("Tortilla Host," 83). Daybreak's arrival, however, reminds the poet that time is pressing; that "*another year . . . arrives/ loses us, passes us by*" (83); that even while "dawn is breaking . . . the sunset builds" (84). To move with the natural rhythm of the cosmos and not be defeated by time, Alurista suggests that we tap the essence of our culture, of our religious backgrounds, and nature itself. He conveys the culture through the synecdoche of food, the "tortilla" in the title, "Tortilla Host," as well as through the command, "eat a plate of frijoles/ and rejoice in/ cebolla" (85). The religious syncretion, which is part of the mestizo heritage, combines "host," again a synecdoche representing the entire communion ritual, with references to pre-Columbian cosmology—for example, Tlaloc and Éhecatl. By fusing Native American religion with Christian motifs, the poet stresses the essential oneness of spiritual belief when viewed from a mestizo perspective. In a related way, Alurista

evokes nature throughout the poem but especially in the pointed pairing of
the homely "Tortilla Host" with the heavenly "a circle round/ the sun
again." The poet also connects the sun's cosmic revolution with the "pace
of our pueblo" early in the poem and then returns to that motion at the end
as well:

> liberation and unification
> pierce our senses
> smell/breathe
> touch the nipples
>     of cornfield mountains
> and drums/*move the movement*
> dream a life
> live a dream . . .
> let tortillas be host to your heart (85; my emphasis)

Through the lyric processes of parallelism and fusion, the sun's revolution
has evolved naturally into the people's revolution, and both were aptly
abbreviated in the "tortilla" and "host" images, once again revealing the
thematic efficacy of Alurista's poetic economy.

A fuller comprehension of the central symbol or rubric of the collection,
"nationchild plumaroja," grows out of an analysis of two other poems
evincing stylistic and thematic concerns found in *Floricanto*. They are "Out
the Alley Our Soul Awaits Us" and "Tal vez porque te quiero" ("Perhaps
Because I Love You"). The Aluristian persona in "Out the Alley" suffers
from the blues, and that explains why his "soul awaits" in "age carved
alleys" instead of on brighter avenues (36). What revives him and transforms his "once lost hopes" to the possibility of joy is *the melancholy itself*,
for it springs from the same depths of his inner being where the unconscious
memory of his cultural past also resides. Because his sadness originates from
the center of his being, it will heal itself because the center of his *raza*
energy is also located there. Hence, "the bongo rhythm" of his "thumping
heart" catches "the wind" (36), an emblem for Éhecatl, the wind god and
one of Quezalcóatl's manifestations, just as his tears "irrigat[e] our cheek-
bone high lands/ pyramids, feathers, and rituals of love," a flood that
unleashes the poet's explicit allusions to Quetzalcóatl, Huitzilopochtli, and
Tlaloc. Although the poem's tone is still slightly subdued at the end, the
speaker no longer suffers the "melancholiac ulcers," for the free associations
stemming from his unconscious have stimulated his emotional recuperation. Thus, the first "wind" of the poem becomes "soft winds" at the end.

Similar transformations affect the "plumaroja" or "redfeather" image in the poem. The image is suggested by the two references to "feathers" midway in the piece and also in the color of "our blood." "Roja" means both "red" and "hot," giving the word a double meaning that the poet usually plays off against the heat of the sun. Moreover, the meaning of "plumaroja" surfaces even more clearly in decoding the following lines:

> quetzalcóatl in life rejoices
> and we walk down age carved alleys
> running to find alma, sangre y aliento (36)

Quetzalcóatl is the "feathered serpent" deity, and the last three words in the citation translate as "blood and breath." The "plumaroja," then, refers to the spirit of Quetzalcóatl, himself a wind spirit, available to all through the air we breathe, the air that oxygenates our red blood warmly.

Finally, Alurista employs the device of apostrophe to convey the essentially sacred/profane nature of his "razared/rojaraza" in "Perhaps Because I Love You." Addressing his beloved "razamia," that is, his conceptualization of today's Chicano *monde* which is interwoven with the *mestizaje* of the past, the poet apotheosizes his people: "molten bronze unto a god/ chicano-*brother, sister* chicana/ *melted into the flames/* [of] razasol" (23). But upon completing the apotheosis—"i kneel before you"—he shifts immediately to a more intimate, even homey tone—"but the people razared/ . . . *heat the beans, the rice/ and the* tortillas" and he wonders "perhaps that's why i love you" (23). In short, it is the synthesis of the sacred and the profane within his *raza* which forms the "nationchild plumaroja." The synthesis exemplified by both the wordblends and the verbal wordplay at the end of the poem also explains the poet's love, or "porque te quiero" (23). Here, both the color and the heat captured in "roja" emerge to complete the ethnopoetic portrait of the nationchild plumaroja presented in the book and which must ultimately be comprehended as a synthesis of pueblo, person, place, process, and poetic perspective.[46] With its blended languages and morphemes, the title thus embodies the blendedness that defines Chicano/a being.

Turning to the new avenues mapped in *Nationchild*, we find that two are especially noteworthy. In theme, there is an intensified interest in religion with a related, generally metaphysical response to social problems, and in technique, there are more frequent and more extreme instances of lexical wordplay, including some examples of concrete poetry. Although aspects of these innovations appear in *Floricanto*, particularly the interest in religion, they do not dominate the collection to the extent they do *Nationchild*.

Christianity appears in *Nationchild* through images associated with Catholic worship and ritual, like, for example, the Cross, chalice, host, and prayer. Never employed straightforwardly, these images either serve a mestizo conceptual aim and/or advance the Aluristian principles of *raza* pride.

> the umbilical chord of my dreams
> craves the *movement that my parents generated*
> in the chalice that
> once held
> to be truly a pachanga
> *our father and* guadalupe
> and the blood of the holy chalice
> the time has come
> for all good men
> to come to the aid of their country
> and to the *mass of colorful flesh* (55)

The poet transmutes the sacred chalice of Christian ritual from a vessel containing the sanctified blood of Christ to one holding the conception scene of the "nationchild." Christianity also appears in the poetry in references to the institution of the Church in allusions which are usually disparaging—for example, "the constipated *brains*/ in the bishop's *skull*" and the incredulous question "*which lord?*" with the bitterly ironic answer, "¡el señor *priest*!/ ¡la señora *church*! . . . that never gave us posada" ("Candle Shuffle," 69–70; also see "When You Have the Earth in Mouthful," 12). However, the majority of Christian allusions are to the miracle at Tepeyac, to Juan Diego, and the Virgin of Guadalupe and her pre-Christian antecedent, Tonantzin.

> if you see tata juan . . .
> *tell him that god is of bronze*
> *that* guadalupe *is* tonantzin
> *and that* san pedro *is* chicano (49)

It is as if the poet finds the Chicano genesis myth not as usually described in the Conquest with the birth of Cortés and Malinche's progeny, but rather, in Juan Diego's vision and the traditional Catholic belief in his vision as a Christian miracle (also see "Juan Diego," 25; "Offering of Man to God," 58; and "Chalice," 60). This more mythical view of history has merit because the military conquest completed by Cortés in 1521 did not win the hearts and loyalties of the Mexicans as did the "miracle" (whether metaphysical or anthropological) at Tepeyac. That occurrence and its promulgation greatly aided in the conversion and subjugation of the natives by the Europeans.

On the other hand, pre-Columbian cosmology appears in the collection through images associated with indigenous deities as depicted in temple art—for example, quetzal/feathers, coatl/serpents, Tonatiuh/sun, Éhecatl/wind, and Tlaloc/rain. Functioning as cultural mnemonic devices meant to trigger the *raza* collective unconscious, these images are part of the recovery of heritage which Alurista believes must precede political action.

> what if we wanted to climb
> to the mountains
> and seek lakes of serpents
> and eagles hunting . . .
> let éhecatl/señor *of the wind*
> change the course
> of our *clouds*
> we need not
> kill sam or sacrifice his hearth
> sam is suicidal
> sam is killing himself
> we need not
> spill his blood
> ("Dawn Eyed Cosmos," 97)

The charge here is to recover one's true self in one's ethnocultural matrix and to forgo revenge against the oppressor, "sam" or the United States. As that recovery is occurring, Alurista would have it meshed with any affirming Christian rituals in our heritage, just as Mary and Tonantzin are one in *la Virgen de Guadalupe*. Then, he would assert, we can confront the world.

> do not ask of the sun
> to give no light
> or ask the moon to hide
> her skirt of stars . . .
> face your fears
> die only once . . .
> learn to live without
> asking your god

> to be kind, gentle
> ("Face Your Fears Carnal," 64)

One obvious implication of this inward-turning spiritualism is that Chicano energies ought to be self-directed on the group and not outer-directed on "the man," "sam," "mr. jones" or any other abbreviated version of "amerika."

Technical innovations in *Nationchild* include frequent instances of wordplay, experiments with morphological combinations, and the use of some concrete forms. The wordplay is natural to Alurista's verse with its emphasis on language as an active agent or catalyst of theme. The wordplay comprises verbal shifts and special coinages that usually lighten the overall tone and effect of the poem, though serious meaning is usually communicated nonetheless. In "Got To Be on Time," Alurista plays with one of his central themes, time, in an effort to defamiliarize it and thus make it more immediate and vivid.

> time, redbrother
> time long gone
> time short coming
> time been walking dead
> the time has come
> to come
> to come
> to the aid of our nation
> aztlán
> aztlán
> land of sometime
> aftertime
> noontime, notime
> afternoontime, suntime
> alltime
> nighttime, moontime
> morning time (68)

By interweaving clichés and slogans with the wordblends, both conventional and original forms, the poet demonstrates his control over time, the merciless tyrant of life. In the same way, in "Blow Up Tight to Fly" he indulges in a wide array of wordblends, all with the base stem "raza," to arouse his "razaroja, razablack" to "find the truth" of life and being *"in the contrasting colors of your skin"* (33), a message that contradicts the white supremacy assumptions of American racism. The morphemic blends appear throughout the collection and, besides those mentioned in earlier discussions, include such novel combinations as goldcoingod, bluebadge man, razanace, islandgreen, padresol, imagesun, and sapobsidiana. Through the frequent use of wordblends the poet achieves a heightened poetic diction that reverberates beyond the text and remains imprinted in one's consciousness.

Another form of wordplay involves lexical shifts that result in semantic or phonological transformations. In "Unidad," for instance, the word and phrase changes disturb our concentration as the poet captures the nuances of political solidarity. At one point, he observes, "estamos unidos/ pero no estados unidos," [we are united/ but not united states (of being)] in a reference to *los Estados Unidos*, that is, the United States (51). Likewise in "Sapobsidiana" Alurista sketches his nightmare of *"obsidian frogs"* and *"machine guns"* that "aim sharp," employing vivid images of ghastly horror that, dreamlike, merge with one another. This merging compares with that of the frogs in his dream: "sapos de obsidiana plague dreams/ . . . *with the help of a* sapobsidiana/ *of stern face/* smiling" (57). These surrealistic examples disclose how the lexical shifts subtly manipulate our understanding by forcing us to follow the poet's extremely private thematic direction.

The concretion of imagery that occurs in these poems appears more overtly in several others. For example:

```
We find ourselves in a shell
        of corporation, military nightmares
        of success, of co in
                co opt
                cut out
                    sp
                        lit
                            go
                                n
                                    e
        . . . life
        is worthless without land
                without freedom   ("I Like To Sleep," 17)

    it is said
                    that motecuhzoma ilhuicamina
        sent***********
                    an expedition
```

                              looking for the northern
                                    mythical land . . .
                              la tierra
                              de
                              aztlán   ("It Is Said," 46; this poem served as the
                                       dedication to "El Plan de Aztlán" drafted
                                       in 1969 at the Crusade for Justice
                                       in Denver.)

In such *Nationchild* poems as these Alurista underscores his theme not only
through the meaning and sounds of the words he chooses, but also through
his arrangement of those words on the page. This coalescence of sound,
sense, and space parallels the poet's use of Mayan symbols as textual
markers in the original edition of *Nationchild* where Mayan numbering was
used instead of Arabic numerals, and it also anticipates his more radical
technical experiments in later books, particularly *Spik in glyph?* In revising
the collection for its second edition (used here), Alurista dropped most of
that arcane symbolism, though he did retain the original five section
headings—Nopal, Xochitl, Serpiente, Conejo, Venado—each unit containing twenty cantos/poems.[47] The Mayan headings both categorize the
sections and "signify the mood and the emotional coloration that should be
assumed by the reader or interpreter."[48]

     From this extended examination of Alurista's *Floricanto en Aztlán* and
*Nationchild Plumaroja* within the context of the earlier discussion of Chicano
poetics, we can see that Alurista was singularly important to the emergence
and shaping of a genuine Chicano poetics. His boldness in incorporating
the fullness of *raza* experience into his work—especially its multilingualism, *mestizaje*, and its pre-American heritage—was recognized as important by readers and scholars of Chicano literature fairly early in his career,
and his boldness and brilliance have also helped guide a number of other
writers in their own conceptions of craft and of *chicanismo*.[49] That he has
continued to write and offer an original and versatile expression of Chicano
being and that he also continues to promote Chicano art through his
publishing and university teaching further establishes Alurista as a major
Chicano poet.

## OTHER PHASE II POETS

     If Alurista's logic of aesthetics catalyzed an authentic Chicano poetics
into being, other poets contributed to its articulation. Either by adding

new elements of form and idea or by applying and extending features promulgated by Alurista, other poetic voices helped define and sustain the field. Some, like Raúl R. Salinas and José Montoya, are notable for a relatively small cluster of memorable titles; others, like Leo Romero and Sergio Elizondo, are noteworthy because of the nature and quality of their styles. With Alurista, each has helped forge a Chicano poetics and in the process has tempered a lyrical art form that has enhanced our insights into self and society.

Helping to temper that understanding especially effectively has been Raúl Salinas who, despite his nearly twenty years as a *pinto*, gained recognition in the early days of the Movement. Gained largely from his active publishing in most of the first-generation Chicano periodicals and anthologies, Salinas' recognition did not arise from a prolific output. For about seven years his 1973 chapbook *Viaje/Trip* served as the only collection of his verse, and although his *Un Trip Through the Mind Jail y Otras Excursions* appeared in 1980, it contained a great many previously published pieces. Despite the small volume of work, it is significant because of the exceptional quality of certain poems and also because of his unique adaptation of the major characteristics of Chicano poetry. To be sure, his verse is multilingual, mestizo, and reflective of ritual, but it is also characterized by his experiences as a drug addict and as a *pinto*, experiences that have produced a multilayered style of striking individuality.

The emblematic framework within which Salinas presents that individuality is the archetypal journey motif which he develops by working from the manifold puns associated with the word "trip." As a noun, "trip" is simultaneously synonymous with journey and also, colloquially, with the effects of drugs on consciousness, a journey of the mind so to speak. As a verb, "to trip" refers both to an accidental fall (e.g., he tripped on the curb) and to an interference deliberately caused by someone else (e.g., he moved his leg to trip the waiter). Because Salinas chose to include "trip" in the titles of both his collections, the word's multiple meanings are obviously important to him. Accordingly, in "A Trip Through the Mind Jail" the poet, at this time a *pinto* in Leavenworth Penitentiary, travels "in the lonely cellblocks of my mind" to an earlier time and space to the "neighborhood of my youth."[50] During his "days of imprisonment" the journey can only be figurative for him, whereas for his audience the journey serves to vivify the poet's literal childhood. Employing fifteen narrative catalogs to describe with evocative concreteness the places, people, and events that constitute his very "flesh," the poet offers his reminiscences to preserve his sanity while a *pinto*, as well as to preserve the "demolished" neighborhoods that "live on, captive, in the lonely/ cellblocks of my mind" (55). His act of preservation thus becomes an autobiographical assertion of "identity," of "a sense of belonging" to

> LA LOMA—AUSTIN—MI BARRIO—
>     i bear you no grudge . . .
> i need you now. . . .
> you keep me away from INSANITY'S hungry jaws;
>     Smiling/Laughing/Crying.
> i respect your having been. (60)

In other words, this "trip through a mind jail," like his "Journey II" and even like Whitman's "Out of the Cradle Endlessly Rocking," follows a map lodged within the poet's memory of his past. In addition, his artist's imagination "grant[s] immortality" to all the recalled bits and pieces of his life, as, for instance, "Andres" of the "Spanish Town Cafe" (57) and the "loud funky music" of "big black Johnny B———" (58). These parts combine to form the mosaic of his life.

The map also contains side-roads to two other kinds of trips: the drug experiences and the accidental falls. In recalling his early adolescence and later the "[n]eighborhood where purple clouds of grass/ smoke one day descended & embraced us all" (58), Salinas makes it clear that the mind-altering trips began early for him. In this poem the allusions to his drug initiation form part of the vast panorama "of my childhood/ neighborhood that no longer exists," and they are no more or no less important than other elements from that "neighborhood." However, if placed within the context of Salinas' poetic corpus, these allusions stand out prominently in relation to the basic fact of his adult life—his incarceration because of drugs (see, for example, "Ciego/Sordo/Mudo" [Blind/Deaf/Dumb], p. 67)—for drugs weave through *Trip Through the Mind Jail* from beginning to end. From the "Dedicatoria's" hope that the book itself "makes up/ . . . [for the] incessant/ (almost incurable)/ illness" of his addiction (16) to the closing piece in the collection with its vivid description of "bitter-sweet Cocaine" and its "stubborn" effect (171), the poet's experience of drugs influences his other life experiences. Consequently, his use of the journey motif is heightened by the linkage to drugs and to his life as a *pinto*. Indeed, most of his finest poetic journeys are not traveled in the Odyssean sense of literally moving from adventure to adventure; instead, they take place in his mind, produced either by memory or by drugs. As a result, his "imprisonment" refers not only to his being locked behind "steel-plated doors" inside "clammy, concrete walls" (41), but also to being trapped in "the timeless corridors of my tormented mind" (79), victim of the same "Hungry Horse" (i.e., heroin) that "silenced" singers "Bessie [Smith]" and "Janis [ Joplin]" (71–72).

The other kind of trip, the accidental falls, in "A Trip Through the Mind Jail" were unavoidable because, as we're told early in the poem, his childhood "neighborhood" is full of "muddied streets—all chuckhole lined" (55), a physical emblem of the social obstacles he faced as a barrio Chicano. From "having cooties in the hair" to "skinned knees" from "chasing" the "Project girls," he and his friends tripped and fell often (56), a foreshadowing of subsequent falls with their more tragic consequences, as in the cases of Lalo and Güero (58), who died violent deaths. In the end and by virtue of the creative act of composing the poem, the poet concludes in affirmation:

> neighborhood that is no more
> YOU ARE TORN PIECES OF MY FLESH!!!!
> Therefore, you ARE. . . .
> my Loma of Austin
> my Rose Hill of Los Angeles
> my West Side of San Anto
> my Quinto of Houston
> my Jackson of San Jo
> my Segundo of El Paso
> my Barelas of Alburque . . .
> Flats, Los Marcos, Maravilla, Calle Guadalupe . . .
> and all Chicano neighborhoods that
> now exist and once existed;
>         somewhere . . . someone remembers. . . . (60)

Here as elsewhere in the poem Salinas uses repetition and catalogs to develop a sense of ritual and of shared space and time between poet and audience. Offered as magical phrases uniting Chicanos across the country, the list of barrio names, some in *caló*, resembles a sacred incantation understood only by members of the tribe addressed in the ritual experience of sharing the poem. The journey metaphor provides a thematic framework for the book and unifies the *pinto* poems with those "of (Partial) Freedom" that were written after his parole.

Several other features also animate Salinas' work and explain its spe- cialness within Chicano poetry. One of these derives from the poet's intense ethnic identity and his recognition of the power of the *Movimiento* from its very inception. In an early piece he asks "where does it all lead to?" and wonders if "the problem" is "social/ cultural/ political" or "economic"— concerns that preoccupy him throughout his career ("Preguntome" [I Ask Myself], 66). He answers many of his questions about social issues in "Los Caudillos" (The Leaders), a poem that may be read as a verse summary of the Chicano Movement's actors and activities during the late 1960s and early 1970s (see Prologue above). The "caudillos" of the title are César Chávez, Reies Lopez Tijerina, Corky Gonzales, José Angel Gutiérrez, and David Sánchez of the Brown Berets. According to the poet, they ignited the "flames of sociopolitical awareness" among the "Bronze People" who are "ubiquitous" and who "at long, long last" began "wresting" political power from the "clutches" of "tyrannical usurpers" (69–70). Salinas' tone in "Los Caudillos" is hopeful and uplifting, quite unlike his tone in "Homenaje al Pachuco" which reveals an ironic, barely controlled rage. Employing a trilingual combination of Spanish, English, and *caló*, the poet addresses "Homenaje" (Homage) directly to "ese loco," to the *pachuco* who dissented from both the dominant society's bigotry and the *raza* community's seeming acceptance of that bigotry. In addressing the *pachuco*, Salinas speaks to himself as well—hence the subtitle in parentheses, "Mirrored Reflections"—for he grew up as a barrio "loco," and his homage is as much an assertion of his personal identity as it is a tribute to the barrio rebels of Chicano culture. The rage surfaces in his mockery of the absurdity of a society that ostracized *pachucos* for being "non-goal oriented" and "alienated" but then eventually saw fit to offer courses on "Pachuco Mythology . . . Language . . . Philosophy" and even on "the Pachuco as Pop-Hero" (97). Angered by the "Oppressive, Racist/ Creativity stifling/ PINCHE SOCIEDAD," Salinas expresses as much concern for "our sister— La Pachuca—of the/ equal *sufferings*" as he does for his "carnales" (87–99). This same concern appears in many of his other poems as a desire for Third World solidarity and coalition-building between the socioeconomically disadvantaged segments of American society and the world's poor.

Inspired and nurtured by his *pinto* identification with enslaved victims everywhere, Salinas' egalitarianism is later put into action when he leaves prison and becomes an active supporter of other social movements. Accordingly, another important thematic feature animating his work is his insistence on synthesis as opposed to nationalism, on Third World solidarity instead of *raza* separatism. As early as the poem "Preguntome," he wonders "when does a rainbow coalition take place?" and suggests that only then can social progress be near. Moreover, his synthetic outlook forces him to pose the question does "aztlán mean utopia?" which in the very asking indicates that Chicano nationalism is not enough for him (66). Throughout Salinas' work appear references to such Third World martyrs as Che Guevara, Salvador Allende, and Sandino, as well as to contemporary U.S. activists associated with a wide variety of ethnopolitical suasions. Summing up this strain in his work, he writes "i have/ become as one/ with struggles of world social movements" ("It's Been Two Years Now," 135), a statement especially reinforced by his poems of Native American solidarity (e.g, 154 and 155) and of socialist hope (e.g., 131 and 144). Uniting his Third Worldism with his *chicanismo* is "Sacrasensación with Flying Colors," which is dedicated to the Royal Chicano Air Force, the artists' collective founded by José Montoya and that parallels Esteban Villa's Mexican-American Liberation Art Front (MALAF), as well as Chávez's UFW, Corky's Crusade, Tijerina's Alianza, and Gutiérrez's RUP. "Sacrasensación" also addresses the "*disease* of our *outer edges*"—that is, heroin—and its "haunting horrores" (163, 165), thereby serving as both "un trip through the mind jail" and "otra excursion" to greater freedom and hope, goals possible through collective action and mutual support.

Perhaps because of Salinas' intimate knowledge of several types of imprisonment, his taste in music is for a form defined by freedom and improvisation, jazz, a form that paradoxically emerged out of legalized American slavery. Indeed, one of his early celebrations of it is titled "Jazz: A Nascence," and it describes the music's cathartic power to "sweep . . . out the mental cobwebs" and to "washaway/musty/dust settled within" (44). In this and other pieces, the poet memorializes such talents as "Satchel-Mouth" & "Joe [Williams] the King," "Charlie O' Jazzbird" Parker, and "John [Col]trane," artists renowned for their technical skill and exquisite creativity. But Salinas' influence by jazz goes beyond the appreciation of an aficionado and to his absorption of its qualities into his poetry. In "Chan/Dan-go," for example, the poet employs Black dialect, hip abbreviations, a broken verse line arrangement, and experimental typesetting to parallel the improvisatory nature of the "FREE-DOM JAZZ DANCE!!!" which inspired the poem (82). Similarly, in "Song for Roland Kirk," subtitled in parentheses "in a minor blues mode," he uses the same techniques found in "Chan/Dan-go" but adds onomatopoeia of instrument sounds to provide elegiac refrains in memoriam to his friend (168–170).

Despite the sparseness of Raúl Salinas' canon and the unevenness of its quality, he and his work deserve a remembered place in Chicano poetry because of the merit of his *pinto* verse with its unique adaptations of the characteristics of Chicano poetics. He used prison as a metaphor for other constraints and constrictions in human society (including drugs), and he balanced the implicit negativism of that metaphor with the affirmation of his major theme—popular solidarity crossing all ethnic boundaries. Interwoven throughout his work, like a saxophonic echo, is his passion for jazz, a particularly apt artistic response for one fully in tune with life's pain and its joy, for one especially sensitive to music and its ritual as the keenest evocation of the human heart.

Like Salinas, José Montoya has published only slightly, but the fine quality of a number of his poems along with the parodic poetry implicit in the Royal Chicano Air Force (RCAF), which he founded, requires that he be considered in this crescive phase. Located in Sacramento, the RCAF is an artists' group which functions as a community-based cooperative. It is concerned with providing a congenial atmosphere for Mexican-American artists and their work and with promoting the legitimacy of Chicano art as another meaningful expression in the universe of art. Originally, the RCAF's name was Rebel Chicano Art Front, but the humor associated with "Royal Chicano Air Force," coined by Montoya, has so insisted itself on the public mind that the nickname has assumed precedence over the original.[51] The issue of whether it is art or life imitating the other arises here with enigma alone surfacing clearly, a fact that does not disturb Montoya. Earlier in his career he joined MALAF, a group devoted "to creat[ing] new symbols and images for *la nueva raza*."[52] These involvements indicate the poet's engagé attitude and activist approach to his ethnicity. Accordingly, his "Early Pieces," "El Sol y los de Abajo," and "El Louie" offer interesting variations on Chicano poetics, variations that further demonstrate the multiplicity of Chicano culture. Like portraits in a gallery, these poems describe people intimately through the disclosure of personal features and idiosyncrasies. Unlike the muteness of painted portraits, however, poems can give an array of verbal insights into habits and behavior. Montoya's poetic profiles—which includes "La Jefita," discussed in Chapter Two— also reflect back on the persona of each poem, the voice that masks the poet's own and in the process reflect aspects of the poet himself.

Emphasizing an oral, anecdotal use of language, "Early Pieces," as the title slang indicates, tells the story of the early sexual exploits of the speaker and his friends. In a barrio dialect replete with such colloquialisms as "ruco," "escamaus," and "vatitos," the speaker describes the adolescent deceptions associated with emerging carnal knowledge which, for men, is commonly a *collective* peer group experience. From the *"told us"* of the first line to the closing scene in "Meño's garage," each stanza refers to the boys collectively. Even their final, individual masturbatory acts lose their individuality in the blithe unself-consciousness of the group spirit.[53] The poem's strength lies in the poet's handling of narrative voice, for he effectively captures both the essentially selfish insouciance of youth and the boyish earnestness typical of sexual discovery. The splendid verisimilitude of the adolescent persona's awkwardness and androcentrism calls to mind the characterizations of Huckleberry Finn and Holden Caulfield.

If the portrait seen in "Early Pieces" is of carefree boyhood, in "El Sol y Los de Abajo" (The Sun and the Downtrodden) the picture is an artist's self-portrait and the contemplative seriousness implied in that undertaking. Opening with a physical description that focuses solely on skin color and its relation to status and power, the poem quickly moves to a definition of the most important features of the speaker/poet's life: "Descendant *I am of the downtrodden/ dragging myself along through life* . . . , I have dragged/ Myself and soul in . . . Search [of] the splendor/ *Of the temples of the sun*" (34). His life is thus defined by paradox—by the yoking of his yearning for the sun with the inescapable reality of his lowly earthbound condition: *"I am of the/ Downtrodden*—find the gutters/ the prisons, the battlefields/ *and the fields of cotton—there you'll find me"* (34–35). But the paradox is only in the eye of those beholders who, like the poem's "patronizing do-gooders" (35), fail to see that the path to the sun is, in fact, through a total immersion in and acceptance of his "vida arrastrada" etched on his mind (36), like Goya paintings with their strong contrast of light and shadow. Accordingly, the three and one-half pages that follow the introduction constitute a total immersion in that life through flashbacks to scenes from the speaker/poet's past. Although the flashback is itself a nostalgic process, the scenes themselves are unromantic in capturing the ambiguities of human nature.

> La curandera, bruja, life-giving
> *Meddler who cured* Don Cheno
> *Of the pain in his navel and the*
> *Fever in his waist—the one*
> *Who gave powders* for lovers *kneeling*
> Praying to a remarkably reasonable
> God that their wives and husbands
> Wouldn't find out . . . (36)

Through recollections like these and through memories of his grandmother's "wrinkled hands" clutching "a hand rolled cigarette" (38) or of his father on "*horseback*," a natural "*guerilla for the cause*" (39), Montoya reaches the conclusion that his own "actions are not yet worthy/ of the ballads." In this realization the inferiority relating to dark skin which opened the poem is transformed into a prideful acceptance of self and culture.

> But Chilam Balam's prophetic
> Chant has been realized—and the
> Dust that darkened the air begins
> To clear y se empiesa a ver el Sol.
>     I AM LEARNING TO SEE THE SUN. (40)

By referring to *The Book of the Chilam Balam of Chumayel*,[54] a Mayan sacred text, the poet asserts the rightness of seeking truth within *raza* culture, even within the ancient ancestral roots unknown to most Mexican-Americans. This assertion also exposes the petty frailty of racist preoccupations with pigmentation and similar features that lack either depth or substance.

That purposeful motivation accounts for much of the power of "El Louie," the poet's most famous work, a poem grounded in the *pachuco* heritage within *raza* culture. The central focus of the poem celebrates the public Louie in all his *pachuco* "roles" in order to honor "el Louie Rodriguez," the man behind the masks who was "class to the end."[55] Written with heavy use of *caló* and born out of the sad occasion of Louie's burial, the poem serves as eulogy for "un vato de atole" (333) from Fowler, a long way from "the big time" of "Los [Angeles]" (334). Still, "we had Louie," the speaker remembers with respect, and with his "tailor-made drapes," customized "Fleetline," and "always [with] rucas," Louie "was as close as we ever got to the big time" (334). But that "big time" was, as the poet implicitly acknowledges, built on illusion—noble, perhaps, but illusion nonetheless. Without diminishing the heroic strains within *pachuquismo*—its rebellion against the cultural norm, its creativity of self-definition through dress and language, its noble endurance of institutional racist violence—the poet casts a floodlight of truth on the essential escapism of *pachuquismo*, an aspect that is frequently overlooked in discussions of this poem.[56] Montoya addresses this fact directly in the poem in a way that does not lessen the honor paid to el Louie.

> En Sanjo[se] you'd see him
> sporting a dark topcoat

playing in his fantasy
the role of Bogard, Cagney
or Raft. . . .

An Louie would come through—
melodramatic music, like in the
*show*—tan tan taran!—Cruz
Diablo, El Charro Negro! Bogard
smile (his smile as deadly as
his *hands*!) He dug roles, man,
and names—like "Blackie," "Little
Louie . . . "
Ese, Louie . . .
Chale, man, call me "Diamonds!"

And on leave, jump boots
shainadas and ribbons, cocky
from the war, strutting to
early mass on Sunday morning. (333, 335)

A quintessential model of the *pachuco*, "Legs Louie Diamonds" like his peers, transformed the natural rebelliousness and idealism of youth into a fashion, a personal fashion of individual, separate identity that, multiplied to all *pachucos*, evolved into cult conformity. By emphasizing the role-playing associated with "ol' Louie" and by describing his successes in terms of the masks he wore and not in terms of any replicable accomplishments in his life (even his reputed war heroics are reduced to "ribbons" and "cocky strutting"), the poet prepares his audience for the abjectness of his death: "He died alone in a rented/ room—perhaps like in a/ Bogard movie" (336). Suddenly we recall the hint given early in the piece that "toward the end" Louie had been "aging fast from too much/ booze *and a hard life*" (333), but, caught up "in his fantasy" we too, ignore the hint until forced to acknowledge it in the "insult" of his death. The poem thus achieves a twofold effect. It is at once an earnest tribute to *pachuquismo*, its participants and its linguistic code, and it is also a realistic portrait of the hollowness of a *pachuco*'s life if the mask is not understood for what it is, a transitional role-playing that must be outgrown if it is to be outlived. The poet—and the reader—understand this, though the "cruel hoax" of "Little Louie's" end indicates that he did not.

Montoya's bilingual idiom, especially its skillful handling of *caló* and other colloquialisms, places his work solidly within the multilingualism of Chicano poetics, just as his lyric portraits of barrio characters conform to the *mestizaje* of that poetics. On the other hand, Montoya's work differs from the Chicano poetic conventions in the absence of distinct ritual features and in the reduction of the non-*raza* Other from a significant role to merely an implied presence in the social ambience. It is as if the poet were seeking to capture a realistic slice of Chicano experience, one as accessible and straightforward as the woodcarving of a New Mexico *santero*, but also one whose thematic density is as complex and enigmatic as the history and objectives of the RCAF.

Two poets whose work belongs in any discussion of a distinct Chicano poetics but whose styles vary from the characteristics of the field described earlier in this chapter are Leo Romero and Sergio Elizondo. Neither has employed multilingual diction to any appreciable degree—Romero relying instead on English predominantly and Elizondo on Spanish—nor has either sought to evoke a strong ritual dimension in his work. Moreover, although both typically find their subjects and themes within the *mestizaje* that defines the work of the other Phase II poets, their poetic approaches—especially in Romero's case—differ markedly from those of others discussed in this chapter. Despite these readily apparent differences and despite the relative paucity of their cumulative work, both Romero and Elizondo have been strong minor presences in Chicano poetry by virtue of their distinctive approaches, the consistent high quality of their work, and their steady creative output for over a decade.

A product of New Mexico, Leo Romero lives and writes there, and the state, as a geographic and cultural locus, figures prominently in his writing. Through New Mexico as metaphor, Romero translates his absorbed understanding, feeling, and experience of *the land* into comprehensible evocations of beauty and meaning. Although his later books, *During the Growing Season* (1978) and *Agua Negra* (1981; both discussed in subsequent chapters), are especially effective and evocative lyric treatments of the land, some of Romero's earliest published pieces may be understood as contributing to the early definition of Chicano poetics. Published in local presses throughout New Mexico, those early poems enjoyed a significant readership in the early 1970s, primarily in the Southwest, and they proved the viability of lyricism at a time when political protest was the norm in Chicano poetry.

Romero's pastoral subjects and themes invite comparison to the fiction of Rudolfo Anaya, also a *manito* (i.e., native New Mexican), whose novel *Bless Me, Ultima* is an acknowledged classic of the Chicano Renaissance. The comparison is a natural, mutually enhancing one, for, like Anaya, Romero is concerned with capturing the nature and essence of the land as a living reality in *raza* culture, even within a modern urban environment. In his first non-campus publication, "The Road to Tres Piedras," for example, Romero used simple, concrete imagery to convey the land's compelling reality and its reflection of interior states of consciousness.

> what a lone lonely
> road
> stretching out
> ever winding away
> with spreading fields
> around it
> with the vastness of an outdoor
> sky around it
> lonely lone road
> away away
> to a needle's point
> on a remote horizon[57]

The poem's title and subject suggest travel, the journeying from one place to the destination of Tres Piedras, a village in the northeast corner of New Mexico. However, the road's stretch through "spreading fields" under "the vastness" of the "sky" evokes instead an unmitigated static loneliness. The "lonely lone road" goes to Tres Piedras, but it looks as if it travels only to a tiny "needle's point on a *remote* horizon" (my italics), a distant speck as tiny and insignificant as the observer perceiving the scene. The poet thus captures the unique character of the Southwest with its endless expanses of unpeopled earth and overwhelming sky and conveys in the process a state of being—loneliness—that is both reflected and intensified by the over-powering natural landscape. In sum, "the spirit of place in the poem is perfect . . . a desert land, a land characterized by sparse growth of sage, snakeweed, and chamisa,"[58] a land where space is at least as significant as human life and the busy-ness it entails, a land that challenges the strength of human will.

Similarly, "Comanchito" contains images of nature that develop into a surreal dream-picture of childhood fear, a dream pregnant with suggestions of primordial experience.

> Dance to the Comanchito
> the moon is in its fullness

Grandma Wake Me
I am having that dream again

Dance to the Comanchito
to the music of centuries . . .

listen to that music
it will connect with your blood

I didn't mean to go so far[59]

In the dream that is the poem, "Comanchito" (Indian lad) and "Indians"
share the same natural world of the "never ending" night, the "sunflowers
without motion," and the "red and orange leaves of autumn." The dream
forces the speaker to "listen to that music" which "will connect with your
blood" and to acknowledge that the "rhythm" of the Comanchito's dance
is in the "blood." That is, the primitive power of nature rises from within
the hidden psyche, and it taps the universal natural energy of earth. The
emergence of this energy in the boy's dream is mysterious and frightening.
The speaker's fear is powerfully captured in the closing lines: "Dance to the
Comanchito/ the rhythm is in your blood/ the Indians are angry/ Grandma
Wake me." The total effect of the poem is Jungian; it demonstrates the
ineradicable reality of the primal connections with earth normally associated with the Indian but which Romero believes yet reside within all
Chicano consciousnesses. One assumes that the "Indians are angry" because
of the despoiling of earth characteristic of our modern age, but, in fact, the
surreal idiom precludes any easy or literal paraphrase as it captures the
preverbal, subrational character of archetypal patterns.[60] This Jungian
quality appears in other Romero poems, notably "In the End It Will Be the
Same as in the Beginning" and "The Desert of Our Remembrance."[61]

The piece that most evinces Romero's vision as a *manito* poet is "Land,"
a poem that directly addresses the meaning of the "tierra obscura"[62] to the
*raza* of New Mexico.

When I say Land
it is the same
as if I were to say Life
It is a long time since
my ancestors came
to this New Mexico . . .
They followed the Rio Grande
not in search of gold . . .

They were after Land
It had been promised them (9)

Presented in a simplicity of language reminiscent of Neruda, the poem develops the equivalence of land-life by showing how *raza* ancestors adapted to the ways of the indigenous peoples: "So much of my food is Indian/ So many of my neighbors" (9). As a result, "the cycle is clearly understood" (9), both in nature and in human life. Toward the end of the poem, however, Romero shifts from pastoral exposition to political statement, from the general inclusive description of the land's importance to a personal interpretation of its subjective meaning. More importantly, he shifts from a delicacy of diction to one that increases in rhetorical volume and intensity, ending with the obscene curse of the last two words.

> With Land I die . . .
> My entire RAZA dies
> I start to scream now slowly
>     TIERRA OBSCURA
>     TIERRA SANGRIENTA
> How long must I scream
> Must my words be English
> Must my dying words be English
> CABRONES JODIDOS (10)

Because the land *is* life, its loss means other losses—language, custom, lifestyle, culture—and ultimately it means "dying" as a victim of the "cabrones jodidos" who took the land despite official treaties and certified deeds and despite the generally tranquil co-existence of Indians and Hispanos.

As these examples of Romero's early work attest, his vision derives from two important sources of inspiration—the modern triculturalism that has characterized *mestizaje* since 1848 and a transcendental philosophy of unity with earth. The Native American/Mexican/U.S. American triculturalism manifests itself in the poet's predominant use of English and in his concern with the nature of *raza* experience in a Yankee society. His transcendentalism appears in his thematic preoccupation with nature and, specifically, with the way humans live in and accept the land. By yoking these two inspirations with a delicacy of language and imagery, Romero achieves a lyricism that is distinctive in Phase I and II Chicano poetry. Moreover, that he largely avoids explicit political argument and ideological didacticism in favor of a quieter, more personal (if, often, surrealistic) rendering of experience further distinguishes Romero from others in this period.

Also distinctive in Phase I and II poetry is the work of Sergio Elizondo, a Mexican-born professor of Spanish whose residency in the United States, like Delgado's and Alurista's, has flowered into strong identification with Chicanos and *el Movimiento*. Elizondo writes in Spanish, not bilingually, and this is the primary feature of his work's distinctiveness in the canon. Although monolingual Spanish is one of the six linguistic modes occurring in Chicano poetry, most poets employ it along with other idioms, either in one text (e.g., Alurista and Montoya), or they alternate its use from text to text (e.g., Delgado and Sánchez). Because Elizondo composes in Spanish and because he subtly integrates into his verse style his vast knowledge of Spanish poetic forms, his work especially suffers from translation and should be appreciated in the original. However, unlike Romero, he devotes considerable explicit attention to the non-*raza* Other, concentrating his poetic eye on viewing "them" from a Chicano perspective. This feature suggests that his work is political, and, indeed, Elizondo engages in extreme social protest, especially in his first book. Nevertheless, his primary focus is the complex energy of *raza* itself.

Elizondo's major work is *Perros y antiperros: una épica chicana* (Dogs and Anti-Dogs: A Chicano Epic) in which, like Gonzales in *I am Joaquín*, he offers a panoramic view of the Chicano. The work is technically not an epic (see pp. 43–44 above), nor did the author intend it to be. As he admitted in an interview, his editors added the subtitle on the basis of extraliterary considerations.[63] Therefore, inasmuch as Elizondo did not write an epic and, indeed, inasmuch as the work's subject, structure, and theme lack epical characteristics, the approach to *Perros y antiperros* here is to regard it as a collection of individual poems sharing a common subject, *chicanismo*, and language, Spanish.

Despite his specialist's knowledge of poetic form and convention and despite his use of sophisticated meters in the work, *Perros y antiperros* gives the illusion of colloquial simplicity, of the vulgate in bronze tone. The speaker of the poem makes clear that his vantage point as participant/ observer/chronicler is personal and anecdotal, and he warns that he is

> . . . not telling what I know,
> but what they told me
> and, as a Chicano, I retell.

> I have no letters in my head
> nor chroniclers at home,
> only anger in my gut
> and strong sweat on my balls.[64]

The effect of this narrative mode is threefold. First, it frees the speaker from the "great man" version of history that constitutes a large part of, to name one example, Gonzales' epic *Joaquín*, a freedom that allows Elizondo's narrator to present a popular, commoners' saga in a style largely devoid of rhetorical flourish or abstruse information. This, too, distinguishes it from *Joaquín* which required a set of notes and annotations to gloss the text. Second, the speaker's role as participant/observer permits him full use of the vernacular with which to vent his frustration and anger against the inequities and injustices life holds for *raza* as an ethnic minority group within a white, monolingual society. The speaker's colloquial idiom laces *Perros y antiperros* with an authenticity that lends the poem a folkloric tenor much as Robert Frost's cultivated rusticity flavors his highly stylized writing. Third, this narrative style gives a universality to the speaker's voice, making him an authentic *raza* everyman. Not many individual Chicanos can identify with Cuauhtemoc or Zapata, but most can share the speaker's ebullience—"I sing my Chicano epic"—and his insecurity in society—"I prattled in English/ I chowed down in gringo" (15)—and other commonplace experiences.

The poet heightens these three effects by fitting *Perros y antiperros* into a dialectical macrostructure. Taken together the collection of poems can be clustered loosely under the rubrics *thesis*, *antithesis*, and *synthesis*, but as the following diagram illustrates, the dialectics should not be forced to include every one of the thirty-three poems.[65] Titles in parentheses indicate a slight deviation from the dialectical taxonomy.

| *Thesis* | *Antithesis* |
|---|---|
| "Perros" | "Antiperros" |
| "Thirteen Stars" | "España" |
| "Epithalamium" | "Grito" |

*Synthesis*
"My Tale"

| | |
|---|---|
| ("Buenos Hijos de La Malinche) | "Pastourelle" |
| | "Chicanos" |
| "Machismo, chismo, chismo" | "My Home" |

("Fathers, Sons; Yesterday, Today")

" 'Marcha' "                        "Mexican Note"
("Que Pedo")                        ("Here Enters Califas")
"Dream"                             "From the Nueces to the
"Death in Texas"                    Bravo"
"Rest"                              "Death"
"Mas Pedo Carnal"                   "Polka"
("Bitch")                           ("Flor")
("Delirium")                        ("Lullaby")
"Murrieta Two"                      ("At Home")
                                    "Murrieta on the Hill"
                    "Rest"

"The Path to Perfection"

That the poet opens with "Antiperros," the antithesis, rather than "Perros," the thesis, may be interpreted as a defiant act. That is, this reversed order permits him to give the *raza* perspective the first and last word. The reversal of the classic dialectic also derives from the poet's belief that any status quo that finds Aztlán *abajo* is topsy-turvy and needs righting. Through this reversed form, then, the poet achieves a parallel between structure and theme. The structural divisions reinforce the poet's thematic interest in the schism between Chicanos and the dominant society. By presenting several sets of antithesis/thesis/synthesis in the poem, Elizondo illustrates one way of neutralizing the cultural schizophrenia common to Mexican-Americans. Moreover, each section itself follows the dialectical model to some extent, so that each one offers discrete reinforcement of the structural whole.

In the first two sections, "Antiperros" and "Perros," the narrator sets out the problem and foreshadows its potential solution. He develops these thematic foci in greater detail in subsequent sections. The opening lines of "Antiperros" succinctly summarize the problem: "Land lost, flame of love/ Land destroyed; I am full of love" (5). As the rest of the poem discloses, the loss of land refers to the invasion of Aztlán by Anglo America in the nineteenth century, culminating in the United States' conquest of space in this century.

        across the tracks
        where they the others live
        in white enamel clinics,
        that cover
        the steel of their lost souls. . . .

> They say that from here
> to the moon they have gone
> to plant insolence
> of aseptic foot on silver sands,
> and a fake rag stiff as death. (5)

The problem, therefore, is Them, the *gringos* and their misuse of power, whether derived from the "bibles on their ass" or their "dungheap of lawbooks in court" (7). But the opening lines also offer the prospect of a solution in the references to love, a theme that is extended throughout the entire work in manifold ways. In these two sections Elizondo equates love with three different activities. It is love that motivates the speaker and his "young brothers" to "sing" this epic in the first place, preserving forever the "pleasure and . . . pain" of *raza* experience which had hitherto existed only orally "without a book" (5). A second form of love appears in the generous hospitality which the speaker's "grandparents" extended to the "hungry" Yankees when the latter first arrived in the Southwest in what was then still Mexico. But the generosity was one-sided, for

> The lands were lost
> to false blue eyes
> and the beggar who came to dinner
> cheated the doors and stayed in my home. (7)

"Perros" closes with a third expression of love, and that is procreative love, the sexual passion and energy that ignites the "flame of love" mentioned in the opening lines and which the poet interprets as an irrepressible source of natural power. These two sections, then, distill down to one contrasting thought: if Anglo power and greed have destroyed the land and have disadvantaged Chicanos for a century and a half, it is the power of love that throughout that time has helped sustain the indomitable *raza* will.

In the third through sixth sections—"España," "Thirteen Stars," "Epithalamium," and "Grito"—the poet presents four short verses to convey the passage of time and the course of history as a multileveled process ramifying in a variety of effects. "España" traces *raza* origins to the "ancient songs" of Spain which give the speaker the strength to challenge today's enemy whom he ridicules as "Bato, / garabato . . . Chilesín / Putín / Son of Rintintín" (11). "Thirteen Stars" describes the sterility of the dominant society's "man-made rituals" from the "melancholy" commercialization of Christmas to the "pretend love . . . of paper hearts" celebrated as Valentine's Day (13). The next short verse, whose title "Epithalamium" refers to a nuptial song in literary convention, continues the disparagement of Anglo rituals to the traditional "white and expensive" June weddings which the speaker reduces to a "symphonic grimace" (13). "Grito" concludes this series of brief verses by again returning to the ancient *raza* past—as in "España"—this time invoking the pre-American indigenous heritage of Mexico symbolized by the "thousand colored Quetzalcóatl bird" (13). Accordingly, in a further dismissal of non-Chicano rites, the narrator cockily asserts that

> My parents
> never made marriage,
>     all they ever made
>         was
>         love. (13)

From his parents' procreative love, which presumably produced him, the speaker moves naturally into his own "*cuento*," the thematically synthetic "My Tale." This section shifts from the universal voice of the folk to the poet's personal voice, a subjective expression of "my Chicano epic," dominated by the speaker's rite of passage to manhood (15). His rite of passage travels the route of World War II in which the speaker fought for the "so-called American democracy" in France and Italy only to return to "Three Rivers Texas" where Chicano soldiers were still "denied burial" because of Anglo racism (15). "My Tale" recounts the speaker's near assimilation into the melting pot of the "trombones and saxophones" of the "Miller band" and the "prattle" of English (15). But, we are told, that assimilation was only part of the aberrant experimentation of youth, and the speaker marks the transition with one line: "A soldier I went, a man I returned" (17). The line addresses the life changes that pushed the speaker to adulthood, and it demarcates a thematic shift in the poem's form. From this point "My Tale" moves to a tender rhapsody affirming *lo ser chicano*, that is, Chicano being. Through synecdoche the poet conveys the speaker's celebration of his culture's *mestizaje*. By citing the dark brown associated with *raza* skin tones as well as the "hot . . . red chile" and the "eyes of the Virgin," Elizondo celebrates Chicano being in its fullness, thereby providing adequate context for the rhapsody.[66]

> Friend: I have everything.
> From now on,
>     the grapes that await me in the fields
>     friends of my harmony,

with tender hands I caress as sisters . . .
Grapes of love
    I feel you leave me;
today I prefer my valiant self . . .
They cannot reach me . . .
I leave them [white bosses] behind
and tell them
you-know-what [¡Chingueasumadre!]
while I paint myself CON SAFOS. (17, 19)

As the passage shows, this section reveals another side of the speaker, one that counterbalances his hostility against the non-Chicano Other which prevails in the first four sections. Here, the tone is joyful, confident, and secure in the knowledge that *lo ser chicano* constitutes a reality of cultural and personal riches, which the "CON SAFOS" (see glossary) assures will be protected.

The first seven pieces just discussed serve as introduction and establish the subject, style, pace, and tone of the collection, with the remaining twenty-six poems adding historical detail and elements of *mestizaje* to the introduction. For example, both "Pastourelle" and "Murrieta on the Hill" deal with the recovery of the true history of Mexican America which has been lost or white-washed by assimilationist educational practices. Likewise, "Chicanos," "My Home," and "Polka" comprise mestizo motifs ranging from quotidian customs to religious beliefs, while "Fathers, Sons; Yesterday, Today" and "At Home" celebrate the family as an integral *raza* unit. Other poems in the collection address such timeless poetic themes as love (e.g., "Mexican Note" and "Lullaby") and death (e.g., "Death" and "Bitch"). In addition, the pattern of dialectics found in the introductory sections carries through most of *Perros y antiperros*. Providing themes of antithesis, for instance, are "Pastourelle," which attempts a rhapsodic recovery of historic "traces of the Mexican" (25), and "Mexican Note," which offers a traditional paean to traditional femininity as an inspiration of masculine love (35). Expressing the thesis through an emphasis on *gringo* perfidy are "Murrieta Two," which focuses on the way "they [Anglos] tried to take away who I [Chicano] am" (67), and "The Path to Perfection," which summarizes the origin of the dominant culture's "plastic" lifestyle and values (71–75). The two synthetic sections are "Fathers, Sons . . . " and "Rest," which neutralize the harshness of the Us/Them antinomy by cohering into soothing lyrics the positive aspects of Chicano experience. The overall effect of this dialectic is to recall the message of Phase I poetry and its focus on sociopolitical polarities. Elizondo's style, however, is generally stronger than that encountered in Phase I work. Moreover, as Erlinda Gonzales Berry suggests, *Perros y antiperros* evinces an attitude and ideology which

> parallel[s] . . . the convictions of nineteenth century Latin American *arielistas*. . . . In a book of essays collected under the symbolic title *Ariel*, the Uruguayan writer, José Enrique Rodó, wrote an ambivalent critique of North American positivism. He postulated that, though Latin American countries appeared inferior to North America in terms of utilitarian materialism, they had not lost sight of the humanistic values inherited from their Judaeo-Classic roots. Consequently, Latin America could boast spiritual superiority over the most [materialistically] progressive nation in the world. . . . This belief . . . still appeals to many present-day latinos.
> We might say that *arielismo* is reborn in Elizondo's poem. . . . [67]

This synoptic overview of Elizondo's major work illustrates *in reductio* the relationship of the poems to each other and how they develop from the first seven in thematically integrated patterns.

One poem, however, because of its lyricism and aesthetic power, warrants closer analysis. It is " 'Marcha'," a thematically and stylistically distinctive piece which falls almost in the exact center of the work—it is number sixteen, and seventeen poems follow it. Its distinctiveness arises from its striking lyrical beauty which, in turn, imparts universality to it. In fact, we can place it among American literature's best war poems. The first stanza presents the subject—the dead returning from Vietnam—in poignant understatement.

> Rataplán, rataplán, rataplán plin plan.
> Rataplán, rataplán, rataplán plin plan,
> Passing by are the faces of the dead
> who, in years of discordant strife
> went to leave their souls
> in faraway lands
> They went dressed in green like children
> going camping at the tender age of fifteen
> But on their shoulders they carried rifles
> (43; my translation for all " 'Marcha' " quotations)

The onomatopoeia of the opening lines explains the poet's enclosure of the title in quotation marks: this is not a real "march"; it is a "parade" of ghosts. In translation, the verse loses the delicacy of its slant rhyme as well as the harmony of its regular meter, but its elegiac tone remains. The second stanza increases the poem's emotional intensity in language and imagery that tap the profound sense of sad outrage at the horror of war.

> Where are the eyes that yesterday beheld the light?
> Today they are hollow bones, shattered windows
> the warmth will shine no more beyond that veil.
> Where is the head of black tresses
> that under the vast sky was my own sunflower?
> Where are the lips that once sang folksongs
> kissed brunettes, blondes, and mothers beneath the sun? (43)

Like Whitman's rhetorical questions in "When Lilacs Last in the Dooryard Bloom'd" or Shakespeare's in Sonnet 67, the nature of the questions makes glib any possible reply. The third stanza interrupts the prevailing tone and thereby keeps the poem from brimming over into the sentimental excess. The poet instead reminisces about the lives once lived by the prematurely dead soldiers: "Those are the chests that at weddings and baptisms/ hurled strong cries of ¡AJUAS! and of song/ . . . that in Texas and Delano/ went . . . to see the Governor" (43). Remembering the "cholos" and the "batos" alive in the third verse is sobering; it is as if the irreversible fact of their deaths suddenly penetrates, and the speaker's elegiac voice changes dramatically to a simple, conversational tone directed to the marchers: "Didn't you say that when you were done/ you wouldn't go picking cotton,/ that instead of hitting the fields/ you were going to be a doctor?" (43). The tonal shift intensifies the loss by underscoring what it means in measurable personal terms, terms that cast a shadow on the future. The young soldiers' deaths have consequences far beyond the immediate loss to families; the impact extends to the general commonweal and future generations. The poem's overall effect, then, as with all fine "war poems," is to weep a poetic prayer for peace.

*Perros y antiperros* established Elizondo's place within the vanguard of the Chicano Literary Renaissance. With Gonzales, Delgado, and Sánchez, he injected a powerful voice of political protest into contemporary American literature, and with Alurista he asserted the Chicano desideratum of a native language other than standard edited U.S. American English if a genuine *raza* literature were to be achieved. He has stated "that the literature of the Chicano has the language that is most suited to the writer, the one he feels more comfortable with. . . . The linguistic variants within Chicano literature simply reflect our linguistic reality."[68] Certainly, his combination of dialect Spanish with sophisticated literary technique constituted an important landmark in Phase II poetry and helped free other writers to compose in the idiom most suited to their purposes and talents. In addition, his use of language serves multiple metaphorical objectives, one of which Marcienne Rocard cites when he observes that "l'espagnol d'Elizondo nous immerge dans un monde coupé de l'extérieur" ("Elizondo's Spanish immerses us in a world cut off from its [white] surroundings").[69] And, of course, his employment of Spanish is a purely political act demonstrating the right of Chicanos to public use of their language. For these reasons, then, and also because of the popularity of *Perros y antiperros* since its first, incomplete appearance in an early number of *El Grito*, Elizondo's is a significant voice *en la poesía chicana*.

As this review of Phase II poetry has shown, the writing in this category has developed beyond the narrower dimensions of Phase I writing with its emphasis on political protest and consciousness-raising about *raza*. Although most Phase II poetry contains discernible and sometimes even pronounced political bases, it is generally more complex thematically and stylistically than the Movement poetry examined in the last chapter. It is also more lyrical in conception and design. For example, titles like Alurista's "fruto de bronce" and "flowers in the lake" along with Montoya's "El Louie" and Romero's "Comanchito" exhibit the characteristics of the poetics defined earlier in this chapter in more refined and stylized ways. They also offer fresh insight into another realm of U.S. American experience, into *lo ser chicano* (Chicano being), and in the process add new facets to our national literature.

The poets read here contributed to a Chicano poetics in manifold ways: Alurista by innovating its multilingualism, Amerindian symbolism, and the possibilities of ritual residing in both the material world and in art forms; Raúl Salinas by exploring the outer boundaries of *pinto* experience and by insisting on fusing crosscultural solidarity into the heart of the Movement; José Montoya through his stylized realism in sketching portraits of barrio characters in a vernacular bilingual idiom capturing the dynamic energy of *mestizaje*; Sergio Elizondo through an unhesitating use of Spanish and sophisticated Spanish poetic meters to convey the essentially Phase I protest message of his verse; and Leo Romero by asserting the acceptability of a predominantly English idiom in Chicano poetics, a feature that looks ahead to the masterly craft of Gary Soto, Lorna Dee Cervantes, and Alberto Ríos, and also by replacing the didactic tone of protest with the quieter but yet forceful tones of lyricism. In these and myriad other ways, these poets enlivened the field with new insight, energy, and honesty that gave crescive momentum to Chicano poetics.

## NOTES

1. Cordelia Candelaria, "Anahuac Again and the Influence of Chicano Writers," *American Book Review* 4:5 (July 1982), 10 [review of Daniel Peters' *The Luck of Huemac*]; and "*Los Ancianos* in Chicano Literature," *Agenda: A Journal of Hispanic Issues* 10:5 (November 1979), 4–5, 33.

2. Felipe de Ortego y Gasca, "An Introduction to Chicano Poetry," in Joseph Sommers and Tomás Ybarra-Frausto, eds., *Modern Chicano Writers* (Englewood Cliffs, N.J.: Prentice-Hall, 1979), 111; also see A. Poulin, Jr., *Contemporary American Poetry* (Boston: Houghton Mifflin, 1971).

3. Other sources that purport to deal with contemporary poetry and that omit any reference to Chicano poetry are Alberta T. Turner, ed., *Fifty Contemporary Poets* (New York: David McKay, 1977); William J. Smith, ed., *Granger's Index to Poetry* (New York: Columbia University, 1978); the 1970–1977 Supplement to *Granger's Index* even congratulates itself regarding its inclusion of "minorities and women"; Karl Malkoff, ed., *Crowell's Handbook of Contemporary American Poetry* (New York: Crowell, 1973); James Vinson, ed., *Contemporary Poets* (New York: St. Martin's Press, 1980); Robert B. Shaw, ed., *American Poetry Since 1960* (Cheadle, England: Carcanet Press, 1973); Donald Hall, ed., *Contemporary American Poetry*, 2d ed. (Baltimore: Penguin Books, 1972); and David A. Evans, ed., *New Voices in American Poetry* (Boston: Little, Brown, 1973).

4. Cordelia Candelaria, "Hang-Up of Memory: Another View of Growing Up Chicano," *American Book Review* 5:2 (April 1983), 7 [review of Rodriguez's *Hunger of Memory*].

5. Donald Hall, "Preface to the Second Edition," *Contemporary American Poetry* (London: Penguin, 1972 [1962]), 37–38.

6. For further insight into (a) Williams' and (b) Neruda's poetry see (a) Jerome Mazarro, *William Carlos Williams: The Later Poems* (Ithaca, N.Y.: Cornell University Press, 1973); Suzanne Juhasz, *Metaphor and the Poetry of Williams, Pound, and Stevens* (Lewisburg, Pa.: Bucknell, 1974); Paul Mariani, *William Carlos Williams: A New World Naked* (New York: McGraw-Hill, 1981); and (b) E. R. Monegal, *El viajero inmóvil* (Buenos Aires, 1967); Amado Alonso, *Poesía y estilo de Pablo Neruda*, 4th ed., (Buenos Aires: Editorial Sudamerican, 1968); René de Costa, *The Poetry of Pablo Neruda* (Cambridge, Mass.: Harvard, 1979).

7. Luis Valdez, " 'La Plebe'," Introduction to Valdez and Stan Steiner, eds. *Aztlán: An Anthology of Mexican American Literature*, (New York: Alfred A. Knopf, 1972), xiii-xxxiv.

8. Valdés Fallis, "Code-Switching in Bilingual Chicano Poetry," *Hispania* 59:4 (December 1976), 884; the quoted definition of "foregrounding" is from B. Havranek, "The Functional Differentiation of the Standard Language," in Paul L. Garvin, ed., *Prague School Reader on Esthetics, Literary Structure and Style* (Washington, D.C.: Georgetown University Press, 1964), 9–10.

132 Chicano Poetry

9. Ron Arias, *The Road to Tamazunchale* (Albuquerque, N. Mex.: Pajarito Publications, 1978), 16–17 [first published: Reno, Nev.: West Coast Poetry Review, 1975]).

10. The modern interpretation of *mestizaje* is influenced by Mexican philosopher/educator José Vasconcelos' concept of *la raza cosmica*, "the race of synthesis, that is integral—made of the spirit and the blood of all peoples, and, for that reason, more capable of true fraternity and a really universal visión." "La Raza Cosmica" in *Vasconcelos: Prólogo y Selección de Genaro F. MacGregor* (México, D.F.: Ediciones de la Secretaría de educación pública, 1942 [1925]), 130.

11. The fiction of Ron Arias and Raymond Barrio along with the poetry of Inéz Tovar and the plays of Estela Portillo Trambley are additional examples of the new *mestizaje* in Chicano literature.

12. *Webster's New World Dictionary of the American Language*, 2d ed. (1980), 1229.

13. For further insight into ethnopoetics, see Jerome Rothenberg, *Shaking the Pumpkin* (New York: Doubleday, 1972) and his *Pre-Faces & Other Writings* (New York: New Directions, 1981), as well as issues of the journals *Alcheringa* and $L=A=N=G=U=A=G=E$.

14. Rothenberg, *Pre-Faces & Other Writings*, 28–36.

15. Ibid., 30–31.

16. In certain respects the eclecticism of Chicano poets (and other *raza* artists, for that matter) compares to the eclecticism of the transcendentalist movement in the United States in the nineteenth century. Transcendentalists like Emerson sought to integrate European sources (like German romanticism, for example) and Oriental philosophies into their native Anglo-American perspectives in a synthetic manner not unlike that of contemporary Chicano writers working with pre-American indigenous sources.

17. For example, Gary Keller writes of "our laureado Chicano poet" in "Alurista, Poeta-Antropologo, and the Recuperation of the Chicano Identity," in *Return*: [Alurista] *Poems Collected and New* (Ypsilanti, Mich.: Bilingual Press/Editorial Bilingue, 1982), xxvii; and Bruce-Novoa writes "to many [Alurista] is the poet laureate of Aztlán," in *Chicano Authors, Inquiry by Interview* (Austin, Tex.: University of Texas Press, 1980), 267.

18. "[T]he phrase *poet laureate* was used as a special degree conferred by a university in recognition of skill in Latin grammar and versification. . . . Independent of these customs and usages was the ancient practice of kings and chieftains, both in educated and barbarous nations, of maintaining 'court poets,' persons attached to the prince's household and maintained for the purpose of celebrating the virtues of the royal family or singing the praises of military exploits. . . . The modern office of *Poet Laureate* in England resulted from the application of the academic term *poet laureate* to the traditional court poet.. . . . The early, primary duty of the laureate was to render professional service to the royal family and the court." C. Hugh Holman, *A Handbook to Literature*, 3d ed. (Indianapolis, Ind.: Odyssey Press, 1972), 399–401.

19. Holman, *A Handbook to Literature*, 401.

20. Alurista quoted in Bruce-Novoa, *Chicano Authors*, 267–68. References to Alurista's personal life are taken from this interview.

21. *El Ombligo de Aztlán* (San Diego: Centro de Estudios Chicanos Publications, 1971), ii; subsequent references to this collection will be made in the text.

22. Bruce-Novoa observes that "[t]o appreciate the totality of [Alurista's] vision and avoid erroneous impressions of him as an exoticist, one should read Alurista's books in toto and in order. They are like programmed instruction manuals. . . . [to] What follows, in *Floricanto* and the other books . . . " (*Chicano Authors*, 265). I concur entirely with this observation, only I start earlier, with Alurista's contribution to *Ombligo*.

23. Keller, "Alurista, Poeta-Antropologo, and the Recuperation of the Chicano Identity," xii; and Juan Gomez-Quiñones, "Preface," *Floricanto en Aztlán* (Los Angeles: UCLA Chicano Studies Center Publications, 1971 [1976]), n.p. Subsequent references to *Floricanto* will be made in the text.

24. Gustavo Segade, "Chicano *Indigenismo*: Alurista and Miguel Méndez M.," *Xalman* 1:4 (Spring 1977), 8.

25. Tomás Ybarra-Frausto, "Alurista's Poetics: The Oral, the Bilingual, The Pre-Columbian," in Sommers and Ybarro-Frausto, eds., *Modern Chicano Writers*.

26. Keller, "Alurista," xlii.

27. The "Flower Wars" were "prearranged military engagements . . . the purpose of which would be to provide a testing ground for aspiring youths and to provide captives for sacrificial purposes." R. C. Padden, *The Hummingbird and the Hawk* (New York: Harper Colophon Books, 1967), 39.

28. Ibid., 26.

29. Keller, "Alurista," xli.

30. Robert Creeley, *Was That a Real Poem & Other Essays* (Bolinas, Calif.: Four Seasons Foundation, 1979), 106.

31. Segade, "Chicano *Indigenismo*," 4.

32. Ibid.

33. See Matt S. Meier and Feliciano Rivera, *Dictionary of Mexican American History* (Westport Conn.: Greenwood Press, 1981), 155–56 for discussion of the Virgin of Guadalupe.

34. Salvador Rodríguez Del Pino, "La poesía chicana: una nueva trayectoria," in Francisco Jiménez, ed., *The Identification and Analysis of Chicano Literature* (New York: Bilingual Press/ Editorial Bilingüe, 1979), 75–76.

35. Alurista quoted in Bruce-Novoa, *Chicano Authors*, 277; italics indicate Spanish words in the original.

36. Bruce-Novoa, *Chicano Authors*, 267.

37. Cordelia Candelaria, "Review of *Flor y Canto IV and V: An Anthology of Chicano Literature from the Festivals Held in Albuquerque, New Mexico, 1977 and Tempe, Arizona, 1978*" in *La Red/The Net* 62 (December 1982), 6–9.

38. Tomás Ybarra-Frausto, "Alurista's Poetics: the Oral, the Bilingual, the Pre-Columbian," in Sommers and Ybarra-Frausto, eds., *Modern Chicano Writers*, 125.

39. The "Hail Mary" reads: Hail Mary, full of grace, the Lord is with thee. Blessed art thou among women and blessed is the fruit of thy womb, Jesus. Hail Mary, Mother of God, pray for us sinners now and at the hour of our death. Amen.

40. Composer Carl Orff is best known for *Carmina Burana* (1937) which combines his fascination with Bavarian folklore, Greek antiquity, and medieval

fairytales and legends. Alurista finds compatible to his own temperament Orff's interest in ancient forms, and he would agree with the composer's belief that "old material . . . [is] valid material. The time element disappears, and only the spiritual power remains." Like Orff, Brazilian Heitor Villa-Lobos also found native folk motifs valuable to his music, and he was bold in his use of Indian and African elements in classical composition in the first two decades of this century. See *The International Cyclopedia of Music and Musicians* (New York: Dodd, Mead, 1964), pp. 1528–31 for Orff and pp. 2311–14 for Villa-Lobos.

41. Made popular by singer José Feliciano, "Light My Fire" was first released as a single recording by The Doors in 1968. A Beatles' song, "Strawberry Fields Forever" first appeared as a single, and later on the album *Magical Mystery Tour*, in 1967. Musician-composer Jimi Hendrix is celebrated as one of the greatest synthesizers of popular music ever. He innovated the use of psychedelic electronic sounds in both rock 'n' roll and rhythm and blues.

42. Ybarra-Frausto, "Alurista's Poetics," in Sommers and Ybarra-Frausto, *Modern Chicano Writers*, 127.

43. Alurista, *Nationchild Plumaroja* in *Return: Poems Collected and New* (Ypsilanti, Mich.: Bilingual Press/Editorial Bilingüe, 1982), 33; subsequent references to this collection will be made in the text. I chose this edition over the original one (San Diego: Toltecas en Aztlán, 1972) because it represents the author's most recently approved edition (see "Introduction," xiv and xxv).

44. Michael C. Meyer and William L. Sherman, *The Course of Mexican History*, (New York: Oxford University Press, 1983), 14–18.

45. Tomás Ybarra-Frausto refers to these wordblends as "neologisms" ("Alurista's Poetics," 126). However, since Alurista consistently changes the combinations from poem to poem and often even within a given poem, they more nearly resemble stream-of-consciousness language where the combined morphemes evince a subliminal process and evoke the connectedness between thought and feeling. Although the poetry is not stream-of-consciousness per se, it is concerned with capturing a similar interior process.

46. See Gary Keller's "Introduction" in *Return*, xxxv-xxxvi, for an insightful discussion of the title symbol, one that emphasizes the "syncretic confluence of religions" embodied in "nationchild plumaroja."

47. Keller, "Introduction," in *Return*, xiv and xxv.

48. Ybarra-Frausto, "Alurista's Poetics," 126.

49. Some of the early critical recognition of Alurista includes Philip D. Ortego, "Chicano Poetry: Roots and Writers," *New Voices in Literature* (Edinburg, Tex.: Pan American University, 1971); Rafael J. González, "Pensamientos sobre la literatura chicana," *Proceedings, National Conference on Bilingual Education* (Austin, Tex.: Dissemination Center for Bilingual Education, 1972); Joel Hancock, "The Emergence of Chicano Poetry: A Survey of Sources, Themes, and Techniques," *Arizona Quarterly* 29:1 (Spring 1973); and Carlota Cárdenas de Dwyer, "Myth and Folk Culture in Contemporary Chicano Literature," *La Luz* 3:9 (December 1974). Writers who have publicly acknowledged Alurista's seminal impact on Chicano poetry include Jesus Maldonado, *Poesía Chicana: Alurista, el Mero Chingón* (Seattle, Wash: Centro de Estudios Chicanos Monograph Series, 1971); Sergio Elizondo, "Myth and Reality in Chicano Literature," *Latin American Literary Review* 5:10

(Spring 1977); and almost all of the writers interviewed in Bruce-Novoa's *Chicano Authors* mentioned Alurista and his work as important to the field and to their own writing, with José Montoya saying "most of what Alurista wrote was a milestone" (135).

50. Raúl Salinas, *Un Trip Through the Mind Jail y Otras Excursions* (San Francisco: Editorial Pocho-Che, 1980), 55. All references to this edition will subsequently be made parenthetically in the text.

51. Bruce-Novoa, *Chicano Authors*, 117.

52. Esteban Villa interviewed by Jacinto Quirarte, *Mexican American Authors* (Austin, Tex.: University of Texas Press, 1973), 134.

53. José Montoya, "Early Pieces" in *El Sol y Los de Abajo and Other R.C.A.F. Poems* (San Francisco: Ediciones Pocho-Che, 1972), 1. All references to this edition will subsequently be made parenthetically in the text.

54. *The Book of the Chilam Balam of Chumayel*, Ralph B. Roys, trans. (Norman: University of Oklahoma Press, 1967), was originally compiled by the Mayan Juan José Hoíl in 1782 in order to preserve the ancient Mayan myths, legends, and prophecies.

55. José Montoya, "El Louie" in Luis Valdez and Stan Steiner, eds., *Aztlán: An Anthology of Mexican Literature*, (New York: Alfred A. Knopf, 1972), 333–37. All references to this poem will subsequently be made parenthetically in the text.

56. Critical discussions that overlook this aspect of *pachuquismo* in the poem include Bruce-Novoa, *Chicano Poetry: A Response to Chaos* (Austin: University of Texas Press, 1982), 14–29; Marcienne Rocard, *Les Fils du Soleil: La Minorité Mexicaine à travers la Littérature des États-Unis* (Paris: Maison-neuve et Larose, 1980), 351–355; and Salvador R. Del Pino, "La Poesía Chicana" in Jiménez, *Identification and Analysis of Chicano Literature*, 84–85. For an illuminating discussion of the subject that neither deifies nor disparages the *pachuco*, see Rafael Grajeda, "The Pachuco in Chicano Poetry: The Process of Legend-Creation," *Revista Chicano-Riqueña* 8:4 (Fall 1980), 45–59.

57. Leo Romero, "The Road to Tres Piedras," *New Mexico Magazine* (Spring 1971), n.p.

58. Mabel M. Kuykendall, "Road to Tres Piedras," *The Taos News* (March 24, 1971), 7.

59. Leo Romero, "Comanchito," *Thunderbird* [University of New Mexico Magazine] (1971), n.p.

60. As Tomás Vallejos points out in his doctoral dissertation, "*Mestizaje*: The Transformation of Ancient Indian Religious Thought in Contemporary Chicano Fiction" (University of Colorado, 1979), the archetypal bond between *raza y tierra* derives from the ancient roots that unite Chicanos and Native Americans both anthropologically and in myth. He points out that modern Chicano writers adapt that bond to figurative effect in their work.

61. Romero, "In the End It Will Be the Same as in the Beginning" and "The Desert of Our Remembrance," *Thunderbird* (1972), n.p.

62. Romero, "Land," *Puerto del Sol* [New Mexico State University Magazine] (1972), 9–10.

63. "Entrevista con Sergio Elizondo," *De Colores* 3:4 (1977), 78.

64. Elizondo, *Perros y antiperros: una épica chicana*, Gustavo Segade, trans.

(Berkeley, Calif.: Quinto Sol Publications, 1972), 9. Subsequent references to this edition will be made parenthetically in the text.

65. There are thirty-three poems in *Perros y antiperros*, not the "thirty-four" claimed by Erlinda Gonzales Berry in her article *"Perros y antiperros*: The Voice of the Bard," *De Colores* 5:1–2 (1980), 46.

66. Rhapsody was a convention of the classical Greek epic where it served as an uninterrupted recitation of extravagant rhetoric and ecstatic sentiment. Elizondo (and Gonzales in *Joaquín*) employ the convention to break the dominant pattern of distress at and dismissal of the Anglo culture in their work.

67. Gonzales Berry, *"Perros y antiperros*," 47–48.

68. Elizondo interview in Bruce-Novoa, *Chicano Authors*, 74.

69. Rocard, *Les Fils du Soleil*, 349.

# 4

# Chicano Poetry, Phase III:
# The Flowering of *Flor y Canto*

As explained in Chapter One *flor y canto* unites two separate images which, in conjunction, give rise to a third meaning. *Flower and song*, from the original Nahuatl *in xochitl in cuicatl*, means *poetry*, even while the phrase calls to consciousness images of blossoms and melody. More specifically, *flor y canto* refers to Chicano poetry, the phrase emerging out of the Chicano Renaissance and out of the first-stage revisionism in Chicano literary scholarship. Accordingly, having described the social protest of Phase I poetry (Chapter Two) and the basic elements and tendencies of Chicano poetics in Phase II poetry (Chapter Three), this chapter presents Phase III Chicano poetry, the efflorescence of *flor y canto*. The compositions discussed here reveal a sophistication of style and technique, an individuality in treatment of subject and theme, and a mature skill and control that signal an inevitably developed form—much as the vivid blossoms of a cactus inevitably flower out of the spiny base.

The flowering of *flor y canto* developed from the poetic forms that preceded it. If Phase I poetry was especially marked by thematic polarities of a sociopolitical nature, Phase III poetry features a polarity describable as subject-I versus object-Other. For example, even the drunken persona relentlessly seeking contact with others in Gary Soto's "Telephoning God" gets no closer than "a gnat circling the ear" of the Other.[1] Moreover, if Phase II poetry was characterized by multilingualism, *mestizaje*, and ritual, the poetry in this chapter is not explicitly defined by those elements, but it is informed by an absorbed knowledge of them. What, then, is salient— what characteristics explain the clustering of poets and poems in this category? There are two primary traits operating here: (1) stylistic skill and lyrical subtlety, and (2) a multiplicity of subjects and themes that range beyond the *raza* concerns visited thus far. Furthermore, out of this second area evolved a narrative voice hardly encountered in Chicano poetry before 1974. It is a private, highly subjective, personal voice quite distinct from the more conventional Chicano poetic personas with their didactic and/or declamatory appeal to the community's shared experience and its condemnation of the dominant culture's abuse of power. The two principal poets discussed here—Gary Soto and Bernice Zamora—exemplify these traits through their fine mastery of craft and through their distinctly personal, lyrical handling of narration.

## GARY SOTO

Recipient of the 1976 United States Award of the International Poetry Forum, *The Elements of San Joaquin* lifted Gary Soto from obscurity to a rung on the ladder of contemporary U.S. poetry. His two subsequent books have further advanced him on the ladder and have brought him greater renown and respect. His work is significant in contemporary letters, and it is central in contemporary Chicano literature. Whether his is viewed as "the most important voice among the young Chicano poets"[2] or whether he is seen as a strong presence with a "certain well-measured universality,"[3] it is clear that his talent rises above the middling norm. Of particular interest is the lean character of Soto's style. His use of language—primarily English—is direct, concrete, and succinct, producing a denuded simplicity of style. However, the suppleness of his diction and syntax belies the simplicity and deepens the surface structure of his meanings to suggest a profundity of idea and emotion not immediately or overtly apparent.

Dedicated to *"mi Abuelita y mi Madre," San Joaquin* discloses the poet's range of interests and prefigures a number of features that are developed to elegant effect in the later volumes. Soto's subjects range from the industrial blight of cities to the lurking threat of violence in contemporary urban life to the ironic beauty of agricultural fields which extract the sweat, toil, and youth of migrant farmworkers, and these are but three from the manifold range in *San Joaquin*. A technique prefigured in this volume and refined later in *The Tale of Sunlight* is his imagistic approach to characterization. The poet manages to evoke complete portraits of his characters by stringing together seemingly random bits of information, images, and tiny vignettes. In incipient form this technique appears throughout the three categories oi his *San Joaquin* poems which deserve special scrutiny: the "field" pieces, the poems of violence, and those we may call poems of negative transcendentalism.

The field poems in *San Joaquin* are set in farm labor fields, and they mesh the raw physical reality of the fields with the mood of the workers who know them intimately. Soto presents the seven field poems in the first person voice of a young man whose suffering has invested him with the sensibility of someone much older and wiser. The speaker emerges in "Field Poem" through a scene that follows him and his brother like a camera as they leave the fields at the end of the day.

> Speaking
> In broken English, in broken Spanish
> The restaurant food,
> The tickets to a dance
> We wouldn't buy with our pay.
>
> From the smashed bus window,
> I saw the leaves of cotton plants
> Like small hands
> Waving good-bye.[4]

The poet achieves this poignancy of deprivation not by explicitly stating the pitiful facts of the two young workers' lives, but by understating the want. The dance tickets "wouldn't" be bought because, we infer, their "pay" must go for family essentials, just as the descriptive detail of the "smashed bus window" brings to mind the neglected decrepitude of the corporate growers' standard means of transport for the workers. Through the personification of the cotton plants, the poet draws a correspondence between the "small hands / Waving good-bye" and the toiling hands of the fieldhands. The adjective "small" is particularly effective because it lingers in the mind as a question— does the narrator have "small hands" too? Are he and his brother children?

Another field poem, "Hoeing," describes the worker's relation to the land that controls him and that appears in the piece as a pervasive part of his being: "Dirt . . . entering my nostrils / And eyes / The yellow under my fingernails" (24). We see what the speaker sees as he works—his hoe crossing his "shadow" as he chops weeds, the "thick caterpillars" that the wind blows into "shriveled rings," and the "sun" warming the "left" side of his "face" (24). But the poem constitutes more than sharply etched description, and Soto manages to take us beyond tableau, however striking or dramatic, with one image and one word in the last stanza.

When the sun was on the left
And against my face
Sweat          the sea
That is still within me  ·
Rose and fell from my chin
Touching land
For the first time (24)

The word is "still," and the image is that of the speaker's "sweat"
symbolically yoked to "the sea." Together the image and the word make
him and his lowly status a firm part of the natural whole. The first two
stanzas describe how the land controls and touches him as he works it, while
the last one shows that he, too, reciprocates. His "sweat" (and tears?)
returns "the sea" to the land, asserting the worker's forgotten place in the
encompassing vastness of earth.

    Another field poem that closes with this kind of image is "Summer."
After answering the question "what was it like?" in the farmworker camps
and then paralleling that form of *campesino* misery with that of "the Projects
in the Eastside," the poet ends with an image that again asserts the reality
of the *campesinos'* place in nature metonymically captured in the reference to
"the Sierras."

And next summer?
It will be the same. Boredom,
In early June, will settle
On the eyelash shading your pupil from dust,
On the shoulder you look over
To find the sun rising
From the Sierras. (26)

Although these images insist on recognizing the worker's place in the vast
continuum of life, they also demonstrate, in the total context of each poem
and in the field poems as a cluster, the insignificance of that human place
in contrast to the awesomeness of nature. The total effect of this imagery
is to suggest that the cyclic inevitability of nature is repeated for humankind in the inexorable inevitability of suffering as an existential condition.
Accordingly, the theme of human insignificance is a dominant one in the
cycle of poems described here as "negative transcendentalism."

    Like the nineteenth-century U.S. transcendentalists, Soto writes obser-
vantly about nature, employing concrete natural imagery to sketch vivid
pictures of the outdoors and of human presence in nature. Unlike those

transcendentalists, however, Soto connects his human subjects to nature not to prove that the mystical transcendence of mundane experience derives from communion with it but, rather, to show that human insignificance is an existential reality *within* and *to* nature. His subjects are part of the natural whole, of the eternal flow of natural time, but instead of being transported to spiritual heights because of that, they merely stand witness to the meaninglessness of the void. As the speaker observes in "Field," after a day's exposure to agrarian nature,

> Already I am becoming the valley,
> A soil that sprouts nothing
> For any of us. (15)

The poet develops this concept of nothingness in "Wind" where mountains and cattle bones are "peeled . . . grain by grain . . . To white dust, to nothing" (16). Here, the subject-I is also blown away by the wind, but the figure is even more reductive.

> Evenings, when I am in the yard weeding,
> The wind picks up the breath of my armpits
> Like dust, swirls it
> Miles away
> And drops it
> On the ear of a rabid dog,
> And I take on another life. (16)

No transcendence here, only existential witness to the indifferent fact of nature. Similarly, in "Rain" the poet conveys the passage of the seasons by contrasting the busy-ness of nature with his own seasonal joblessness.

> When autumn rains flatten sycamore leaves,
> The tiny volcanos of dirt
> Ants raised around their holes,
> I should be out of work. (20)

With the "autumn rains" and the ants' preparations for winter, the speaker knows that the season will "tighten" the "skin of [his] belly / And there will be no reason for pockets" (20). Rather than giving cause for hope and spiritual transcendence, nature's regular cycles confirm the negative truth of the farmworker's transient life and dependence on seasonal work. Likewise, nature in "Avocado Lake" serves only as a backdrop for death by drowning—not a purposeful, transcendental dying that unites the dead

with the All, but a "willows"- framed death where "what remains of him"
is the regurgitated "phlegm" of his dying "now, at daybreak . . . drift[ing]
beneath the surface" of the lake (30). These examples show Soto to be
intensely part of the unromantic modernist spirit of our century. They also
distance him from Chicano poets (like Alurista and Romero, for instance)
who find sublime purport in *raza*'s relation to land and nature.

Further widening the thematic distance between Soto and other Chicano
poets are his poems of violence or the threat of violence as elements in the
contemporary consciousness. Other Chicano poets incorporate violence and
conflict into their writing, but theirs is almost exclusively related to
political and collective arenas like police brutality against *raza* or the high
percentage of Chicano deaths in U.S. wars or the exploitation of workers
through corporate greed. Soto's, on the other hand, concerns the widespread phenomenon of criminal violence in modern urban society. He
writes of the fear of, the fact of, and the fantasy of violence inflicted on the
individual by pathological strangers in a menacing environment. "The
Underground Parking" exemplifies this category of *San Joaquin* poems. It
describes an assault on "your wife" by "a man who holds fear / Like the lung
a spot of cancer"—that is, the fear is malignant and spreads like disease that
hurts and contaminates others. It describes a rape "under arms of tattoos,"
a "kick in the mouth," and an "ice pick at the throat" (5). Ironically, the
speaker sympathizes not with the victim and her terrified "whimper," but
with the assaulter and his fear: "I could give him the bread of my luck / And
a prayer," says the speaker before admonishing

> If your fist closes, open it.
> If you curse, swallow your tongue
> Because you won't have nothing to say,
> Not a kind word to lead him
> From where he squats, waiting. (5)

The poet is not concerned with punishment, which he suggests only
worsens the assaulter's pathology; he is interested in *transformation* through
kindness, the more difficult response. It is here, perhaps, that the poet
reveals his romantic side by assuming that a trace of humaneness exists
inside the criminal sadist's heart.

Like "The Underground Parking" which is partly addressed to "you," in
a blend of second and third person verbs, "The Morning They Shot Tony
Lopez, Barber and Pusher Who Went Too Far, 1958" is addressed in the
second person to the dead Lopez. The narrative voice describes in graphic

detail and vivid realism "what happened when they entered the back door" and "you were too slow in raising an arm" (11). What happens is that Lopez is murdered. Soto adeptly draws eerie parallels between inanimate images and human feeling, images that leave a haunting trace of fear and discomfort in one's consciousness. The speaker tells, for example, of "your pockets turned inside out, hanging breathless as tongues" and of "the earth you would slip into like a shirt" (11). The closing lines masterfully link the murdered Lopez to the fetal Lopez being born exactly one lifetime earlier.

> When they entered, and shot once,
> You twisted the face your mother gave
> With the three, short grunts that let you slide
> In the same blood you closed your eyes to. (11)

The parallel of the Barber's bloody death with his blood-smooth birth reduces both to mere markings on the physiological continuum of life. Certainly the speaker can find no other meaning. As a group, these poems demonstrate the poet's need to treat the everpresence of violence as another common element of life (in San Joaquin) that must be understood within the multitudinous flux of experience.

Not content with recording plausible acts of violence and kneading original metaphors in and around them, Soto also writes of the threat of violence which lurks ubiquitously like an expected shadow of the city night.

> Because there are avenues
> Of traffic lights, a phone book
> Of brothers and lawyers,
> Why should you think your purse
> Will not be tugged from your arm
> Or the screen door
> Will remain latched
> Against the man
> Who hugs and kisses
> His pillow
> In the corridor of loneliness?
> ("After Tonight," 8)

We are not ever entirely safe from harm, the poem avers, and certainly not immune to death's visit. "Because blood revolves from one lung to the next,/ Why think it will/ After tonight?" (9). There are good answers to these troubling questions, of course—like, for instance, life cannot be lived

without the expectation of a future—but the poet's rhetoric suggests that
the answers are less important than the process of self-examination generated by the questions. The poet strings together a number of items familiar
to suburbia, things of comfort that give an illusion of security like
"sprinkler[s] turning," central heating, and "siamese cats . . . against your
legs" (8). "But remember this," he cautions, those are trifles in comparison
to "the splintered wrists" of enslaved workers or the reality of life that is
as vulnerable as "blood" circulating within fragile veins. He would dis-
comfit and frighten us into remembering the difference in values.

Although these three categories of poems in *San Joaquin* are the best of
the volume, also of interest are Soto's portraits of *raza* life, which constitute
another set of "elements of San Joaquin." (Parenthetically, the poet uses
"elements" in the title in its scientific meaning referring to irreducible
substances that cannot be separated by ordinary chemical methods and also
in two more colloquial senses. "Elements" also refers to the constituent
parts of a whole and to "the elements" of weather and climate which he
usually employs in the compound senses of geophysical and sociocultural
climates.) "History" and "Remedies," are *raza* portraits which focus on
"Grandma" with her "paisley bandana" and "face streaked / From cutting
grapes / And boxing plums" ("History," 41). She is brought to life by the
vividness of the weave of elements and images—like the "spears across the
linoleum floor," the "secret cigar box," and the "pepper . . .
beet . . . [and] asparagus" hidden in "her blouse" (40). In writing about
her, the poet's English in one place shifts easily to vernacular Spanish (40),
and the wonder is that that shift does not occur more frequently in these
poems, for in several contexts it is clearly the natural and the aesthetically
desired idiom. The reason for the dominant English in these *raza* pieces
may perhaps be explained by the poet's confession that

          . . . I do not know
     The sorrows
     That sent her praying
     In the dark of a closet.
     The tear that fell
     At night
     When she touched
     Loose skin
     Of belly and breasts.
     I do not know why
     Her face shines . . .

> Only the stories
> That pulled her
> From Taxco to San Joaquin,
> Delano to Westside,
> The places
> In which we all begin. (41)

He does not know why; he can only recall and describe what he recalls. Unlike "History," simple verisimilitude characterizes "Remedies" (Note: not *remedios*, the expected colloquial term which would be more appropriate in this context). Here the poet recalls Grandma's cures "for a cough . . . color blindness . . . a canker" and "for a sty" (42), objectively describing her curandera's practices. But he offers none of his typical probing images or remarks or, even, a word to give artistic perspective to the description, and this absence of texture diminishes the poem's quality.

Two portraits of *raza* life that do contain artistic perspective and that thus enhance the narrative poetic style are "Emilio" and "Copper," the former profiling in third person a neighbor recollected from the poet's past and the latter recalling in first person a period in the poet's life. Described "on the porch, alone" in the evening, Emilio "watches" the neighborhood activities "until night sends [the children] home" (39). The observer's viewpoint interrupts the description toward the end of the poem when we omnisciently enter Emilio's mind.

> . . . He lies
> Thinking of Mexico—a woman sweeping,
> Farmland that suddenly rises
> Into small hills of grass—
> While the moon starts down
> In a darkness that will not repeat itself. (39)

These closing lines explain what objective description cannot, that the subject's aloneness is not temporary but a chronic state of being and also that he is not really "at home" as we originally believe, for his home, Mexico, is actually *inside* him, in mind and soul. In another vein, "Copper" describes the speaker's and "Leonard's" days of "collecting copper" from "alleys" and abandoned "trucks" for re-sale "on the Westside" (43). Especially effective in this piece are such evocative details as "the short-throated pipes furred in oil" and "today we are . . . glowing before a snowy TV," pictures that evoke their precise referents. The poet's perspective appears here in the last three lines with the "spotted . . . glow/ Of copper, the only light needed/ To show the way back" (43). The point here is that

at the time in their lives remembered in the poem things were uncom-
plicated and did not require a brighter "light" to lead "the way back." By
implication, we expect that such simplicity is no longer part of their
present lives, an awareness that is made possible for us by the narrator's
intrusion upon the realistic description.

Gary Soto is one of a tiny number of Chicano poets to have consistently
published in long-established, non-*raza* little magazines, and he is the only
one who has done that and also had four books released by a mainline
academic press, University of Pittsburgh. Moreover, to appear in *Poetry* and
in *Revista Chicano-Requeña* as he has testifies to both the quality and range
of his poetic vision and style, as many others have noted.

*Elements* is an extraordinary work by a Chicano poet who has mastered . . . his
form, has found his voice, and who has the life experiences to provide meaningful
content. Thus, it is an important work because it avoids both the . . .
bombastic/rhetorical statements which too often plague Chicano poetry, and the
lifeless cocoon of pretended intellectual and emotional achievement, the tired
elliptical little descriptions of what is seen out the window (to paraphrase Baraka)
that characterises much of American contemporary poetry.[5]

Furthermore, even the reviewers who have strong reservations about some
of the poet's mannerisms (e.g., frequent enjambements and overstuffed
descriptive tableaux) nevertheless find his work important enough to
command serious critical analysis.[6] The main reason for the literary
credibility that his work has earned among diverse audiences stems from the
logic of aesthetics effectively realized in his poetry. It reveals an individuality, self-identity, experience, and craft so seamlessly unified that the
poems' tight integration of parts cannot be disturbed. Such artistic control
is rare, and his later books bear out the complexity of its source.

## BERNICE ZAMORA

Although Bernice Zamora has been publishing in alternative periodicals
since 1970, her first book, *Restless Serpents*, did not appear until 1976. The
warmth of the reception for her book has not been diminished by the
absence of a sequel, though it would be received with great interest. "Her
poetry is strong and sure of itself,"[7] writes one reviewer, whereas another
is attracted to "Zamora's power [which] lies in the intensity of the strife
between love, a metaphor for all the life impulses, and the rigid limits, in

any of their varied façades, which restrict life."[8] In addition, her poetry manifests Phase III characteristics in its general stylistic competence and occasional brilliance, as well as in the multiplicity of subjects and themes that range from Aztlán motifs to frequent allusions to art, religion, and death. Also in keeping with this category of poetry is the intimacy of the poet's narrative voice which appears variously in the agony of self-examination, in the combined joy and confusion of love and passion, as well as in her observant wonder at the multifariousness of life.

Serving as a rich emblem for the entire book, the title poem and image contain the fundamental thematic crux of the volume. The poet introduces the serpent metaphor first in "Stone Serpents" where it expresses the basic condition and state of mind "of the weary wealthy."[9] Although we normally associate serpents with the subtle intelligence and evil of the snake in the Garden of Eden, as well as with a common human revulsion to reptiles, the "serpents" here are "carved" into the "balustrades" outside the "castle of the weary wealthy" (66). They are thus inanimate as "the stone" they are made from and as impotent as the "rusting treasures" cached inside the unused "temple" of the dead aristocracy. Oppositely, the figure in the poem "Restless Serpents" lives in the freedom of unfettered action— "coiling, / recoiling, pricking / the master's veins" (74). These serpents dominate their environment and elicit the solemn diligence of human attention, for, as the poem's epigraph notes, "the duty of a cobra's master / is fraught with fettered chains" (74). Taken as metaphors for two kinds of *modi operandi*, approaches to living, or attitudes toward life, the dichotomy between "stone" and "restless" serpents symbolizes the difference between impotence and decay and vitality and creativity. And this dichotomy relates not only to the political concerns of wealth and poverty, but also to the personal concerns of "spite," "pain," and "the soul" (74, 66). Moreover, because many of Zamora's poems treat themes of love and sexuality, the antimony also captures elements of the erotic and of sublimated sexuality. In a great many of the volume's poems, the poet addresses this contrast by exposing sterility on the one hand and by celebrating vital energy—even the confused, chaotic, and sometimes mad vitality within one's subrational being—on the other. Such dynamic vigor requires scrupulous care, the poet indicates, and the treatment she recommends is found in art: "Lyrics, / lyrics alone soothe / restless serpents" (74).

Several of the poet's "soothing lyrics" deal with the subject of art, and most of these capture, intertextually, the dynamic energy of either particular poets or their fluxive subject matter. "And All Flows Past," for example, dedicated to U.S. poet Theodore Roethke,[10] pulses with the excited energy characteristic of his "greenhouse poems," while her "Orange-throats" borrows his zoological diction and imagery. Like Roethke in the greenhouse pieces, Zamora flashes back to her childhood in "And All Flows Past."

> when my brother drove us in his pickup
> truck across Siloam prairie after a late autumn snow storm.
> It was a ride in and out of the self—
> romping in four-wheel drive,
> seducing frozen cedars to chip off sap, and
> searing fence posts to ghostly stumps of lost conifers,
> when, fending with the assurance of Absalom,
> we raced at eighty miles sideways. (68)

The speaker uses the highly charged motion of riding the pickup as synecdoche for the conventional journey motif which nicely suits the idea of rite of passage suggested in the "ride in and out of the self." Despite the mechanical nature of the trip, the erotic diction underscores the budding sexuality of pubescence through the description of the roller-coaster thrill.

> Our unclipped heads searched for
> hidden ravines where wheels could get
> lodged in pits. Father-rocking traction
> would lull us for a throttled charge up
> the gorge and jack-knife turn onto the blinding
> white sea plain fenced to a mountain. . . .
>
> At floor-board urge the truck careened . . .
> while our axled bodies climaxed. . . .
>
> Ignoring the mountains advance, we whip-
> lashed toward that hour known
> to all darting offspring. (68)

The poem thus imitates the emergent sexuality of Roethke's greenhouse pieces, both poets finding part of the puzzle explaining adult personality in a commonplace event located in the far reaches of memory. Furthermore, the poem demonstrates again how art is the only preserver of the manifold "all" that "flows past" in a lifetime.

Also displaying "restless serpent" vitality are two poems, "Pico Blanco" and "California," alluding to U.S. poet Robinson Jeffers.[11] Zamora addresses "Pico Blanco," written in the second person, to "you, Jeffers," and she comments on the philosophy of Inhumanism which he articulated throughout his poetic corpus. In brief, Jeffers believed in the progressive deterioration of the human race which, to him, was infinitesimally minor in the grand scheme of nature. As an alternative to the egocentricity he saw underlying most isms, he offered a theory that rejected human solipsism and promoted "transhuman" acceptance of nature. Eventually, nature evolved into the center of his particular mysticism.[12] Zamora's "Pico Blanco" rejects Inhumanism even as it recognizes the firm basis for Jeffers' dissatisfaction with religious orthodoxy and the sociopolitical status quo. Adopting the mask of Cassandra, the classic madwoman in Euro-Western literature and the title figure in the Jeffers poem Zamora challenges, she attacks the earlier poet's promise that God can be reached through a total immersion in nature. Posed as Cassandra in the California coastal mountain peak, Pico Blanco, Zamora's heroine "strain[s her] eyes/ to catch a glimpse of the 'great king'" Jeffers eyed during his own visionary walks through nature (32). Unsuccessful in finding what he had found, she gives up the search and concludes "these are the stewards of *your* estate," but, she suggests, not of hers (32). The *human* victory does belong to her, however, when her Cassandra asserts her power to "chip" away at nature and to be conscious of her actions.

> "Poor bitch," you say. Indeed I am;
> but I am not mumbling to my people
> or to my gods. I am chipping the
> crust of the Pico Blanco.
> Your stewards could help—or you,
> Jeffers; then you and I could vacillate
> breaking the crust—You and I, Jeffers. (32)

Ultimately, her optimism and independence are greater than Jeffers' in that he perceived himself and Cassandra as the prophets of "truth," ignored and, even, "disgusting" to both "men and gods." Zamora, on the other hand, underscores the importance of continually "chipping" away to expose the truth regardless of the response.[13] Furthermore, as the citation shows, the poem's "restless" energy animates its intertextual relationship to Jeffers' poetry, presented here as an argument against Inhumanism, and it also evokes the creative dynamics that inspired the poem. In these ways, Zamora recasts Jeffers' work in essential ways, forcing us to reconsider our experience of the original poem, much as Eliot's discourses on the Metaphysical Poets forced reconsiderations of their work.

Zamora's second major allusion to Jeffers is her poem, "California," written as a modified sonnet sequel to his "Roan Stallion." Rich with "restless serpent" energy, Zamora's "California" and its intertextuality have received significant critical attention which illuminates the present discussion.

"California" attempts a dialogue with its parent poem. . . . the heroine of "Roan Stallion," California is married to Johnny, an Anglo gambler and drunkard who uses her to satisfy his lust. Johnny brings home a roan stallion. . . . [and] One night California becomes the center of physical, sexual warfare between Johnny and the horse. Johnny, lusting to do with California what he has seen the stallion do with his buckskin mare, wants to sexually abuse California; but since [she] presumably has had a liberating experience with the stallion, she repulses him and escapes to the corral. . . . California, armed with a rifle provided by her daughter, aims and kills [Johnny's dog] Bruno. The stallion tramples Johnny . . . [and] California fir[es] three bullets at the horse.
     . . . The first two lines of . . . Zamora's poem are the two final lines of "Roan Stallion."[14]

The quoted passage summarizes the plot action of "Roan Stallion" and explains California's motives and motivations as spouse-victim turned avenger. Focusing on California allows Zamora to move inside the character's consciousness so that we can learn her reaction to the violence that left "[t]wo gods . . . at my feet; I have / shot one, and that one killed the other" (21). With tired irony she explains how "both . . . beasts" tortured her: "Each in his turn . . . laid over me splitting hairs, splitting atoms" (21). But although Johnny and the roan were "beasts," she does not separate herself from them completely, for they are "all of us pools in the moonlight" (21). Moreover, just as the horse's fate was irrevocably tied to "the wind [nature] and rein [man]" and just as Johnny's fate was tied to "the night [eros] and wine," so too is California's fate "inexorably bound by the fetters ('corral') of her very human ('wailing will'; 'bloody') circumstances."[15] Nevertheless, by enspiriting California with new life and voice and by going beyond "Roan Stallion" to memorialize the woman's perspective, Zamora performs a "feminist act that exposes the limitations of her male precursors"[16]— in this case, Jeffers.

Zamora alludes to the earlier poet in two other pieces, "'The Extraordinary Patience of Things'" and "Phantom Eclipse," which indicates the extensiveness of his influence on her. However, these two poems lack the textual vitality of "Pico Blanco" and "California." Both poems emphasize the dynamic energies that define interrelational tensions between the I and the Other, whether other persons, other poetry, nature, or even the warring sides of the self. These contrastive tensions also show obvious kinship to the restless serpents metaphor of the title.

The "stone serpents" half of the sterility/vitality antinomy appears effectively in two short poems about art, "Without Bark" and "Metaphor and Reality." Written "after" German novelist Hermann Hesse,[17] "Without Bark" dispenses with the hydraulic energy of the previous titles, employing instead a quieter, calmer diction and imagery. "If the trees in the background/ remain sombre, let it be," observes the speaker, casting her eye on what "is forbidden to us," on the "broken, splintered branches" that "rattle songs in the wind" (34). The scene here—the mood and tone— recalls the still lifelessness of "Stone Serpent," and it also brings to mind Hesse's solemn existentialism in *Steppenwolf*. The poet seeks to capture the eerie surrealism of Hesse's fiction as if to demonstrate its salience to Chicano consciousness. Also suggestive of the sterility of the "stone serpent" as well as the relevance of art to life is "Metaphor and Reality," a piece hinged to an explicitly literary metaphor.

> Working in canneries or
> picking beets is the
> metaphor of being,
> of being as it has been
> in the scheme of things. (71)

Assembly-line work and stoop labor, declares the speaker, is not real "being," only an unreal "metaphor" of it. Who or what, we ask, experiences true being? Her answer, simply and directly stated, is complex in its ironic abbreviation of social class:

> As it is, the dream remains
> for you who sit easily with
> Grendel and Godzilla
> as they pick their teeth
> with your children's bones. (71)

The holders of power experience real "being," but their abuse of power transforms them into atavistic beasts. For example, the monster Grendel from the Old English saga *Beowulf* and the modern movie monster Godzilla share the brutality that they inflict on helpless victims. The worse cruelty, however, belongs to those who "sit" comfortably by while the essentially feudal monsters of industry or bureaucracy or politics feed on the helpless, distorting their life experiences into mere metaphors of reality.

Moving from Zamora's art poems to a cluster focusing on the hidden
subjectivity of the self, we again find the stone/restless serpent antinomy.
Describing her childhood, for instance, "Angelita's Utility" unmasks the
"I" in unflinching honesty.

> It is not enough I am
> A child of poverty—
> A child among twelve—
> A poverty among indigence;
> It is not enough I
> Acknowledge my impotence,
> My gainlessness, my
> Inutility . . . (69)

Coupling her self-perception of ugliness with her childhood experience of
poverty like this draws attention to the way poverty often produces negative
self-esteem among its young victims. The speaker feigns stoicism—"I rest
prostrate . . . / Let me live this way"—to mask her debilitating guilt,
shame, and yearning for punishment.

> Prostrate I can taste
> The ground I disgrace;
> Naked I can feel the
> Confusion I caused . . .
> Let me die this way. (69)

Like the "stone serpent balustrades . . . of the weary wealthy" Angelita
suffers an *in*utility that is as unbearable as the unborn "child" in the
"rusting" castle (66). Interestingly, the intense yearning for self-
punishment connects with the youthful speaker's fascination with
the self-flagellating *penitente*[18] rites of the Colorado San Luis Valley where
the poet grew up. The persona calls the rites "irresistible" in "Penitents,"
and her scrupulously detailed description certainly justifies the
adjective.

> Once each year *penitentes* in mailshirts
> journey through arroyos Seco, Huerfano . . .
>
> Brothers Carrasco, Ortiz, Abeyta
> prepare the Cristo for an unnamed task.
> Nails, planks and type O blood are set
> upon wooden tables facing, it is decreed,
> the sacred mountain range to the Southwest. (8)

The speaker goes on to describe how the "Nahuatl converts . . . flog one another," their rosaries wreathed around their bodies. Besides the self-punishment, her fascination stems in part from the ritual's antiquity, symbolized in the *"alabados"* which "are heard" rising "from the mountains" and their geological ancientness (8). The poem ends on a note of irony as the poet points out that "all is sacred in the [San Luis] valley"— but only "for one week" (8). Although "Penitents" describes a great deal of activity, the repetitive, decadent nature of the ritual itself likens it to the decayed, impotent order of "Stone Serpents" as well as to the "impotence" and desire for self-punishment in "Angelita's Utility."

Altogether different in tone and idea are a number of other personal poems that disclose the poet's range stretched broadly. "Gata Poem," written entirely in Spanish except for one line, addresses the eternal subject of the mating game. Unlike Shakespeare's sonnets or Marvell's "To His Coy Mistress," Zamora informs her treatment of the subject by her feminism (which surfaces more forcefully in several other poems, notably "Pueblo, 1950" and "Sonnet, Freely Adapted"). In "Gata [Cat] Poem" the feminine speaker describes a romantic appeal made by *"a perfect man, a Chicano"** (16). His form is so strikingly beautiful that the speaker's description momentarily jolts into English in the fourth line: "He glistened in the sun like a bronze god," but notwithstanding his godlike beauty, the "perfect . . . Chicano" behaves like an ordinary man trying to seduce a woman. The speaker listens to the bold lover's florid, passionate appeal and then considers whether or not to join him. The poem's last line presents her decision—"Y me fui." As others have observed, the line is ambiguous, for it can mean "and I went [with him]" or "and I left [him]."[19] However, the line's ambiguity enhances the poem by capturing the complex mysteries and uncertainties, the acceptances and rejections, the starts and stops, of romantic love and the sexual mating game.[20] In short, at a given moment the speaker "went" with the "bronze" lover, while at another she "left" him, depending on how responsive she, as a *"female cat dressed in black,"* felt at the moment (16). In its subtle richness, ambiguity, eroticism, and wit, "Gata Poem" is one of the most successful poems in the entirety of Chicano poetry and has enjoyed widespread critical acclaim.

Another poem treating the mating ritual between lovers is "Plumb," written in a less obscure, imagistic style.

*Italicized lines indicate translations from the original Spanish.

> Before we ate
> While I was putting
> The snowshovel away,
> I saw two robins. . . .
>
> From the window
> I studied the robins
> Keeping each other warm
> While you instructed
> Me in Hemingway;
>
> It was a fine day for learning. (38)

Like so much of Zamora's writing, the erotic here is implicit, hidden within other layers of meaning. The title, for instance, can refer to the intellectual "plumbing" of the depths of Hemingway's fiction, or it can refer to physically "plumbing" the body's sexual depths. The robins' "keeping each other warm" serves as appropriate correlative to the lovers together inside "learning."

In contrast to these love poems is "Bleating," in which the poet struggles to identify what she believes metaphysically and what her true "yearn-[ings]" are (70). She would like "to pray / for an existence / on edge with / any other," an existence beyond the merely physical (70). But "cliff-hanging . . . is not the way," for her, "nor is . . . stacking / Babel skyscrapers / (out of desperation) / toward arbitrary clouds" (70). Despite the intellectual comfort a firm, orthodox metaphysics might bring her, the visceral truth of her desires is simpler.

> I yearn instead
> For goat's milk,
> piñons, and the
> absence of color
> In this painted corner. (70)

The world's multiformity is too much with her, and she herself would be cleansed and revived with less—with the small but sacred facts of her plain and simple southern Colorado origins. The title's aural pun can now be understood: like a stray goat she is "bleating" for home and because of that she would like to "bleed" the busy "color" out of her private "painted corner," settling instead for the comparative blandness of piñon and goat's milk.

The fourth (of six) section(s) in *Restless Serpents* is titled "So Not To Be

Mottled," and the last poem in that section bears the same title. The five-line poem may be viewed as a summative gloss on the volume as a whole, one that simultaneously accepts and rejects the foregoing dichotomous, stone/restless serpents, analysis of Zamora's work.

> You insult me
> When you say I'm
> Schizophrenic.
> *My* divisions are
> Infinite. (52)

The seriocomic tone of the lines, with its opening "You," draws the audient/critic immediately into the poem and, ironically, into dichotomous conflict with the "I." By directly addressing her work's two-sidedness Zamora acknowledges the applicability of that opinion. Moreover, by challenging the notion of simple duality with the self-mocking assertion that "*my* divisions are / Infinite," the poet appears to acknowledge its validity as well. The import of the title, with its explicit rejection of a multicolored life, implies her tacit acceptance of a dualistic black and white worldview. On the other hand, the asserted infinity of her "divisions" accurately describes the wide range and multiplicity of her subjects and her approaches to them. This flexibility has been noted by others: "Zamora demonstrates a lyrical ability . . . [to] fus[e] various literary traditions with social content. Her poetic expression transcends any one tendency by . . . writ[ing] well in a strictly [U.S.] American literary tradition, or as a Chicana recalling images of her past, as a Chicana criticizing Anglo society, as a woman looking into a man's world, symbolically treating a theme [with and] without sexual or ethnic ties, or simply [by] developing an anecdote."[21] Ultimately, "So Not To Be Mottled" reflects both the contradictions and consistencies of the poet's multifarious verse.

Like a sarape with its multicolored threads, Zamora's importance in Chicano poetry is multithreaded. She is important, first, for making intertextual reference a significant part of her method. Although other Chicano poets— namely, Alurista, Raúl Salinas, and Ricardo Sánchez— speckle their writing with allusions to other artists, especially in music, literary allusions are noticeably rare in the vast bulk of Chicano poetry. By exploiting her Chicana identity, Zamora transmutes conventional literary allusion into an original form of lyrical expression. A second important aspect of her work is the skill and versatility of its crafting, which in several poems discloses consummate poetic ability. Finally, given the "triple jeopardy" of Mexican-American women in U.S. society, Zamora is important both as a *woman* and as a *Chicana writer*, for she has managed to use the "triple joys"[22] of Chicano experience as a filter for her poet's imagination and vision. As a consequence, she adds indispensable feminist and feminine threads to the still largely androcentric tapestry of contemporary American literature.

## OTHER PHASE III POETS

Another poet who adds significantly to *flor y canto* is Lorna Dee Cervantes, a Chicana who invigorates her skillful verses with the rich resonance of womanhood, a state of being she perceives as large and expansive enough to circumscribe the diversity of human experience. Concerned with capturing the manifold quality of personal experience, including its most private aspects, Cervantes textures her work with vivid details from everyday life. Her verse also reveals a powerfully evoked *chicanismo* comprehended as both a literal part of her self-identity and as an external source of metaphor.

Because of the consistent fineness of her work and because the subject of her poetry is inclusive and wide-ranging, Lorna Dee Cervantes fits comfortably within the Phase III category of writers. Alurista has described her as "probably the best Chicana poet active today,"[23] a tribute to the consistency of quality evident throughout her career from her earliest work to its culmination in *Emplumada*, her first published volume. Discussed in the next chapter, "The Circle of Poetry," where its style and themes inhabit a more congenial environment, *Emplumada* discloses a talent that is fresh, forceful, and multifaceted. This chapter seeks only to introduce her work by discussing some of her contributions to the Flor y Canto Festivals, gatherings that offered all Chicano/a writers—the novice as well as the widely published— a forum, an audience, and, later, a printed outlet for their work. The anthology from Flor y Canto IV and V contains five pages of Cervantes' poems, the second largest amount of space afforded a poet in the book, signifying the early recognition of her promising talent.

"Self-Portrait," an eight-line piece arranged like a prose poem, contains images and ideas that characterize much of Cervantes' most memorable work. For example, the first two words, "I melt," reflect her persistent description of herself as fluid and changing, shaped by her surroundings, her personal history, and her culture. In the first four lines she appears to shift identity four different times, but the shifts are actually only variations

of her fundamental Indian-ness, that part of her mestizo identity symbolizing her emergence from primally ancient roots.

> I melt into the stone Indian features of my face.
> Olmec eyes. I am an old brown woman of the moon.
> I am the milk raw woman side of Ométéotl.
> Quetzalcóatl has his sex in me. His long cock
> is a soft pink plume of subtle poetry.  . . . [24]

It is as if she is looking into a mirror where her reflection reminds her of
the chiseled "Olmec eyes" found on the giant pre-Aztec sculptures of
Yucatán. That image in turn suggests the universally acknowledged visage
of the "moon," seen here not as the proverbial man-in-the-moon but as an
"old brown woman." This figure contrasts sharply with the vital fertility
of the "milk raw woman" half of the androgynous deity Ométéotl, supreme
creator of the universe in Aztec cosmology. The contrast sharpens even
further in line 4 with the reference to Quetzalcóatl and his maleness, which
the female poet also subsumes. By encompassing female, male, and
androgynous aspects in a final mystical "melting," the poet captures the
creative power of the artist who synthesizes all reality like a shaman "on a
pyramid . . . [making] slow sacrificial love" with experience (55). "Self-
Portrait" thus evolves into a subtly etched picture of *mestizaje* interwoven
with androgyny.

In "Caribou Girl," a thirteen-stanza poem presented as a narrative
account of the title character, Cervantes again relies on Native American
motifs to image the mystical wisdom she sees inherent in keeping in touch
with primitive origins. The poem demonstrates this wisdom through the
speaker's description of all of Caribou Girl's special features like her
communication with "the crows who spoke/ and sent her poems" (51) and
her "vision" of the "four great hawks"—features that imbue her with "the
serenity of a mockingbird,/ the justice of a crow, the/ strength that a blue
jay has" (52). But the narrative is hardly as straightforward in its exposition
as this paraphrase might suggest. It opens and closes with the speaker
"plung[ing] like a frantic lifeguard" into the water to save Caribou Girl as
"she slips from the rocks" which the speaker knows "will drown" her (51,
53). These water and drowning references remain unexplained as we learn
of the narrator's "love" for "the girl some thought/ too strange, too dark,
who spoke in words/ from her own mythology, her own sanity" (51).
Moreover, the intermittent dialogue spoken by Caribou Girl defies conventional paraphrase.

He is a Great-Brown.
He is a Too-High.
He can make mountains and smoke.
His footsteps leave visions of God
Quetzalcóatl
and the Holy Ghost.
Amen. (52)

Such enigmatic mysticism and the fusion of Catholicism with Aztec belief, along with the speaker's close identification with Caribou Girl and her "balance of hooves/ and the wade through ice," give the poem the quality of an impressionistic interior monologue.

The speaker's clear understanding of and exceptional sensitivity to Caribou Girl hint that the narrator-I and Caribou Girl form a compound persona for Cervantes' consciousness. Perhaps Caribou Girl represents the speaker/poet's child, much as the boy in "Out of the Cradle Endlessly Rocking" represents Whitman's artistic consciousness in youth. And just as Whitman's child-persona identifies with birds, which function as an apt emblem for the future singing bard, so too do the many bird images function in this poem, while the caribou, a reindeer-like North American animal characterized by branching antlers in both sexes, suggests both the poet's essential bond with earth and her omniscient androgyny. This interpretation would mean that the plunging and drowning of the first and last stanzas refer to a lyrical descent into the subconscious where logic and grammar rules are suspended and dreamlike symbolism dominates, producing a kaleidoscopic action comparable to Alice's mythopoeic descent into the Wonderland of the cave. The poet knows that she must welcome and cherish the Caribou Girl in her, for she represents her art, emotion, and intuition. Yet, the poet cannot exist solely within Caribou Girl's environment, for, like Narcissus falling into the pool of his own reflection, "she will drown." Appropriately, the poem ends with "I'll have to leave her/ for another breath before/ I plunge again" (53).

Less explicitly mythopoeic in "Free Way 280" (as in her popular "Beneath the Shadow of the Freeway"), Cervantes nonetheless still writes of identity— its nature and her quest for it—and her shiftings in and out of a variety of selves. "Free Way 280" captures the changes time and technology have brought to her old neighborhood now "conceal[ed]" by the "raised scar" of the "freeway" (54). The poem's most important revelation, however, is that the physical impediment of the highway cannot hide or destroy the irrepressible life of the people uprooted by the "grey cannery." Instead,

new grasses sprout, wild mustard reclaims.
By a skinny creek a small boy
pulls at his sister's trenzas,
skips a flat rock across the green pools . . .
The old gardens come back revived.   . . .
Viejitas come here with paper bags to gather greens. (54)

These descriptions celebrate the traditional life of *el pueblo* and how that life asserts itself in spite of the most imposing obstacles set against it from without. Ironically, the speaker once sought to escape the vitality of her past: "Once I wanted out, wanted the frigid lanes/ to take me to a place without sun" (54). But no longer. By discovering that the social forms and culture of the displaced people resist extinction, the speaker also discovers that she, too, is linked to these resilient forms, and from her epiphany comes the hope that "I'll find it, that part of me/ mown under/ like a corpse/ or a loose seed" (54). By equating the lost part of herself with the forgotten "corpse" and the tiny "seed," Cervantes levels her individualism to the size of negligible objects which, despite their insignificance, contain within themselves the kernel of viability that will transform the sterility of the asphalt highway into a "Free Way" of life.

Alurista is credited with introducing the concept of Aztlán to the Chicano Movement and, hence, to contemporary U.S. consciousness in the late 1960s.[25] By the mid-1970s the concept had become an established part of Movement rhetoric, and, more significantly, it had become a household word among *raza*. As explained in the previous chapter, Alurista's innovations and influence were as significant in literature, specifically poetry, and he helped promulgate the notion of *flor y canto* as well. His poems from the mid-1970s, collected in *Timespace Huracan* and *Spik in glyph?* evince the same inclination to explore and experiment, to innovate and take risks, that characterized his earlier writings. Disappointingly, however, both books fall short of the quality of *Floricanto en Aztlán* and *Nationchild Plumaroja*, and at times they even project a mannered abstractionism suggestive of parody. Still, the books merit consideration because the experimentations in them are always bold and often interesting and because Alurista is so important in the field.

Composed of seven sections arranged according to what Gary Keller calls "ritual genre" classifications,[26] *Timespace Huracan* contains sixty-five poems addressing three major subjects—Amerindian typology, a *raza* utopia, and, to a lesser degree, the Movement. The Amerindian typology continues the

poet's earlier interests manifested in his first three books. We encounter the
*tunas*, *nopales*, maize, and eagles signifying the pre-American indigenous
order, and we again find a wealth of Nahua and Mayan terms and names.
The typology is intended to resurrect the luster of our native *"raíces"* and
to demonstrate the "timespace" continuum that exists as an historical and
mythic reality in Alurista's worldview. The second major subject, a *raza*
utopia, proceeds from Alurista's earlier ritualistic incantations to his
"nationchild" to discover itself and its soul in the greatness of its autochthonous heritage rather than in the "thick gasoline vapor" and
"fun-filled . . . filthy bourgeoisie" of U.S. society. Although Alurista is
somewhat romantic about Amerindia, he does not advocate a revival of
primitivism. Rather, he seeks to awaken among *raza* a prideful recognition
and acceptance of the Mesoamerican heritage which has been stifled for over
400 years. The poet aspires to the transcendent ideals of, for example, peace
and humanism, but he is vague about the process of achievement or, even,
what they are precisely (see "La Paz" and "Hamacas brisas"). Like a minister
of the sacred, Alurista preaches and chants as if to charismatically lift his
flock to a higher level of Amerindian purity without bothering with praxis
(e.g., "Solar alma libertá," "Razaunida," and "Adiós, adiós, adiós").
Regarding the third major group of poems in this volume, the Movement
poems suffer from a general didacticism and vagueness of idea despite
occasional concrete images and references. Their repeated detraction of
"amerikan injustice" in the same words and phrases eventually becomes
hackneyed and uninspiring (e.g., "Amerindian Circle," "Wachinton d c"
[1–4], and "Hacendado"). One yearns for the Aluristian inventiveness of
"When Raza?," "Address," "Tata Juan," and "Got to Be on Time," to
mention four memorable pieces from *Floricanto* and *Nationchild*.

Stylistically, *Timespace Huracan* extends to abstract extremes the experimentation with form seen in *Nationchild*. It is odd for a poet who has so
actively promoted the essentially oral, communal, and ritual dimensions of
poetry to present a large number of pieces that are essentially visual and
print-centered. For example, "Dogs Bark Cantos" and "Soft Winds," two
concrete poems, cannot convey their visual shape in performance, and
without at least comprehension of their printed shapes their denuded
imagism fails. Similarly, "A Oír raza" and "A Pelear," to cite two of a large
category, gain part of their total effect from their typography and another
part from the fact that they are "reversible"— that is, they can be recited
from the top of the page down or vice-versa. Although that may be
interesting, in performance these features are virtually meaningless. What

is more, these technical experiments seldom counterbalance the lyrical and semantic thinness of the words and verses themselves.[27] The same holds true for the section titled "Ojos de Dios" where the poet clusters ten variations on the haiku which, unlike the classic haiku, are essentially minimalist word pictures that are too condensed and lacking in contextuality to compel much interest at any thematic level.

Although this negative criticism applies to the bulk of *Timespace*, Alurista's talent is such that the book is not uninteresting. His vision, energy, and creativity are pervasive even if the earlier control and craftsmanship are lacking here. Four pieces meriting individual reading are "Wachinton d c [5]," "What It Is," "Cantares arrullos-5," and "Ollín." Each in its own way showcases the poet's stylistic trademarks without reducing them to parody, and each discloses a technical maturity that builds on the three earlier volumes.

The first two of these four poems employ a similar rhetorical framework, one that depends on the repetition of phrases modified slightly from line to line for conceptual transition and for emphasis. Accordingly, the fifth segment of the cycle "Wachinton d c" opens thus:

> departing to raza origins
> > returning to raza ends
> > > *we return to the beginning**
> *we begin with the return*
> > *from northeast to southwest . . .*
> > > from the program
> > > > to the channel
> > > from the pool
> > > > to the river
> *we return, depart* (63)

The cumulative effect of the repetitions and slight modifications is, on one level, to build a circular, self-reflecting logic and on another to achieve subliminal impact. The circularity devolves around the question of the space of identity—where are "raza origins" and "ends" and where is "aztlán"? The poet draws a circle from historical "beginnings" to "ends," from the geographical "northeast" to the "southwest," from "life" to "death," and so on until he reaches the logical conclusion that "here" and "there" are, in fact, identical. He therefore finds an intersection of alpha and omega.

*Italicized words indicate translations from the Spanish.

```
aquí nomás
      en la tierra
            bajo el sol
aquí, no más allá
      más allá en el sol
            sobre la tierra—allá, no más aquí
[here only
      in the land
            beneath the sun
here, no longer there
farther over there in the sun
      on the land—there, no longer here] (63)
```

(Because a translation into English cannot capture the subtlety of Alurista's use of language, the original is supplied for comparison.) Within the context of its cycle—concerned with a social advocacy mission to the nation's capital—the poem asserts the persistence of fundamental, natural human reality in the face of bureaucratic machinations ("la chichi mecánica").

Constructed in the same rhetorical framework is "What It Is / Is / What It Does," a poem that manages to suggest philosophical weightiness through the simplest, most straightforward diction. "What it is / ain't / what it was. / neither is it / what it will be. / what it is / is / what it does" (67). The poet never specifies the referent of "it," leaving its specification to us. However, the last six lines suggest that "it" pertains to the relation between ethics and conduct.

> *from the saying*
>
> *to the doing*
>
> *quite a stretch*
>
> *finished stretch*
>
> *doing the saying*
>
> *saying and doing*

Because maxims or sayings ("dichos") characteristically concern a culture's ethical values, the closing lines indicate that "it" concerns values, and because "dicho" is linked to "hecho" (the deed done), the lines also have to do with deeds of conduct. In shifting from English to Spanish for the last third of the poem (a technique frequently seen in *Timespace*), Alurista uses language metaphorically to suggest that English is satisfactory for raising problems and questions, but Spanish is imperative for supplying answers and judgments.

Also effective as a poem, though stylistically different from the previous two, is the fifth piece in the "Cantares arrullos" [Lullaby Songs] cycle. This poem focuses on the qualities that make the Native Indian experience special, and it does this by echoing the style and imagery of Indian expression. The poem opens with "the death of morning rises with the sun,/ and moon appears to be grandmother/ of the night" (88). It goes on to catalog items associated with "the breath of pueblos" before shifting from those specifics to a statement of the abstract.

> *cultivated life*
>> *with patience*
>>> *with love*
>>>> *with the flames that*
> *illumine stars*
>>> *coloring voicetones* (88)

By making clear in the first part of the poem the precise terms underlying the abstraction, the poet fuses his utopian ideal with elements of the mundane. His point is that the ideal can only be attained through immersion in the real, in the merging of the sacred and the profane. The shift to Spanish holds through to the end, signifying that the linguistic choice itself is meant to evoke the style and imagery of Amerindia. Appropriately, the poem ends with a specific reference to a pre-American deity, the god of rain: *"welcome rains of Tlaloc's fire"* (88). That the reference is oxymoronic emphasizes the poem's other synthetic, unifying imagery where opposites are merged as one.

   Illuminating the title *Timespace Huracan* is the poem "Ollín" which takes its title from the Mayan concept of motion as a basic component of matter. The poem appears in diagonal typography on the page, and it concerns a utopian time/space "where all the people sing / . . . *the melodies and rhythms / that move inside / hearts*" (71). The utopia exemplifies the *carnalismo*, love, and solidarity which Alurista believes reside as a latent power in the human heart. The opening lines refer to "time" and "space," and Ollín appears in the "rhythms" moving inside "hearts." "Ollín" also relates to *Huracan*, meaning "hurricane," an image evocative of natural energy and power and, in combination with "Timespace," indicates Alurista's belief in the potential power of *chicanismo*, which the book seeks to unleash among *raza*. As with the titles of his previous books with their synthesis of disparate concepts and their blending of separate morphemes into one, *Timespace Huracan* links two dimensions and then unites the resulting

English wordblend with a Mayan term. As a consequence, the poet achieves a synthesis of parts constituting a genuine *mestizaje*.

Quite differently, *Spik in glyph?* extends the poet's experimentation, especially linguistically, to an esoteric level that reduces communication and impedes comprehension. The poet plays games with language, mixing Spanish and English dialects with a phonetic orthography and exploiting the homonymic correspondences between the two languages. For example, the first thirteen pieces in the collection bear quasi-numerical titles 1 through 13, but their spelling develops double entendres recognizable to the bilingual reader.

| | |
|---|---|
| "juan" | John and "one" |
| "tu" | You and "two" |
| "tree" | Arbol and "three" |
| "for" | Preposition and "four" |
| "fi" | "Five" in dialectal syncope and the interjection, fie |
| "seex" | "Six" in Spanish pronunciation and seeks |
| "se ven" | They're seen and "seven" |
| "e it" | And it and "eight" |
| "na in" | Not in and "nine" |
| "ten" | Ten |
| "ee le ven?" | And they're seen? and "eleven" |
| "tu el" | You [are] he and "twelve" syncope |
| "tracy" | "Trece" and name and "thirteen"[28] |

The aesthetic problem is that despite these puns the titles add little (or nothing) to their poems. The word and letter games suggest an imagination working in the service of its own interior apparatus, not for art. The book's title warns us of this in its punning bilingual query which we can paraphrase as "do you/ can you speak in hybrid hieroglyphics?" The doubling of "spik," normally a defamatory epithet for "Hispanic," as the English verb "speak" also derives from the phonemic value of the four letters: / s p i k /. By phrasing the title as a question, the poet covers his tracks to some extent because, presumably, a negative reply could explain a negative response to the poetry; that is, if a reader does not communicate or comprehend "in glyph" that itself would explain any negativity toward the book's verse.

What *Spik in glyph?* does contain to a limited but welcome degree is evidence of a personal voice, of the lyrical persona that has been largely absent in Alurista's corpus. His has been a consistently bardic, omniscient, teaching voice, one that, despite all the poetry, has kept the poet as a private person distant from his audience. Several poems in this volume are touched by a welcome narrative intimacy that distinguishes them as a departure for the poet. The poem, "i," for example, opens with a refreshing self-reference that immediately draws one closer to the images.

```
        i am tired
             of chasing coyote
   with a prayer stick
                  feathered
        plumed and colored
                     continent, unbound (47)
```

These lines hint at the poet's possible desire to seek new subjects for his art, to travel new avenues of theme and symbol. However, instead of pursuing this personal track to evoke in recognizably human terms why the speaker is "tired," the poet moves away from the first person subjective voice to adopt his characteristic third person bardic voice: "coyote keep blue/ deer away/ and children wail the waning/ moon" (47). By obscuring the speaker's perceptions and feelings, the distancing weakens the overall effect of the piece. Similarly, "my" begins with the speaker's revelation that "my eyes/ cannot stand/ white light/ at night" (41), but instead of continuing in this intimate vein he slides into the third person "someone remembers," ending the poem on a note of remoteness.

Oppositely, sustaining the personal voice more effectively are "here" and "do u remember," where the poet allows the interior, personal perspective freer development. In "here" the poet communicates his fascination with the "magical" power of "word[s]," and he suggests both the emotional and physical effect they have on him.

```
   here is a word
   a magic word
   to me at least
   a sacred sound
   for long i've known
   and kept so close
   it hurt my lungs
   to breathe alone (39)
```

By injecting a personal I into the poem this way, Alurista immediately diverges from his usual method of describing his subject omnisciently. He thus achieves greater immediacy and lyrical power than what is possible in the didactic mode. Moreover, he more sharply conveys his mystical appreciation of words (e.g., that they "heal minds and hearts" [39]) through the subjectivity. Also in the personal voice, "do u remember" succeeds as a reminiscence because the speaker does not veil himself behind the mask of prophetic bard.

> do u remember
> the parody of trembling laughter
> through the parks clouded by moonlight . . .
> > and the thunder
> > > mushrooming
> > > huracanes
> > do u remember
> > > under our feet
> > life sprouted on wet dark
> > > earth, do u (45)

Because the memories bear the surreal qualities of a nearly forgotten past, the images and the event are not identifiable in specific terms, but that obscurity does not interfere with the accessible fact that there was something very special about the night two persons were caught in the rain together in the city ("asphalt," "neon," and "celluloid"). The emergence of this personal dimension adds lyricism to the collection and saves it from withering in an airless atmosphere of esoterica.

One reviewer writes about Alurista's esoteric post-*Floricanto* style:

. . . lo que se advierte en muchos de los poemas es que en el afán por afirmar su voluntad de estilo, el poeta se encierra en un hermetismo insólito producido por retruécanos artificiosos y sutiles malabarismos, de manera tal que el mensaje poético no puede llegar al pueblo . . . cuando a las palabras les falta la enjundia, la poesía se convierte en un ejercicio banal.[29]

[ . . . what is noted in many of these poems is that, in an eagerness to affirm stylistic freedom, the poet encloses himself inside an unusual secretiveness produced by artificial puns and convoluted subtleties, consequently the poetic message cannot be communicated to the audience . . . when words lack substance, poetry becomes a banal exercise.

(My translation)]

This observation is astute. The fact that the poet has remained a respected figure among Chicano writers despite the dropping off in quality of these later volumes reconfirms the greatness of his earlier work.

## INÉS TOVAR

A woman whose work and presence furthered the flowering of *flor y canto* is Inés Tovar, who has been greatly influenced by Alurista's style. In "Chicano-Hermano," a poem from *Con razón corazón*, she addresses him as her "hermano," and she quotes a line from his "Tal vez porque te quiero" (*Nationchild Plumaroja*; see above, pp. 98–108). Indeed, the title "Chicano-Hermano" comes from the forth line of Alurista's poem. Part of his influence on Tovar's writing has been his use of Amerindian typology in his verse, for she strongly identifies her own Indian roots with herself as a writer.

I would like to ask one thing . . . please point out my double heritage: I am a Chicana/Nimipu . . . poet. My mother is full blood Nimipu; her people are much better known by the French-imposed name "Nez Perce." Anyway it means a lot to me to have this acknowledged, and possibly the fact that I am Indian sheds some light on my writing.[30]

Another aspect of Alurista's influence relates to Tovar's unharnessed use of Spanish and bilingual idioms in her verse. Spanish appears to be her preferred language, and Alurista's pioneering role in freeing Mexican-Americans to employ their natural idioms inspires her. As she says to him in "Chicano-Hermano": "*I am grateful to you for the destiny / You put before us . . . that song captivated my heart.*"[31] Alurista's linguistic experiments in his writing also influenced Tovar and help explain the title of her first book, *Con razón corazón* ("With Reason Heart" or, more idiomatically, "Do It Right, Heart"). Like Alurista, Tovar finds possibilities of meaning in language where others perceive only commonplaces. Hence, she could see the semantic tension residing in *corazón*—that is, *cor*/with and *razón*/reason—and locate in it a figure to cohere poetic themes ranging across a variety of subjects. That the Spanish word for "heart" results from a combination form literally meaning its opposite, reason, suggests to her an etymological inclusiveness and semantic tension capable of accommodating themes dealing with marriage and mothers as well as with revolution and love.

Two subjects that the poet treats especially distinctively in *Con razón corazón* are love and the metaphysics of reality. In "Realidad I" she brings both of these subjects together for a provocative treatment of the nature of being. Using the conceit of an argument between two lovers—"Animo" (Soul or Will) and "Desesperación" (Despair)—vying for her affections, she presents the conflict as a personal quarrel. Without indicating that the conflict is anything other than that of a classic love triangle, the first stanza opens *in medias res*: *"Not even if you both were so wonderful/ Fighting for my love"* (13) would I be able to choose either of you, the speaker announces. Even after introducing "Animo" and "Desesperación," the speaker's tone remains private and intimate, as if these terms might be *cariños*, special words of endearment between lovers.

> *You, Soul {of mine}, want me to love you*
> *For your happy and well-favored appearance . . .*
> *Well, {and} you near friend*
> *also want to possess me*
> *You, Despair,*
> *with your calm and smooth manner* (13)

Toward the end of the third stanza, however, the metaphysical nature of the dispute emerges clearly. Her true lover and "mero mero amigo," she declares here, is *"Death / who has always been faithful to her"* (14). Death's *"constant attention"* has *"won"* over the action-less conduct of the other two lovers who *"got tangled in words / And whose dialogue didn't include me"* (14). But as the speaker contemplates the lover-Death's everpresence in her life— *"you are always at my side"*—she suddenly realizes that "he," too, is another lover who must be denied, and she feebly asserts *"no way will I go with you* [either]" (14). "Realidad I" ends with four lines that return the metaphysical issues back to the terms of a lover's quarrel: *"But, / Pinche powerful Death / Who sent you? / Who gave you permission?"* (14). The poem illustrates a paradox of life in which the constructive energy of both soul and will seem in constant tension with the destructive energy of despair. For Tovar both polarities share space along the same axis between life and death. Moreover, by combining personal love with metaphysical abstractions here, the poet conveys the intimate, subjective quality of the dilemma—its existence within the innermost nature of her individual being.

Accordingly, Tovar's love poems are seldom simply that. In other words, she weaves the love theme in and around unexpected subjects. For instance, in "Poema" she opens on a purely metaliterary level, concerned with the source of her creative energy, her muse.

> *Sometimes my poems*
> *rush at me*
> *like willful lunacies*
> *like birds*
> *clouds*

> *and waves*
> *of the* nada
> *of life*
> *of the* meta (26)

At this point she shifts rapidly into the subject of *"you,"* and she emphasizes the shift by codeswitching into English for one line. Not romantically coded, however, her love is understated as faith: without you *"I wouldn't believe in the* movimiento / *you know* / *you and I* / *we are* / Revolución" (28). Tovar keeps her idea deliberately ambiguous in order to sustain a multiplicity of meanings, but the intimacy of the tone, together with its placement on the same page as "Guerrillera Soy," another love poem, accentuates the love theme. "Guerrillera Soy" (Guerrilla I Am) presents a more explicitly romantic message through its diction and personal images, but even here the central metaphor relates not to romance but to revolution. *"With every drop of my blood,"* says the narrator, *"with every breath . . . and in every demonstration of love . . .* guerrillera soy" (28). By employing *"demuestra de amor"* instead of "acción" or "prueba," the poet underscores the poem's dominating symbol of guerrilla activism, for *demonstration* refers at once to an *act* (of love) and also to a political *demonstration.* As with "Realidad I," then, Tovar's ingenious conceit in "Guerrillera Soy" allows her to emphasize the integrality of both love and revolution within her personal identity.

Other pieces in *Con razón corazón* that deserve singling out include "Compañero," a brief verse dialogue with *"solitude,"* and "Rezo," a long personal prayer addressed to a composite Mother Goddess. "Rezo" (I Pray) is especially interesting in its meshing of feminism (which Chicana scholars trace farther back than either the contemporary women's movement or American suffragism; see note 22 above) with traditional feminine reverence. Variously praying to *"our mother of queen / mayan goddess tears"* and to *"sainted mother of indian goddess woes,"* as well as to the *"beloved mother of the solitude / of mestiza daughters"*—the poem sanctifies Mexican-American women and the oppressed but unvanquished spirit of our foremothers. The closing verses stress the humanness of the *"goddesses"* whom Tovar addresses in chantlike phrases and repetitions reminiscent of Alurista.

> *help us reverent mother . . .*
> *grandmother*
> *help us*

*mother*
*help us*

*daughter*
*help us*

*sister*
*help us*

*woman*
*help us* (26)

Also suggestive of Alurista's influence is the wordblend "casaztlán" occurring near the end of the poem. Like her mentor, Tovar also includes
references to *mestizaje* via La Malinche, the Virgin of Guadalupe, Tonantzin, and La Llorona. Overall, the poem conveys the poet's view that *la vida
chicana*, understood in both generic, culturalist terms and female, gender-
specific forms, merits apotheosis because it has been naturally sanctified
through suffering (25).

If Bernice Zamora represents the stylized Phase III poetry written by
Chicanas in the mid-1970s, Inéz Tovar represents the more popular, less
strictly literary variety. Tovar's directness in treating her subjects gives her
work a freshness and clarity that make the poems accessible, and although
some of them appear oversimplified (e.g., "Para Teresa" and "Chiflazones")
most usually disclose a conceptual or figurative development that is rich
and subtle. In addition, her artistic worldview is colored by what one
Hispana critic describes in the poetry by Chicanas as "a complex perspective
which involves an internal tension generated by ideological positions, a
feminist attitude which debunks cultural myths, and a personalized treatment of human experiences."[32] Certainly, the Tovar poems analyzed here
evince this perspective as they struggle to name, define, and project
Chicana identity.

An overview of Phase III writing reveals that it brought two important
dimensions to the canon of Chicano poetry. Although these dimensions
were not totally unknown in the earlier phases, they were, at most, of
tertiary significance and, often, accidental features when they appeared.
The first important dimension is the subjectivity evident in Phase III
poems, the personalizing of voice and reference in a way that reflects the
post-modernist flavor of twentieth-century literature. The subjectivity is
not *ombligo*-gazing, despite Alurista's often cited image of "el ombligo de
Aztlán." Rather, it is an inward turning in search of the lyrical poetic self

through which the poet can filter external experience and the materials of the world. As a result, these poems evince an I-ness absent from most of the earlier Chicano poetry, and although this tendency has not produced confessional poetry, it has informed the work with greater immediacy and intimacy. The second important dimension concerns the more *inclusive range* of subject matter within Phase III verse. Soto, Zamora, and Cervantes here, like Cárdenas and Ríos later, considerably broaden the range of vision beyond a narrowly defined *mestizaje* or *chicanismo*. To add feminist issues and women's themes as well as attention to urban violence, its origins and consequences, as Zamora and Soto, respectively, have done is to strengthen the canon through greater, wider representativeness. Sown together with the major features planted in Phase I and II, these two dimensions contribute new weight and substance to *flor y canto*.

## NOTES

1. Gary Soto, "Telephoning God," *The Elements of San Joaquin* (Pittsburgh: University of Pittsburgh Press, 1977), 10.
2. Peter Cooley, "I Can Hear You Now," *Parnassus* 8:1 (Fall/Winter 1979), 304.
3. Arthur Ramirez, "Review of *The Tale of Sunlight*," *Revista Chicano-Riqueña* 9:3 (Verano, 1981), 73.
4. Soto, "Field Poem," *The Elements of San Joaquin*, 23. Subsequent references to this edition will be made parenthetically in the text.
5. Juan Rodríguez," Review of *The Elements of San Joaquin*," *New Scholar* 6 (1976), 273.
6. Cooley, "I Can Hear You Now," 310-11. For a more denunciatory view, see "Interview with Ricardo Sánchez" by Rafael Castillo in *Imagine: International Chicano Poetry Journal* 1:2 (Winter 1984), 25.
7. Joe Olvera, "Review of *Restless Serpents*," *American Book Review* 2:2 (October 1979), 20.
8. Bruce-Novoa, "Review of *Restless Serpents*," *Latin American Literary Review* 5:10 (1977), 153.
9. Bernice Zamora, *Restless Serpents* (Menlo Park, Calif.: Diseños Literarios, 1976), 66. Subsequent references to this edition will be made parenthetically in the text.
10. See Theodore Roethke's *Collected Poems* (Garden City, N.Y.: Doubleday, 1975). Also see Richard A. Blessing, *Theodore Roethke's Dynamic Vision* (Bloomington: Indiana University Press, 1974).
11. See Robinson Jeffers, *Roan Stallion, Tamar and Other Poems* (New York: Modern Library, 1953). Also see Arthur B. Coffin, *Robinson Jeffers: Poet of Inhumanism* (Madison: University of Wisconsin Press, 1971).
12. Jeffers articulates these views throughout his poetry and in a number of prose writings. See his Preface to *The Double Axe* (New York: Liveright, 1977), and

his Foreword to *The Selected Poetry of Robinson Jeffers* (New York: Random House, 1938).

13. Cf. Jeffers, "Cassandra," *The Double Axe and Other Poems* (New York: Random House, 1948), 117.

14. Marta E. Sánchez, "Inter-Sexual and Intertextual Codes in the Poetry of Bernice Zamora," *MELUS* 7:3 (Fall 1980), 55–68.

15. Cordelia Candelaria, "Another Reading of Three Poems by Zamora," *MELUS* 7:4 (Winter 1980), 102–3.

16. Ibid., 104.

17. See Hermann Hesse, *Siddhartha*, Hilda Rosner, trans. (New York: New Directions, 1957); and *Steppenwolf*, Basil Creighton, trans. (New York: Holt, Rinehart & Winston, 1961). Also see Joseph Mileck, *Hermann Hesse: Life and Art* (Berkeley: University of California Press, 1978).

18. Although not as flourishingly active as they once were, *penitente* sects occur throughout the Southwest, primarily in northern New Mexico and southern Colorado. See Matt S. Meier and Feliciano Rivera, *Dictionary of Mexican American History* (Westport, Conn.: Greenwood Press, 1981), 274–275; and Marta Weigle, *The Penitentes of the Southwest* (Santa Fe, N.Mex.: Ancient City Press, 1970).

19. Sánchez, "Inter-Sexual and Intertextual Codes," 64.

20. Candelaria, "Another Reading of Three Poems by Zamora," 104.

21. Francisco Lomelí and Donaldo Urioste, "Review of *Restless Serpents*," *De Colores* 3:4 (1977), 81.

22. Chicanas experience "triple jeopardy" "(1) [as] members of an ethnic minority in a white dominant society, (2) as women within Chicano culture, and (3) as women of color in a society where racism and sexism are significant social factors." Fortunately, the triple jeopardy is counterbalanced by the "triple joys" found in "(1) the triculturalism of Spanish, Indian, and U.S. American features, (2) Spanish/English bilingualism, and (3) the well-documented feminist roots of our history." Citations from Cordelia Candelaria, *Mexican-American Women, Triple Joy/Triple Jeopardy: A Program of Study for High School Teachers and Students*, 1983 Grant Application, U.S. Department of Education.

23. In a conversation with me at the National Conference of Teachers of English, Denver, Colorado, November 19, 1983.

24. "Self-Portrait," *Flor y Canto IV and V*, Festival Committee, eds. (Albuquerque, N.Mex.: Pajarito Publications, 1980), 55. Subsequent references to Cervantes' work in this anthology will be made parenthetically in the text.

25. Luis Leal, "In Search of Aztlán," *Denver Quarterly* 16:3 (Fall 1981), 20.

26. Gary Keller, "Alurista, Poeta-Antropologo, and the Recuperation of the Chicano Identity," Introduction to *Return: Poems Collected and New*, (Ypsilanti, Mich.: Bilingual Press/Editorial Bilingüe, 1982), xxxviii.

27. Alurista, *Timespace Huracan* (Albuquerque, N. Mex.: Pajarito Publications, 1976), 59. Subsequent references to this edition will be made parenthetically in the text.

28. Alurista, *Spik in glyph?* (Houston, Tex.: Arte Publico Press, 1981), 5–16. Subsequent references to this edition will be made parenthetically in the text.

29. Alfonso Rodríguez, "Review of Alurista's *A'nque: Collected Works, 1976–79*" in *La Palabra* 3:1–2 (Primavera, 1981), 146–47.

30. Letter to Cordelia Candelaria, Posted Fresno, California, October 22, 1982.

'31. Inés Hernandez Tovar, *Con razón corazón* (San Francisco: Milagro Books, 1977), 29. Subsequent references to this edition will be made parenthetically in the text.

32. Miriam Bornstein, "The Voice of the Chicana in Poetry," *Denver Quarterly* 16:3 (Fall 1981), 33–34.

# 5

# The Circle of Poetry

This chapter taps the primordial symbol of the circle and its immanent presence within the mestizo roots of *chicanismo* and draws a figurative ring around the poetry of the ages to demonstrate that Chicano poetry is tightly centered within it. Symbolically, the circle is fundamental as a universal emblem of wholeness, connections, unity, and eternity. As perceived by artists and philosophers throughout history, circularity is essential both as a recurring pattern in nature and as a recurring idea by which to order our multiphenomenal world. Emerson, for example, saw "the life of man as a self-evolving circle,"[1] whereas Melville compared our ability to see beyond the obvious to "circles on the water, as they grow fainter, expand . . . like the rings of Eternity."[2] Commenting on the business of the novelist, James observed that "universally, relations stop nowhere, and the exquisite problem of the artist is eternally but to draw . . . the circle within which they shall happily appear to do so."[3] And commenting on "the power of the world," Black Elk said that it "always works in circles, and everything tries to be round," just like the "life of a man is a circle from childhood to childhood and so it is in everything where power moves."[4] Accordingly, poets use circularity to image the temporal cycles of nature that combine, after all, into the endless generations that make eternity, as well as to represent the spatial forms that constitute matter and energy.

This chapter especially seeks to show how Chicano poetry lies (logically, if not actually) within the full mainstream of world literature and how that fact makes the poets considered here particularly accessible to all readers. These poems have a certain familiar sound and sense that connects them to other poetic traditions and movements, but, importantly, their force derives from the absorbed Chicano identity of their authors—as the water from a mountain spring derives its purity from the multivaried recesses of its surroundings. In addition, these poems disprove the charge that contemporary ethnic literature is necessarily parochial and limited to a homogeneous audience without relevance to non-Chicanos. However, my purpose is to demonstrate not that this poetry is generic or assimilationist, but rather that its absorption of the distinct particularity of *chicanismo* allows its universal aspect to emerge, much as Shakespeare's absorption of Elizabethan England makes it accessible and even universal. To achieve the chapter's purpose, the poems are clustered around particular themes instead of according to individual writers. This approach allows full discussion of their relatedness to each other and to the spirit of world literature. Of course, given the limitations of space, the theme clusters can only be selective, not exhaustive, and readers are encouraged to pursue their acquaintance with the poetry beyond these covers.

## NATURE

The elements of nature and human apprehension of them could well be the oldest subject known to poetry. Nature's ubiquity and awesome power have occupied human intelligence and the imagination throughout time. From folklore to belles lettres, from one hemisphere to another, from age to age, nature has held a focal place as subject and theme in the creations of the imagination. In Chicano poetry, however, as in much contemporary poetry, nature is not a primary focus. It is instead a part of a total landscape of experience, one that is often used as a foil for the poet's expression of a private emotion or particular ideology. As previous chapters have shown, poets like Alurista, Zamora, and Delgado have been resourceful in exploring natural imagery for adaptation to uniquely *raza* purposes. Four poets whose recent books have generated considerable excitement in Chicano literature and who return to nature repeatedly in their writing are Gary Soto, Alberto Ríos, Leo Romero, and Lorna Dee Cervantes. Although their treatments vary from the pastoral to the ironic, they all share a remarkable sensitivity to the lyric possibilities nature still holds despite the weary cynicism of the modern temperament.

The titles of Gary Soto's three major volumes of poetry allude to nature in one form or another. *The Elements of San Joaquin* (1977) includes the natural elements of the San Joaquin Valley, and a large number of the poems in the book specifically deal with those features. Two later titles, *The Tale of Sunlight* (1978) and *Where Sparrows Work Hard* (1981), again allude to nature, and the poet threads the title images through the poems— though with a very delicate, restrained needle. Not concerned with redundant sketches stressing nature's power and beauty, Soto depicts nature from a resolutely human, frequently ironic perspective. For instance, he presents "The Leaves" in *The Tale of Sunlight* entirely from the perspective of "[t]he raked leaves" and their desultory "[d]rifting . . . south."[5] He carefully avoids any trace of anthropomorphism until the very end of the poem, as he centers our awareness on the "leaves shuffl[ing] off / Like shoes . . . Drifting, they / Rubbed the soft belly / Of earth, loosening / Its hold on rock" (29). Besides the precise description of the leaves blown along in disorderly fashion, what holds our interest is the sharpness of the poet's metaphors.

> Blown into fences,
> They scattered
> Like ants
> And followed
> What the ants followed . . .
> They crossed orchards,
> A stand of trees
> They never saw,
> Scratching an alphabet
> In the damp ground.
> Climbing the foothills
> Under a rumor
> Of rain,
> The leaves left
> For a new wind (29)

As we follow the description of the leaves' upheaval, we realize that the poet focuses as much on the force behind the upheaval—the wind—as on the leaves themselves. The poet thus uses nature to address the subject of causality and the inevitability of certain effects resulting from particular causes. The simplicity of such causality is limited, Soto suggests, only to tangibles, to physical stimulus-response patterns, and he conveys this in the personification of the closing lines.

> And the brightness
> They [the leaves] would see
> Was their own
> As they moved south
> Toward the jeweled fire of snow. (30)

By shifting from the purely descriptive to the invention of subjectivity for
the leaves, the poet implies that perception, at least, can remain outside the
will of external causes.

"The First," another poem in this collection, weaves the subject of the
destruction of nature with that of the destruction's effect on simple
"villagers," and through the interweaving develops the theme of primal
loss. Nature in "The First" is decidedly sentient with human capabilities—
" . . . the river / Gloved its fingers / With leaves / And the autumn
sunlight / Spoked the earth / Into two parts" (36). The personification here
is relevant to the poem's first word, "After," a preposition that carries only
one temporal meaning. The substance of the poem concerns what happened
"*after* the river gloved its fingers" (my emphasis). Because wearing gloves
is a human feature, just as spokes are associated with wheels, the first two
anthropomorphic images in the poem connote the alteration of nature by
people and their technology. The rest of the poem extends the connotation
further by comparing the effect of nature's change to the change experienced by "the villagers" who had co- existed easily with nature in the past.
They had been forced to undo "Their houses, / Thatch by thatch" because
"the earth / Was not as it was" (36). Through reductive irony, Soto reveals
the theme at this point in the description of what the "earth" now is:

> . . . the iguana
> Being stretched
> Into belts,
> The beaver curling
> Into handbags;
> Their lakes bruised
> Gray with smoke
> That unraveled from cities. (36)

The irony lies in the fact that the villagers "were the first / To leave"
because of these changes and, not surprisingly, their departure was "unnoticed. . . . For it no longer / Mattered to say / The world was once blue"
(37). After so much devastation, the poem suggests, no one would think
to wonder at "the first" human casualties resulting from the human-caused
loss in nature.

In both "The Leaves" and "The First," the poet's characteristic short,
two- to three-beat lines (i.e., dimeters and trimeters) are especially well
suited to his subject and theme. Too short to sustain more than an image
or a fraction of a thought, the lines create a feeling of disruption, of things

broken off suddenly. This feeling converges with the upheavals caused by "the wind" in blowing "the leaves" away, and it merges also with the disjunction and fragmentation resulting from the world's loss of "blue" in "The First." Moreover, Soto's short, trochaic lines call to mind another U.S. poet fond of that length and meter, Gary Snyder, who also consistently writes about nature. Although Soto's verse lacks the Japanese-influenced delicacy and mystery of Snyder's, both share the restraint and subdued emotional coloration associated with Japanese poetry.

More clearly in the British-influenced American grain is the writing of Alberto Ríos, the 1981 recipient of the Walt Whitman Award presented by the Academy of American Poets. He also was the first winner of the Western States Book Awards for his short story collection, *The Iguana Killer*. In poetry Ríos prefers the longer units of rhythm of the free verse line, finding greater flexibility and naturalness in it. In *Whispering to Fool the Wind*, his award-winning book, he frequently writes in cadences reminiscent of modernist Wallace Stevens with the densely packed descriptive language and imagery characteristic of Stevens. Two of these poems, "Winter along the Santa Cruz" and "Camp of the Third Night," address nature themes with a stark power reflective of modernist technique.

To capture the solemn dormancy winter brings, Ríos in "Winter along the Santa Cruz" uses figures that reduce nature and its seasonal changes to less than human size. The "snap and turn" of daring "squirrels" becomes "the motion that spins a child's wooden top,"[6] thus reducing their activity to the comprehensible science of physical energy. Similarly, the change winter brings to the Santa Cruz River and its environs cuts nature to subhuman dimension.

> . . . the river sand is still, like heavy cream
> left out too long, assuming the color
> death requires, still and stretched:
> severed long arm lying, crooked at its elbow,
> white with the last summer pulses
> of rain through its hard and thinning arteries
> sucking in liquid instinctively, feeding
> on itself, first from its fingers, then wrist (66)

Through personification the poet transforms the power of nature into manageable, familiar terms. Nevertheless, even though the poet shrinks the river's grandeur to a mere cannibalistic appendage, it—as a metonym of nature—still serves as a mirror of human moods and psyche, as attested in the following description of the early morning fog.

> the river consumes everything but the clear sweat
> of its own effort, visible in the early morning,
> beads carried off by the wind and the redbirds
> and the sailors who are lost. (66)

These closing lines, especially the last one, suggest that the emblematic reductiveness of nature is an externalization of the speaker's own feeling of abandonment and loss—like that of "the sailors."

Ríos more explicitly parallels interior moods with the external materials of nature in "Camp of the Third Night" where he extends the metaphorical value of "apples" in interesting ways. The poem's opening image draws the traditional Judeo-Christian connection between apples and sin.

> The green apples fall hollow and flat
> picked out by the sparrows
> like the bulbous eyes of fat men who have
> sinned so that their graves are left
> shallow, obvious and mounded up
> for the animals of all worlds. (32)

With fine subtlety Ríos continues the biblical allusion to Genesis with "I dream of / the apples, of the origins of hollowness" that take "everything in from the imagination / of the earth, leaving its parts dry" (32). He concludes this thematic thread of the poem with the bitter recognition that "this fat story of the apples" has become "more real than anything / we can remember" (32). In this respect, the poem offers an ironic and bitter gloss on Genesis 3 which, the speaker suggests, casts an "evil" moralistic shadow over a humanity that desiccates "the earth." The poem's grotesque imagery precludes our perceiving nature as a serene landscape, and the dark tone insists that we experience nature as an extension of the speaker's dark mood as he and (we assume) his lover "catch the night of this place / forcing it into our bodies" (32).

Another poet who captures the dark mystery of nature through images of night is Leo Romero (see Chapter Three above). In his volume, *Agua Negra* (Dark Water), Romero focuses on the many varieties of impressions and sensations contained in his native New Mexican environment, and he delicately connects them to the mythic elements of native Southwestern cultures. For example, "You Listen to the Chickens" evokes a haunting mystery through the anthropomorphizing of nature.

> At a certain time
> you can see the darkness
> step from behind the trees
> in the mountains
>
> And very soon
> it is at your doorstep . . .
>
> And again you hear
> that *other* breathing
> Those measured footfalls
> cautious as a prowling moon . . .
>
> This late at night
> you listen to the chickens[7]

Through elliptical references and unstated associations, Romero evokes a dread that is as palpable as it is pervasive. The speaker's intense discomfort at the encroaching darkness makes him a part of the very cause of his fear. Even when "[a]ll you can do / is shut the door," the night forces itself into the narrator's consciousness where it dominates his thoughts as he is compelled to "listen to the chickens" (20).

In "Weaving the Rain" Romero captures the vastness of New Mexico by describing the manifold effects of nature: "I smell the first rain of this spring / . . . I am reminded of a feeling I had yesterday / . . . I was overcome by a sense of enormous space" (41). The immensity of the empty blue western sky as a natural surrogate of space is a commonplace to New Mexicans and visitors to the state. As in the previous poem, although the speaker perceives nature as a separate dimension, it insists itself to such an extent that it becomes internalized within him. "I caught a whiff of a wind / carrying rain, and *I felt* the grama grass / moving around me" (41, my italics). The poem's personification underscores the union of humankind and nature that is basic to Romero's worldview. Personification also explains the poem's title:

> Outside the wind is weaving the branches
> with their sprays of young leaves
> and flowers
> The wind deftly weaving the rain
> into darkness
> as the trees wave (41)

By both humanizing nature and by making it an intimate part of human consciousness, the poet asserts the unity of the two even in contemporary post-industrial life with its diminution of the natural. Ultimately, however, Romero's pictures of nature's beauty subtly evoke the awesome power manifest in its dominion over space and time.

Nature also figures importantly in the work of Lorna Dee Cervantes, a Chicana who writes in a much more personal voice than that heard in either Romero's or Ríos' poetry. Cervantes usually develops a distinct subjective I-persona in each of her poems to achieve an intimacy reminiscent of Confessional Poetry. In this way, the point of view in her work is quite distinct from the impersonal, often epic voices heard in Phase I and II Chicano poetry. A review of the individual titles in *Emplumada* discloses several poems with emphatically personal points of view—as the following titles indicate.

Uncle's First Rabbit

For Edward Long

For Virginia Chavez

From Where We Sit: Corpus Christi

Poem for the Young White Man Who Asked Me How I,
     an Intelligent, Well-Read Person Could Believe
     in the War Between Races

To My Brother

For All You Know

Como lo siento

[Etc.]

Accordingly, Cervantes' treatment of nature partakes of this subjectivity in interesting, powerful, and often unusual ways.

In "Emplumada," the book's last poem, the poet moves from a consideration of nature as *a mirror of the passage* of time to a representation of nature as *a means of escaping* time. To mirror the decay that time brings, Cervantes employs floral imagery:

> When summer ended
> the leaves of snapdragons withered
> taking their shrill-colored mouths with them.[8]

Shifting from objective description to a comment on the unpleasantness of summer's end, the narrator (uncharacteristically speaking in the third person) iterates, "She hated / and she hated to see / [the flowers] go" (66). In a reflexive effort to avoid other "withered" commonplaces of summer, she then lifts her eyes to gaze "above the fence" and spies

> two hummingbirds, hovering, stuck to each other,
> arcing their bodies in grim determination
> to find what is good, what is
> given them to find. Those are warriors
>
> distancing themselves from history. (66)

In the hummingbirds' mating, in their determined union, in this most primal procreative act, the narrator finds respite from the passage of time. For a moment (as in Marvell's "Coy Mistress"), "[t]hey find peace / in the way they contain the wind / and are gone" (66). As the final words ("and are gone") show, however, even that primal union cannot prevent nature's end from approaching, for, in the final analysis, only the poem can outlast time. Like Emily Dickinson's description of the way hummingbirds trace a "route of evanescence," this poem pays homage to the fleetingness of life.

That this piece is both the volume's title poem and the last one in the book evidences a specialness that relates to the book's central theme. The poem conveys the fragility and transitoriness of lived experience and suggests that art—poetry here—is the only real way to gain "distanc[e] from history." The book's lexical inscription ties these two qualities together aptly:

em • plu • ma • do *v.m.*, feathered; in plumage, as in after molting

plu • ma • da *n.f.*, pen flourish (unnumbered inscription page)

Nature's plumage and humankind's use of plumes for writing make the term "emplumada" uniquely descriptive of Cervantes' approach to poetry, for the plumage that molts with the passing of the seasons represents lived experience and the pen flourish symbolizes the permanence of literature. This wedding of the temporal with the eternal occurs in other Cervantes poems that focus on nature.

For example, "Starfish" sketches a vibrant portrait of "[t]housands of baby stars . . . lovely in the quartz and jasper sand" (30). What is "lovely" about the starfish to the poet is the natural artistic "talent" that propels them to create "terrariums with their bodies" and that then leads the speaker to "dry them, arrange them / Form seascapes, geodesics," in short,

to make art out of nature. But even this innocent beauty must die, the
poem suggests in the closing lines:

> In the approaching darkness . . . we left hundreds of
> Thousands of flawless five-fingered specimens sprawled
> Along the beach as far as we could see, all massed
> Together: little martyrs, soldiers, artless suicides
> In lifelong liberation from the sea. So many
> Splayed hands, the tide shoveled in. (30)

Only the poem survives to testify to the starfish's beauty and the speaker's
encounter with it.

The poem in the collection that most strikingly coheres Cervantes'
personal voice with her interest in the relation of nature and lived experience to art is "The Anthill," a compact piece of figurative density. The
poem presents the speaker's recollection of the childhood discovery of sexual
pleasure in homoerotic terms that call to mind Section Eleven of Whitman's
"Song of Myself."

> My palm cupped her mouth
> As I kissed her, the flesh
> Of my hand between us.  . . .
> After school, my friend's throat
> Ringed with daisies, so pale
> And like me; I couldn't stand it—(7)

By interweaving the girls' physical experience with their discovery of "the
anthills," the poet achieves a wonderfully reverberating *double entendre* in
which the pair's search for "the Queen / Hiding in the dank recesses"
parallels their search for eros hidden within themselves exploring together.
The incessant motion of the "thousands" of ants around them suggests the
persistent erotic energy at work inside their young bodies.

> After school, we'd cross
> The fields of wild mustard
> To the anthills . . .
> All those bodies moving.
> An army of soldiers who had it
> In for me. I could taste
> Our salt. They could smell it. (7)

"The Anthill" ends on a disturbing note of violent recklessness that raises
a number of ambiguities. In the end the ants are left "defending / Their

missals as we kicked in / The nests to find her, and recover / The soft white packets / Of her young" (7). Is Cervantes implying that adolescent libido is so powerful it cannot be restrained? Or that the chromosomal bond of sex with violence means that the latter always hovers near the surface of sexual expression? Certainly, the ending conveys the feeling that the force of awakening sexuality suppresses other human traits like compassion, empathy, and sensitivity to the sanctity of nature. Finally, the destruction of the anthill yokes sex (love?) with death as surely as the poet yoked the beauty of nature with time and death in "Starfish" and "Emplumada."

## DEATH

"Death," wrote Whitman, is the "word of the sweetest song and all songs . . . strong and delicious,"[9] thus describing the subject with an exuberant optimism characteristic of Emersonian transcendentalism. In this view of death, Whitman and the transcendentalists were influenced by their absorption of Oriental philosophies with their emphasis on an unbroken death/life continuum. Some Chicano poets (notably Alurista and Delgado) share this mystical perception of death which derives from their own absorption of Native American or Indianist attitudes toward the subject. Still, it is Emily Dickinson's manifold rendering of death that offers the thematic variety needed to account for the treatments of death in Chicano poetry. Sometimes she perceives a world and life beyond the present; sometimes death invites thoughts of despair or of a kind of clinical physical end, and other times she is indifferent or merely curious about it. Chicano poets equal that range of treatments and even extend Dickinson's to the arena of politics, an area of human discourse virtually outside her themes of interest. As with their approaches to other traditional poetic subjects and themes, Chicano poets offer a distinctive quality that derives from their ethnic experience in the United States.

Leo Romero apprehends death unromantically as a fearsome thing that shadows our lives every single day. Despite its frightening inevitability, death has its own life-giving beauty for Romero. In "The Goat's Cry," for instance, the poet describes the speaker's frightened horror as a child when he witnessed the butchering of *un cabrito*, a young goat, one of the dietary staples of Southwest Chicanos, especially for ritual celebrations like weddings, baptisms, and feast days.

            My grandmother took the young goat
            and slit its throat
            Delicate cords cut in the glass air
            I fled from the sharp knife
            from the gush of hot blood
            which had stained my grandmother's hands
            which the earth drank greedily
            In the air the goat's cry
            shattered clouds
            opened and closed blue doors
            I cowered inside the house (*Agua Negra*, 8)

Through a synesthetic description of the goat's cry, Romero shows how the slaughter dominates the boy's consciousness. Besides "shattering clouds" and "opening and closing doors," the cry also "fill[ed] the sky like smoke" and sounded "jagged as broken glass" (8). Later, Romero places the boy's fright and pity in appropriate perspective as he recalls the scene in adulthood and acknowledges the necessary and proper place in life of the *cabrito*'s death.

            . . . the goat's cry finally left the sky
            and my grandmother was calling me
            to wash my hands
            to drink of the blood
            which she held in a pan
            A pool of life
            bright life (8)

That the "hot blood" becomes a "pool of life" indicates the poet's perception of the relation of death to life as circular and mutually generative. The poem thus captures a range of sentiments (from the boy's fright to the man's understanding) that transforms them into insight.

A similar treatment of death appears in Romero's "End of the Columbus Day Weekend," even though the subject and style differ markedly from that in "Goat's Cry." "End of the Columbus Day Weekend" tells of an evening's car trip across New Mexico "[t]raveling nonstop" over "[t]wo hundred and fifty miles" (11). Written in the present tense and presenting images of the road and landscape, the poem opens with an ambiguous "It began"—a storyteller's opening like "once upon a time"—and the rest of the poem provides the referent(s) of "it." Part of "it" is the sheer tedium and frustration of "a winding / canyon road" with "elk hunters / in front of me and behind me" and an uncooperative radio offering only "Christian stations / and static" (11). But the heart of "it" is the journey which the speaker travels within his head and which is introduced obliquely in the third stanza's leap away from the literal.

> I drive carefully
> wary of what the car lights
> may suddenly reveal, that creature
> half man half coyote
> causing cars to swerve
> off the road without warning (11)

Traditionally in Mexican folklore, the "half man half coyote" figure represents death, a subject that now gains control of the tenor of the poem. Importantly, it is introduced in the context of love.

> All the darkness of the plains
> makes me think of death and love
> And I think I sense a little
> of the fear my grandmother
> must have felt when she died (11)

From here on, Romero intertwines love and death just as he alternates impressions of the speaker's external trip with images from—in Raúl Salinas' phrase—his "mind jail." Just as the poet bound the child's horror at the *cabrito*'s killing with the "pool of life," here his characteristic bent leads him to bind death with "the darkest side / of love, that will not let you go" (13). Most effective in conveying the death/love linkage is the last stanza.

> And all the way to Clovis
> I count the dark spots on the highway
> that once were rabbits . . .
> I think of the dark side of love
> and how its pain can seem
> as endless as the darkness of the plains
> And how terrible it is to be caught
> by love, a love like the one
> these rabbits knew, a love
> that demands everything, a quick
> burst of light and a speeding wheel (12–13)

We now comprehend the opening "it" as encompassing the speaker's entire trip—on the road, in the mind and imagination, and through memory and retrospection. We understand that "it began" before the "end of the Columbus Day Weekend" and that "it" will continue after it into the future.

Similarly concerned with the dark, deadly side of love is Lorna Dee Cervantes in "Uncle's First Rabbit," a narrative poem covering "fifty years" of Uncle's life. As with the speaker in Romero's "Goat's Cry," Cervantes' protagonist "still hears" the "terrible singing" of his first killed rabbit "just like a baby's" (*Emplumada*, 3). Instead of associating the animal's death with the "pool of bright life" found in "Goat's Cry," Cervantes links violence to the absence of affection.

> He remembers how the rabbit
> stopped keening under the butt
> of his rifle . . .
> He cried all night and the week
> after, remembering that voice
> like his dead baby sister's,
> remembering his father's drunken
> kicking that had pushed her
> into birth. (3)

The Uncle's painful boyhood memories of domestic violence stir his recollection of the brutality of war, which he experienced as a common foot soldier. In the third stanza, both forms of remembered violence mesh into one bitter act of catharsis and revenge on the wrong victim.

> . . . At war's end, he could
> still hear . . .
>                   Ten long hours
> off the coast of Okinawa . . .
> He pounded their voices out
> of his head, and awakened
> to find himself slugging the bloodied
> face of his wife. (4)

Cervantes thus suggests that the same organic connection linking nature's storms to natural climatic causes also links violent human natures with early formative causes. Accordingly, along with the violence another thread weaves throughout the Uncle's story—his "dream of running" away, of escaping the violence in order to "forget." Even in the ghastly ending with its mental cruelty which occurs when he is sixty, we find the escape dream repeated, the boy's desire of "running [away] . . . he'll / take the new pickup to town, sell it, and get the next train out" (5). Thus, we can see that Cervantes, too, draws a circle in her poem, signifying a continuum, a connectedness of time and experience, but this one is a single well-traveled rut of hurt.

Another poet who addresses death in his poetry is Reyes Cárdenas who writes some of the most inventive post-modernist verse in the Chicano poetic canon. Boldly experimental, Cárdenas' poetry creates its own terms and categories, and, especially in the early work, is not amenable to straightforward explication. "La Autobiografía de Reyes Cárdenas," for example, comprises thirty-seven sections containing short verses that range from the nonsensical ("Stephen F. Austin was a cartoonist whose / real name was Walt Disney") to the solemn (*"This goodby is for all the sad / things that happen in Los Angeles"*).[10] Such variety and range create an automatic thematic tension reminiscent of Whitman's inclusive catalogs of opposites in *Leaves of Grass*. As a result, "La Autobiografía" (to be discussed in the Epilogue) has the American epic quality associated with *Leaves of Grass*, Hart Crane's *The Bride*, William Carlos Williams' *Paterson*, and Allen Ginsberg's *Howl*. In his later book, *Survivors of the Chicano Titanic*, Cárdenas modifies this natural urge to explore vast bardic panoramas and produces instead a volume of poetry that is simultaneously focused and narrow, provocative and profound.

Death in *Survivors of the Chicano Titanic* is literally about death and dying; Cárdenas ignores the metaphysics of the subject and concentrates on it solely as an important variable of ideology. This perception of death appears succinctly in "Totem" where he relates his concern for the world's dispossessed poor to his speculation about the origins of greed and cruelty.

> The long history
> of death is
> nothing compared
> to the long history
> of the injustices
> that cover not
> just our own
> 3hird World, but
> our whole tight
> little world.[11]

Most of the poems in this book address the sociopolitical inequities that govern the lives of most of the world's inhabitants, and in this context death, to Cárdenas, is another unfairness meted out with disproportionate harshness and frequency to *los de abajo*. For them "[t]here is nowhere / to go, there is / no escape door" (24). The poet has no faith in political solutions, for, he implies, the injustices stem from a fundamental genetic flaw in the species. Thus, his hope can only be

> that somehow
> the repairmen,
> the chromosomes,
> will figure out
> something as
> soon as possible.
> Before these
> pebbles cease
> being cups,
> before these roots
> become vampires. (24)

Obscure though the last five lines be, they suggest that, unless there is a fundamental transformation, people will continue to exploit people until the final, cannibalistic dead-end ("vampires") is reached.

Cárdenas immediately follows "Totem" with a piece titled "And Now, the Translation," a poem that uses irony to superficially reverse the attitude toward injustice, violence, and death developed in "Totem." "What a comfort / injustice really / is, the pure / rump of mankind" (25)—writes the poet, this time offering the viewpoint of the perpetrators of injustice. Employing a mock-joyful tone to suggest the pleasure that the powerful receive from their oppression of the weak, he lovingly traces the "echo that / shootings kindle / bouncing in the canyons / of the cities." In both "Totem" and " . . . the Translation," he describes the "long history of death" and of "injustice" as forming a circle from human experience to the roots of that experience, a circle that propels itself by the sheer force of its historical momentum. The second poem makes the circle explicit by showing how the powerful victimizers—blithely called "the trigger-set"— are themselves victims of their cruelty. They, too, will know "the terror of / being swallowed" by death's grave, and here the poet closes the circle by repeating with heavy irony the poem's opening line at the end, "What a comfort" (25). In other words, the only "comfort" to be found in an unjust death is knowing that tyrants must also suffer dying.

Like Cárdenas, Leroy V. Quintana, a poet from New Mexico, writes of death and injustice and of the repetitive continuum that turns them into a revolving wheel of experience. And like *manito* Leo Romero, Quintana focuses on the local color materials of New Mexico in his poetry. Unlike Romero, however, Quintana's poetic lens is more documentary as it seeks to picture and preserve (at least in art) the life and habits of a culture that has resisted the encroachment of modernity and Anglicization. Quintana's two volumes of poetry, *Hijo del Pueblo, New Mexico Poems* (1976) and *Sangre* (1981), evince an elegant simplicity and evocative power in which Frank Waters, dean of Southwest letters, found "treasures of emotional meaning" and "a new and valid record of [Chicano] tradition."[12]

Despite the forementioned resemblance between Cárdenas and Quintana, the latter poet's handling of the subject of death and injustice is only slightly ideological. In one untitled poem, for instance, Quintana outlines a grandmother's dying "in poverty" and shows how that fact fit into the speaker's life. With the spirited energy recommended by Dylan Thomas in "Do Not Go Gentle into That Good Night," the last words of the grandmother in this piece are

> curses
> her last wish
> that they
> tell the governor
> she cursed his
> welfare and commodities
> cursing[13]

The dead woman's cursing brings to the speaker's mind his own "Eighth grade" swearing "before mass . . . outside the church," a recollection that moves attention away from the dead woman's angry dying. This topical shift continues to the end:

> that year the nuns
> told us to pray
> for peace in the world
> and that base times rate equaled percentage
>                    (21st unnumbered page)

Through this easy free-association, Quintana understates the unpleasantness of death and makes his ideological point elliptically rather than frontally. By contrasting the nuns' promotion of "peace in the world" as an abstract principle with the minute particulars of the grandmother's "poverty," the poet illustrates the sterility of institutional models for dealing with human needs. By equating the nuns' call for peace with their teaching of arithmetic, the poet undermines the genuineness of the spiritual message.

Quintana explores the impact of death on "the small town / where I was raised" in the first three untitled pieces of *Hijo del Pueblo*. The speaker connects the occurrence of death with certain expected responses from the community. He says "we always knew / when somebody on our side / had died" because certain expected things would happen: "The bells / of the Iglesia . . . would ring / and the old ones would mention / don Ricardo or Doña Martinez" (first unnumbered page). Similarly,

> When Grandma died
> doña Marina,
> our neighbor, said
> she remembered
> the small birds
> that came and perched
> on the ledge of the hospital window
> she said the same thing
> after Grandpa's funeral          (third unnumbered page)

The speaker associated death with specific responses, and the implication is that just as surely as the responses occur so too does death. These lines and images have an ethnographic clarity about them that resembles a primitivist painter meticulously detailing the habits of the folk. Quintana works his poetic verisimilitude from the very life of the village people, *el pueblo raza*, capturing their stoic perseverance and specialness with the awe of the native son ("el hijo del pueblo") who is both part of it and, by virtue of his writer's distance, outside of it. Here, as elsewhere in Chicano poetry, death as lyric subject reveals the multifarious richness of *flor y canto*.

## LOVE

Love is probably the quintessential subject of poetry, popularly associated with romance and courtship from the ancients (e.g., Sappho, Pindar, and the biblical "*Song* of Solomon") to such artifacts of today's popular culture as the greeting card and country western recordings. Although it could be said that love is to poetry as clay is to sculpture, twentieth-century belletristic poetry, especially in English, seldom speaks of love at all. There are no extended love sonnet sequences, coy mistresses, enamored pastoral voices, or love-inspired Don Juans in the canons of any major poet writing in English in this century. Whether it is the influence of post-World War I existential angst or the experimentations of modernism and post-modernism, contemporary American verse manifests a diminished interest in love as a fecund topic for poetic expression. To a large degree Chicano poetry shares this characteristic. Although love enters the poetry, it is not a prominent current except as abstract theory—for example, in Alurista's declarations to "his" *raza* or Elizondo's faith in the love-motivated energy of Chicano solidarity. Love does, of course, appear in the poems discussed throughout *Chicano Poetry*—indeed, it is present in the nature and death poems treated earlier in this chapter—but in this section it is the primary topic of the poetry.

For example, Gary Soto writes of love in a few poems in "The Manuel Zaragoza" section of *The Tale of Sunlight*. Manuel, the persona through whom the poems are presented, is a Mexican bartender given to some introspection and a great deal of action. The poem "Graciela" sketches Manuel's expression of love from the ecstasy of his wedding night to the fact of his first child's stillbirth. A short piece, "Graciela" opens with Manuel's reaction to his

> Wedding night
> Graciela bled lightly—
> But enough to stain his thighs—
> And left an alphabet
> of teeth marks on his arm.
> At this, he was happy.[14]

Love brightly colors their life together, even though "They worked long hours / hoeing crooked rows of maize / Evenings she wove rugs . . . To market in Taxco" (49). Soto marks the transition from the bliss of the couple's "liv[ing] well" with one word, "However," in the twentieth line. After this we follow Graciela from "the seventh month" when, "rising like a portion of the sun / something knotted inside her" (49). Despite the midwife's *remedios*,

> The child did not ease out.
> Days later she turned
> Onto her belly
> And between her legs
> Unraveled a spine of blood. (49)

The poet offers no further comment; Manuel does not sentimentalize or seek comfort in the bottle here as he does in other poems. Our final image of Graciela reminds us both of her needlework—the "unraveled blood" between her legs recalling her "wove[n] rugs" and "embroidered curtains"—and of their love and the blood "stain[s on] his thighs" on their wedding night.

In "Catalina Trevino Is Really from Heaven," Manuel's lust cannot be confused with love, and yet love animates his passion for Catalina, his partner in adultery. He effuses about "[t]his wonderful woman" who excites him to describe his fervor in playful figurative language:

> We danced . . .
> My crotch puffed
> Like a lung
> And holding its breath. . . .
> I opening her
> Like a large Bible,
> The kingdom of hair. (55)

She even moves him to "[w]hisper . . . a line / Of bad poetry" (55). With lusty abandon he invokes religious imagery to show how much he cherishes Catalina and his passion, calling to mind a Donnesque conceit. Here as in the other pieces in the "Manuel Zaragoza" section, unrestrained emotion dominates, and the energy and enthusiasm of love spark the speaker's imagination. These qualities paint the poems in vibrant hues, making special and blessed certain facets of the lowly bartender's life.

Contrasting sharply with these depictions of love is "Her," a Soto poem from *Where Sparrows Work Hard.* "Her" captures the poignant feelings that reawaken between lovers reunited after a "ten years" separation. The speaker recalls the stages of his pain at the time of their first separation: "First I forgot your voice, then the photo you gave me. / When a leaf fell I no longer / Thought of you."[15] They meet again in spring, traditionally a time of renewal but reversed for them into a time to "grow sullen with beer" (57). Soto leaves unstated the barriers to their permanent reunion, but we sense the end of love in every reductive line of the piece. At one point, for example, the speaker takes her hand "[a]nd it is little more than a warm glove." Even his recollection of their earlier love is couched in uncertainty and unpleasantness:

> I take [your hand], *trying to* say what it meant . . .
> To lean you in a corner in East Hall

> And touch between buttons
> *As you shivered like a machine, fearful*
> That someone would see us. (57, my italics)

The final stanza completes the poem's chronology of their relationship which began in the past of his forgetting, continued to the past of their love, and ends with "Tonight . . . I fail with the light . . . You hug me like a suitcase / And then send me walking / Slowly back, down a side street" (57). But the poet does not conclude "Her" with that trite, movie image of unrequited love; he instead follows the speaker's consciousness to "a balcony" where "a girl / is singing to the banging of spoons" (58). This final image suitably transforms the lover's serenade to a one-sided song experienced by only half a couple.

One-sidedness in love figures similarly in Alberto Ríos' "The Pioneer Hotel Fire" from the poet's *Whispering to Fool the Wind*. In surreal fashion the poem offers a series of love images about a woman from the perspective of a man's fantasy. Left deliberately ambiguous is whether or not the scene envisioned describes a dream or a literal event experienced by the speaker. The object of the speaker's fancy is an "[O]lder" woman "pretty in a nightgown" who is trapped on the ledge of a burning hotel (53). With this as the donnée of the poem, Ríos then develops the speaker's infatuation in the highly charged language of passionate love.

> . . . he sees her
> run over the crowd
> into his secret arms,
> falling at first but then turning . . .
> on a comfortable couch in mid-breath
> so that he can be there with her
> in secret . . .
>             allowing herself
> to be taken down in an electric moment (53)

As Ríos develops the poem, he subtly shifts our interest away from "the Pioneer Hotel fire," from the woman on the ledge, and even away from whether or not the scene actually happened, and moves to the intensity of the speaker's private excitement.

> kissing and biting still breathless
> she is shouting, yet not that exactly,
> trying to shout but

lost in the almost and almost and
then two short single personal explosions.

As the passage reveals, the narrative shift from external events to his private
agitated passion is suddenly and strangely interrupted by the phrase "yet
not that exactly." This unexpected break suggests that the poem concerns
a man's masturbatory fantasy, for the strange interruption occurs right
before the climactic instant. Given the intense passion of the moment, it
is an odd comment to offer between commas at this particular time because
it stops the couple's lovemaking and reintroduces the question of the exact
nature or realness of the event. At the end of the poem the only certainty
is that someone, presumably the male speaker, felt sexual "fires" inside the
"Pioneer Hotel."

Lorna Dee Cervantes' treatment of love differs markedly from that
sketched above by Ríos in that she explicitly addresses the love shared by
two people. In "The Body as Braille," for instance, she describes a woman's
reticence in responding to a lover's expressions of love.

> He tells me, "Your back
> is so beautiful." He traces
> my spine with his hand. . . .
>
> . . . I'm in love
> but won't tell him
> if it's omens
> or ice.
>
> *(Emplumada, 57)*

The brevity of the piece makes it hard to tell if her holding back ("won't
tell him") results from shyness, coyness, or a desire to tease his passion
along. The poet offers a small clue in the middle stanzas in the lines about
"the white ring / around the moon" which her *"abuela"* called "a witch's
moon" and which "[t]he schools call . . . / 'a reflection of ice crystals'"
(57). This clue reveals that the speaker finds herself caught between the
mysterious folklore of her grandmother and the equally mysterious science
of the schools. Perhaps Cervantes intends to suggest that the speaker cannot
respond actively to her lover because her mind and heart are filled to excess
with all she has been taught.

Not as brief or elliptical as "The Body as Braille," "For Virginia Chávez"
tells a powerful story of the relationship between two women whose loving
friendship develops over time and which the poet presents by focusing on

their development into adulthood. The long poem has three movements. The first movement images their friendship as girls when they first discovered boys.

> We were never told what they wanted
> but we were bold.  . . .
>                     They were such
> dumb hunks of warm fish
> swimming inside us,
> but this was love,
> we knew, love, and that was all
> we were ever offered. (16)

As the girls shared pubescent secrets, we share the poet's irony at the likely nature of the "love" that was "offered" them. The first section of the poem captures the recklessness of adolescence, and it offers a rare glimpse into the rite of passage of girls, something seldom encountered in literature. Another stage of the friends' development occurs in the teenage period when the speaker introduced Virginia to poetry, her own and that of "Byron, Donne,/ the Brownings: all about love" (17). Whereas the first section emphasized similarities between the two, leveling them into one "life we thought we'd live together," the second movement begins to reveal their differences. The speaker is becoming the teacher, the intellectual, while Virginia is "proud of the woman blooming out of . . . fourteen lonely years." We later learn that she remains trapped in her traditional gender role.

The third thematic movement of the poem opens with "the years that separate," and it discloses that the friends have indeed traveled separate paths. Two precise figures summarize the chasm that "the years had brought between us: my diploma and the bare bulb/ that always lit your bookless room" (18). The speaker's interest in books and her independence contrast sharply with her friend's indifference to books and her conventional dependence on marriage. Despite the differences, however, their loving friendship matures with them and remains intact. Consequently, when the speaker finds Virginia beaten up by her husband, "the blood/ pushing out of you/ in purple blossoms," her love for her friend surfaces spontaneously and powerfully:

> With our arms holding
> each other's waists, we walked
> the waking streets

back to your empty flat,
ignoring the horns and catcalls
behind us, ignoring what
the years had brought between us:
my diploma and the bare bulb
that always lit your bookless room. (18)

"For Virginia Chávez" opens with the pair's discovery of sexuality and the beginning of their transition from childhood. It ends with emphasis on their womanhood and the flourishing of their friendship through two lifetimes of vast changes.

Reyes Cárdenas also writes of the kind of love that transcends the vicissitudes of routine experience and that is "more costly than . . . money" (*Survivors of the Chicano Titanic*, 23). For example, in "Prices" he writes of the love that motivates martyrs, referring specifically to Oscar Romero, the theologian of liberation who, while saying mass in El Salvador in 1980, was murdered by killers hired by the country's fascist rulers. Equating Romero's life with the "price" that must be paid "for peace," Cárdenas pays homage to the greatness of the dead man's "benevolen[ce]" that warmed the world until the very moment of his death when he

even asked
forgiveness for
those who could
never possess half
of your love
for the people.
The misguided
whose lot will
never involve
freedom or love. (23)

Cárdenas' poetics of politics presents Romero's love as a paradigm of ideal affection that must be sought even in personal relationships. An example of this "ideological" love is the poem "Aztec Sacrifice," which opens dramatically with "As if sleeping together meant we/ could do something for the hungry" (61). "Aztec Sacrifice" argues that all human action should mirror the martyred Romero's, should sacrifice personal comfort, and should connect with the struggle against human oppression. For Cárdenas that is ultimately how love is demonstrated.

Celso, the I-persona of Leo Romero's *During the Growing Season*, would quarrel with Cárdenas' narrow, ideologically focused definition of love. Romero develops Celso's character in Part II of *During the Growing Season* where Celso's penchant for supernatural flights of mind and his habit of stumbling into eerie experiences in the dead of night, usually involving the dead, make him a slightly amusing, warmly grotesque figure, one that is carved out of the genuine timber of an isolated New Mexican village (like a minor character in *Bless Me, Ultima* or *The Milagro Beanfield War*). Celso would quarrel with Cárdenas' political interpretation of true love because, as the poem "Moonstruck," reveals, Celso's experience of love is thoroughly irrational, emotional, and sexual. Like the pastoral lover of old, Celso, the speaker of "Moonstruck," directly addresses his beloved, Fideligna. But she spurns him and ignores his declarations, leaving him with "a hole/ deep and straight as a well . . . where the heart should be."[16] His sleepless nights and visceral pining lead him to ask, "am I crazy/ to be so much in love with a ghost/ a spirit that glides through the night-sky" (24). At this point we assume his language to be figurative, but that view changes at the end. Despite his suffering, Fideligna, in keeping with the archetypal reserve of the classic "coy mistress," still does not respond to him, and he is left with the

> . . . fear
> that if I could grab hold of this love
> it would turn to ice
> And that there is nothing, nothing
> which could ever fill this emptiness
> that displaced my heart (25)

Ordinarily, that kind of emotional pathos would evoke compassion, but the closing lines cited above so closely resemble in passionate rhetoric the ending of "A Widow's Dance" that we are left to wonder about the authenticity of Fideligna's form, for in "A Widow's Dance" Celso uses nearly the same language to describe a drunken hallucination. We are thus forced to ask, is she a mortal creature or another figment of his fiery imagination? With Celso, the latter is probable, but Romero's purpose through his simple character is to show that love is a basic human essential, even to a foolish sot like Celso.

As this discussion shows, *raza* poets treat the theme of love with the same post-modernist *un*romantic anxiety we associate with other twentieth-

century writers. With few exceptions the poems here forsake the moonstruck lover's conceit to tell, usually explicitly, of sexual discovery and
sensual pleasures, of unfulfilled dreams and ended love affairs. Moreover,
the pieces that do contain moonstruck lovers end with strange reversals that
undercut the sentimental elements—for example, Manuel's stillborn baby
in Soto's "Graciela" and the hallucinatory unreality of Celso's romantic
"interludes" in Romero's work. Love in Chicano poetry, like nature and
death, exhibits all the complexities, confusions, and occasional clarities of
contemporary experience, and the filter of *mestizaje* and *chicanismo* intensifies
these qualities all the more richly.

## NOTES

1. Ralph Waldo Emerson, "Circles," *Essays* (First Series), 1841, collected in
Reginald Cook, ed., *Selected Prose and Poetry*, 2d ed. (New York: Holt, Rinehart &
Winston, 1969), 111. In this essay, Emerson recasts St. Augustine's idea that the
microcosm of humankind can, through total surrender to God, reflect the godly
purity of the universal macrocosm.

2. Herman Melville, *Moby-Dick*, Luther S. Mansfield and Howard P. Vincent,
eds. (New York: Hendricks House, 1952 [1855]), 473.

3. Henry James, Preface to *Roderick Hudson* in *The Art of the Novel* (New York:
Charles Scribner's Sons, 1962 [1907]), 5.

4. John Neihardt, ed., *Black Elk Speaks* (New York: Pocket Books, 1972
[1932]), 164–65.

5. Gary Soto, "The Leaves," *The Tale of Sunlight* (Pittsburgh: University of
Pittsburgh Press, 1978), 31. Subsequent references to this edition will appear
parenthetically in the text.

6. Alberto Ríos, "Winter Along the Santa Cruz," *Whispering to Fool the Winds*
(New York: Sheep Meadow Press, 1981), 66. Subsequent references to this edition
will appear parenthetically in the text.

7. Leo Romero, "You Listen to the Chickens," *Agua Negra* (Boise, Idaho:
Ahsahta Press, 1981), 20. Subsequent references to this edition will appear
parenthetically in the text.

8. Lorna Dee Cervantes, "Emplumada," *Emplumada* (Pittsburgh: University of
Pittsburgh Press, 1981), 66. Subsequent references to this edition will appear
parenthetically in the text.

9. Walt Whitman, "Out of the Cradle Endlessly Rocking," *Leaves of Grass*,
lines 180–181.

10. Reyes Cárdenas, "La Autobiografía de Reyes Cárdenas," *La Voz Poética del
Chicano* (Berkeley, Calif.: Quinto Sol, 1974), 15 and 19.

11. Reyes Cárdenas, *Survivors of the Chicano Titanic* (Austin, Tex.: Place of
Herons Press, 1981), 24. Subsequent references to this edition will be made
parenthetically in the text.

12. Frank Waters, "Introduction," *Hijo del Pueblo, New Mexico Poems* (Las Cruces, N.Mex.: Puerto Del Sol Press, 1976), n.p.

13. Leroy V. Quintana, "[He told me]," *Hijo del Pueblo*, 21st unnumbered page. Subsequent references to this edition will be made parenthetically in the text.

14. Gary Soto, "Graciela," *The Tale of Sunlight* (Pittsburgh: University of Pittsburgh Press, 1978), 49. Subsequent references to this edition will be made parenthetically in the text.

15. Gary Soto, *Where Sparrows Work Hard* (Pittsburgh: University of Pittsburgh Press, 1981), 57. Subsequent references to this edition will be made in the text.

16. Leo Romero, "Moonstruck," *During the Growing Season* (Tucson, Ariz.: Maguey Press, 1978), 23. Subsequent references to this edition will be made parenthetically in the text.

# Epilogue: The "Eyes" of Chicano Poetry

To convey the multiplicity of forms, themes, and meanings characteristic of Chicano poetry, let us return to the tradition of popular song where, as explained in Chapter One, the poetry had its origin (see above, "Chicano Literary History"). Here, however, the return to song is metaphorical for, in this case, the reference is to only one specific song, "Cielito Lindo," which is as embedded in American folklore as "Home on the Range." "Cielito Lindo" is familiar to both Hispanics and non-Hispanics who can usually sing, if not the entire song, the simple refrain.

> De la Sierra Morena, Cielito Lindo, vienen bajando.
> Un par de ojitos negros, Cielito Lindo, los contrabando.
> Ay, Ay, Ay, Ay, Canta y no llores
> Porque cantando se alegran, Cielito Lindo, los corazones.[1]

The "Ay Ay Ay Ay" of the refrain is especially well suited as a summative metaphor of Chicano poetry because it emerges from the folk, the original source of the poetry. It is a punning summation predicated on the multiple meanings captured by the one sound "Ay," a homophone that reflects the bilingual range and multicultural richness of Chicano poetry. First, there is the *eye* of the poetic seer who, like a prophet, offers a personal lamp to illuminate our experience of the world. Second is the *I* of the poet's self, the artistic persona, which is shaped into parables of symbol and insight that transcend the writer's ego. Chicano poetry also presents the *¡ay!* of pain and suffering evoked by the poet's depiction of *tristezas* from Chicano history and mundane Chicano experience. Fourth, there is the *hay* (i.e., the "there") representing the poet's locus of interest whether barrio, campo, llano, or any of the other sites in or relating to Aztlán.

This section, then, presents the expected conclusions about the material presented in Chapters One through Five, but it is done clustering the poems around the homophonic "eye/I/ay/hay" of the poetry. In this way, we capture the rich possibilities of both the bilingual idioms of Chicano literature and the multiculturalism of Chicano experience. It is also shown here that one does not *discover* Chicano poetry in a static, one-dimensional encounter. Rather, its dynamic nature enfolds us in an on-going process of *discovering* that leads eventually to the discovery that the multiple "eyes" of the poetry also include the I of the discoverer—you and me.

One poet who has written several poems that manifest the eye of the poetic seer is Alberto Ríos in *Whispering to Fool the Wind*. His "Belita," a piece about an old dying woman named Belita, looks ahead to dying and death and captures with sensitive precision the changes in sensation that accompany old age.

> The faces and the hands of her grandchildren
> had grown too big to fit through her eyes.
> She learned to keep bowed her head
> because . . . faces she could not [recognize], not even
>     . . . her own
> which fit her now like a wrinkled handkerchief,
> like the brown, unlaundered, unironed handkerchief
> she kept always in her hands because her grandchildren
> had given it to her . . . [2]

As the poem develops, Ríos shows us how Belita's diminished physical capacities return her to the narcissism of childhood where everyone and everything are perceived solely in relation to the self. Then at the end of the poem his prophetic eye moves beyond agedness to the future that is her death. He accomplishes this through a barely perceptible shift from the old woman's consciousness to that of her mourners, a shift that informs us of her death.

> She remembered her friends suddenly as children,
> how they had played Death like this because ahead
> only dinner waited for them . . .
> Now it was her turn, and quickly her own eyes
> closed . . .
> But those eyes are not her own.
> She cannot recognize any longer the little head,
> covered now by that handkerchief, kissed by the children. (9–10)

Like other poets before him, notably Wallace Stevens in "The Emperor of Ice Cream," Ríos writes of death with fresh power, forcing us to experience it and its certain futurity in ways that make it palpable in the living present.

Similarly, in "Sleeping on Fists" Ríos portrays the abject suffering of a drunk and his grimly patient wife in such a way that we, too, experience something of their misery. The poet's prophetic eye penetrates beneath the obvious aspects of suffering to the underlying purity that gives such inevitable agony its integrity. Like a prophet who probes what is to come, Ríos' persona can enter another's skin to share his or her feelings and soul in a way that clarifies what the future holds in store. For example, he shares the drunk's discomfort as he is dragged along the ground "[h]is uncombed head felt like one/ in a bunch of fibrous coconuts" (48), and he aptly evokes the queasiness produced by liquor when the drunk feels like "the state of life one imagines to exist/ in the sea: wet and slow and nauseous" (48). Into this "insolid middle of the seas at storm" comes the "clam and lofty eye" of the drunk's wife who had also "measured a hard life . . . harder even" for she "had been forced . . . to care" (49). To convey the way both halves of the couple share in the misery as well as its cause, Ríos extends the sea metaphor to include the wife as "clam" in the husband's drunken, bleary eyes. At the same time, he avoids cliché by employing "clam," not "calm and lofty eye," thus jarring conventional expectation just as the drunk jars the commonplace habits of his wife. The poet steers far from bathos by so sensitively understanding the couple's life together that he even knows what they know:

> So this was their way, she nodded.
> He to be drunk, and herself
> to take charge of him . . .
> But these were their functions, she
> decided, and all else was without meaning,
> the celebration of sadness
> must take this form. (49–50)

By seeing to the core of suffering, to its inevitability, the poet transcends the immediate, the obvious, the *apparent* real and penetrates the hidden, the obscure, the *essential* real.

In a completely different style of poetic prophecy is Reyes Cárdenas in *Survivors of the Chicano Titanic* where his ideological interpretations of the future are bleakly pessimistic (e.g., "State of the Union" and "Poema Sandino"), or violently optimistic homages to the revolution (e.g., "El aeropuerto de Managua" and "Hit and Run"), or startlingly incisive in their clear-eyed honesty (e.g., "Aztec Sacrifice" and "June 25, 1980 Driving to the Future"). Concerned with the persistence of exploitation and its oppressive by-products, Cárdenas examines middle-class complacency and Third World deprivation and shows how the former breeds the latter.

> Luxuries peak in
> vehement districts,
> imposed like
> unfortunate oracles,
> hardened in the wind.[3]

In other words, the creature comforts enjoyed by the few portend an inescapably "unfortunate" future in which the "vehement" many will seek to topple their exploiters. He is also concerned with the potency of words and of poetry to effect radical changes in experiential reality. As with other poet-activists, Cárdenas seeks to pierce through the thickened layers of materialism which generations of affluence have produced among his compatriots, making them insensitive to the subsistence-level suffering of the vast majority of the world and insensitive, too, to their own basic humanity. Ultimately, he concludes "[a] million years from now we'll/ still be mining words together" (62), as if to say that the process of poetry (of art?) transcends and outlasts the material world of experience.

The eye of Cárdenas' prophecy appears explicitly in "Oracles," a post-modernistic piece that fuses the ordinary with the extraordinary.

> In the tub you
> only wash away
> the apocalyptic;
> the cyclops of
> useless precautions. (33)

The poet levels the catastrophic, "the apocalyptic," to the recognizable size of a bath and exposes the futility of one-eyed, unseeing "precautions" against quotidian problems and dangers. He asserts that lifestyle and individual circumstances themselves serve as "oracles, hardened in the wind," the lifestyle determining future outcomes. Consistent with his Marxist ideology, Cárdenas believes that material "luxuries . . . support themselves on Achilles' heels," vulnerable to the "[s]omeone [who] crawls/ along with a knife" and who would challenge the unearned luxuries of the powerful (33). The fusion of modern egalitarianism with traditional mythology (apocalypse, Cyclops, Achilles) forces our awareness of the long persistence of human exploitation throughout history.

In "Light at the End of the Tunnel" the poet invests new meaning and power into the title cliché, a favorite expression of the political establishment in recent years. He transforms the phrase into a pessimistic epigram of a future built firmly on the blindness of the past. Opening with a straightforward "[t]here is no secret cipher/ to talk of injustice," the poem builds figuratively as it describes the injustice of "the poor at the bottom" of the "pyramid" that is the town (37). The answer to "how things got this way" is known to a

> . . . few that see the light
> at the end of the tunnel,
> and step out to be
> bathed in it, must step
> back into darkness
> if all are to survive. (37)

The true seers, says Cárdenas, adjust themselves to the "darkness" and retreat from the light of truth and knowledge, to remain blind with the predominant majority. Nevertheless, the poet insists that conformity cannot eliminate from the few the "glow" in their "eyes" that remains from their visionary probing to the truth, to the "light at the end of the tunnel." Now transformed, at the end of the poem the title refers more to the light of the prophet's vision than to the procrastination of political promises.

In "Lagrimas" Cárdenas again employs the eye figure—this time "los ojos"—to reveal the future and how it is inextricably yoked to the past. Written entirely in Spanish, "Lagrimas" ("Tears") captures the multiple functions of eyes—to see, to weep, to perceive the revolution—by focusing on the inutility of tears. The first stanza suggests their inutility, for *tears "never have made/ anyone free"* (43, my translation). The second stanza extends this perception further by blaming the helpless sentimentality of *weeping* for *"maintaining them* [the privileged few] *where they are . . . on top!"* Moreover, by deprecating the value of Father Hidalgo's famous cry of freedom, "el grito de Dolores," which is historically seen as marking the start of the Mexican Independence Movement, Cárdenas undermines hero worship of revolutionary leaders given to charismatic rhetoric and symbolic flourish. He suggests that they inspire "tears only." Instead, he would have the masses imagine a genuine revolution of action in which "guerrillas/ *come out of the eyes,*" not tears, for weeping is like "*blow*ing guerrillas away [to the wind] through the eyes" (43). To Cárdenas the poet is a visionary revolutionary who illuminates our experience of the world by casting light on the sociopolitical determinism that he believes defines it. He equates tears and guerrillas, pyramids and towns, the apocalypse and baths to disclose how the extraordinary resides in the very ordinary.

Slightly different in prophetic content but with similar symbolic technique, Gary Soto in "The Point" measures the universe through commonplaces like a chicken's eyes, lint, and a streetlight.[4] Developed around Molina, the poet's lowly persona, the poem rhymes images rather than sounds. In the first ten lines, Soto rhymes "[t]he moon going orange" with the "chicken . . . eyes/ Blown deep/ As targets," and these circumferences in turn rhyme with the "circles" the chicken makes around "[i]ts droppings" (5). That these images mirror cosmic turns and revolutions is made explicit in Molina's perception of the stars as "the galaxy/ Of lint tilting on its axis," indicating that Molina is a man given to wondering "Why?"

> Why the cloud
> That never rained,
> The sleep that is something
> More than sleep?
> Why the crowd found
> Flat as a glove,
> Its beak open on a yawn?
> Nothing answered . . . (5)

In frustration that nothing is answered and also at his "poverty" and "his hunger," Molina takes "six rocks . . . And bursts a streetlight/ That won't come to the point" (5). Here Soto shifts from rhyme to pun, from the points of the orbs and circles to *the* "point" of the phrase "come to the point"— that is, to get specific. And what is "the point"? The closing lines express it lyrically:

> The sky swallows
> Hard on the echo
> And Molina's eyes are lost
> Between the blue of two stars. (6)

Molina projects his agony on the aloof cosmos represented by "the sky" as Soto merges his protagonist's vision with the heavens, simultaneously illustrating the unavoidable unity of the one with the all and, in his characteristic reverse transcendentalism, the futility for Molina of seeking profundities in nature where the one can only be "lost" in the endless, eternal "blue."

As these few verses disclose, especially in the context of the poetry examined in all the preceding chapters, the "eyes" of Chicano poet-seers peer into death and drunkenness (Ríos), into political motives and political futures (Cárdenas), and into the existential reality that A, after all, only equals A (Soto). That these eyes see the strange residing in the ordinary typifies any artistic eye; that they also recognize the ramifications of both the strangeness and the ordinariness suggests a visionary insight. And the clarity of their visions of the world cannot but illuminate our own.

Turning to *hay*, one Spanish homophone of "eye," we focus on place, the lexical meaning of *hay*. We examine both the *there* that the eye perceives and the *where* in which the action occurs whether barrio, campo, llano, alma, or any actual or imagined locus of life. Except for historic landmarks, places usually do not transcend their ordinary function or value except in the memories held about them as settings for the people and occasions shared there. The poems in this cluster describe, define, remember, praise, and even denounce certain loci of experience that seem etched ineradicably within the poets' internal *hay*—that geography where mind, heart, soul, imagination, and memory intersect like lines on a map.

Gary Soto's poem, "There" in *Where Sparrows Work Hard*, offers a particularly effective introduction to this section, for it presents a nostalgic but unsentimental rendering of place.[5] In "There" the speaker returns to a childhood home and playground only to find that the "yard" and "the pinned wash/ White in the wind" have been replaced by "the filth of bottles, gutted mattresses,/ A dead cat on its rack of weeds" (56; also compare Cervantes' "Free Way 280"). The speaker's pilgrimage to the locus of his early life reveals the vast deterioration taking place "there" since the time he heard the "Rattle of bees in a shoe box" to the present and the "raffle of snagged papers" in the "tumbleweed," that certain sign of neglect and abandonment. But the carious condition of the yard cannot destroy the lived past there, and memory revives the speaker's "brother, his voice over my/ Shoulder" (56). Curiously, Soto employs the indefinite article in describing the sibling ("I'm looking again/ For *a* brother" [my italics]) as if his brother might turn up accidentally "behind a shed or the blue caravan of bushes" like a missing shoe (56). The poem ends with a tinge of muted humor and soft irony. Gathering up the artifacts from his visit "there,"

objects that might represent the speaker's childhood interests, the narrator
muses—

> I have much to show—
> Bent nails and a pair of pliers.
> This coffee-can, pressed to my ear,
> Is a way to the sea . . .
> Wind in the China tree, and it's just over there.
>                                    (56; Soto's ellipsis)

In other words, given the unexpected decrepitude of this early home, the
speaker must do what his brother used to do: "Look . . . for the rain that
ends beautifully."

More acerbic in its recollection and caustic in its humor, "TV in Black
and White" succinctly depicts the collision of three loci of experience—the
world of "The rich on TV," the literal world of affluence with its "Gin in
the afternoon," and the speaker's world of farmwork in "a vineyard/ That
we worked like an abacus,/ A row at a time" (11). Soto describes the fantasy
world of television as totally real in its contrast to the world of the workers
in the *campos* who, devoid of other forms of recreation, "were sentenced to
watch" as "Ozzie Nelson" played "golf" in "his eighth season" while the
farmworkers

> . . . hoed
> Fields flagged with cotton
> Because we understood a sock
> Should have a foot,
> A cuff a wrist,
> And a cup was always
> Smaller than the thirst. (11)

Transforming the idea of "world" from an abstraction of universal place to
a sentient conspirator that "still plots" its classist divisions of misery, Soto
justifies his harsh metaphor with familiar examples of the unfair social
conspiracy: "Piano lessons for this child,/ Braces for that one" and so on
(11). Nevertheless, concludes the poet, despite the domination of televised
scenes of comfort and affluent centers of power, the poor will not always
continue in passive toil, for "if the electricity/ Fails, in this town,/ A store
front might/ Be smashed" as the powerless seize the only form of power
available to them. In the end the popular image of television's heroes living
in eternal unalloyed bliss provides Soto with the meat of his subtly abrasive

humor. Just as the rich feed on the labors of the poor, so too will the poor seek retribution whenever the moment offers itself, and thus "if someone" steals "a black and white TV,/ It's because we love you Donna [Reed],/ We miss you Ozzie" (12).

The arbitrariness of fate suggested in the previous poem's depiction of unfair social stratifications also appears in Soto's "The Map" in *The Tale of Sunlight*. In "The Map" Soto's character, Molina, exercises his imagination in order to conquer the arbitrariness of his birthplace in a torrid heat zone where "the sun's whiteness closes around us/ Like a noose" (7). Through the use of such images of weather as "thermometer," "fog," "snow," and even the "map," Soto captures Molina's preoccupation with the heat at "noon" as he "squats" in the "uneven shade of an oleander." He also shows how Molina escapes the heat by fantasizing about the other places he marks on "the map" with "a pencil": "He dots rain over Bogota, the city of spiders,/ And x's in a mountain range," and, most importantly, he finds

> Where the river Orinoco cuts east,
> A new river rises nameless
> From the open grasses,
> And Molina calls it his place of birth. (7)

Thus, to Molina the unpleasant reality of *hay* can be transcended effectively by the fertile fictions of his mind and imagination.

Imagination of a weirdly impressionistic kind dominates Reyes Cárdenas' "Images of Boston" in *Survivors of the Chicano Titanic*. In its unharnessed random associations and nearly unfathomable surface semantics, "Images of Boston" recalls the impressionistic catalogs of "La Autobiografía de Reyes Cárdenas," the poet's early tour de force published in *El Grito* (discussed below). Certainly, place figures prominently in "Images of Boston" where Cárdenas seizes U.S. poet Robert Lowell, literal heir of generations of New England's literary aristocracy, as the archetypal representative of Boston. He then invests his unique image of the poet with a variety of unlikely associations.

> The hamburghers
> can't translate Robert Lowell.
> Thick little gringo.
>
> In Boston
> the billboards of his
> automobiles also remind

us of meat.
( . . . *Chicano Titanic*, 17)

We are not surprised that Cárdenas reduces the bourgeoisie (i.e.,
" . . . burghers") to the commonness of ground beef, but his reductive
description of Lowell startles because of its irreverent dismissal of the
traditionally most esteemed strand of the U.S. literary tapestry. And yet
the facile irreverence is on target, if slightly obscure. The reference to
"automobiles" that "remind us of meat" calls to mind the tragic car
accident with Lowell at the wheel that critically injured his then wife,
writer Jean Stafford. In the same way the third stanza's mention of Lowell's
"wives," "shark fins," and "nervous breakdowns" remind us of the eminent
poet's well-known personal upheavals. If Lowell represents all that is
blueblood Boston as well as the *crème* of contemporary U.S. literature, then
the poem's speaker must "sit out the game" on the "sidelines [that] are
probably pants," which cover "Lowell's guts" (17). These lines sneer the
Chicano poet's rejection of the traditions Lowell personifies and his rejection too of those Yankee values associated with Boston, one of the cradles
of the country's definitive social and literary forms.

A range of sentiments and ideas more various than the pejorative reduction of "Images of Boston" characterizes the poet's "La Autobiografía
de Reyes Cárdenas." Comprising thirty-seven sections spread over four
books, the first entirely in English and Books Two-Four in monolingual
Spanish, "La Autobiografía" bears the features of post-modernistic writing. Each section contains a number of usually one-sentence stanzas most
often in simple declarative syntax, and particularly in Book One, the tone
and meanings resemble the absurdist nonsense of Ionescan dramatic
fiction.

2
. . . The Spanish-American War was Napoleon
landing on the shores of Rhode Island.
The Korean War was Charlemagne
killing King Kong in Crete. . . .

The Vietnam War was Alexander the Great
looking for a horse throughout Maine. . . .

6
. . . I build houses for Randolph Scott, the
San Francisco T.V. repairman. . . .

> My mother, Davy Crockett, makes hamburgers.
> She's waiting for me at the door.[6]

The poet's reduction of all subjects into a toybox of equivalent nouns to be equated at random reflects the post-modernist urge to defy conventional logic and the kind of Eliotic exegesis that looks for complex meanings under words like an archaeologist turning dirt for potsherds.

Interestingly enough, references to place pervade "La Autobiografía." In the opening section, for example, Cárdenas enumerates five kinds of poets, and each reference is modified by a place name.

> The Texas poet is a Mexican who breaks
> horses for William Wordsworth.

> The New York poet is an Iroquois who
> seeks a girl named Marie Sandoz. . . .

> The Wyoming poet is Benjamin Franklin,
> the best known surrealist doctor. (10)

These geographical adjectives heighten the absurdist non sequitur of, say, a pillar of yankee patriotism like Benjamin Franklin practicing surrealist medicine in Wyoming. Similarly, section 4 centers on "George Washington," and each of the poet's whimsical references to the historical figure deals with particular places: "I picture him in Texas bathing in the Rhine,/ but I can never picture him in Iowa./ No matter how hard I try" (11). The pointed whimsy serves paradoxically both to revivify "Washington" by placing him in unexpected situations and locales and to undermine the historical facts usually associated with him. As these examples show, in his early work Cárdenas clearly perceived place as integral to definitions, whether of the self or of culture or of ideology, and whether strictly literal or emphatically figurative.

Other sections of "La Autobiografía" display his comedic voice. For instance, section 3 of the poem is singularly slapstick in its outrageous allusions to poet Lord Byron and actor Audie Murphy, and its place names function to heighten the comedy. Likewise, the second stanza in section 7 uses *place* to underscore the foolishness inherent in taking *places* too seriously.

> I like to pretend I am Currier and Ives
> climbing the Matterhorn until I reach the
> face of Millard Fillmore or until I touch
> noses with General Custer. (13)

Currier and Ives, of course, are famous for their quaint renderings of rustic
settings, whereas the Matterhorn represents a traditional challenge of
natural topography as well as its more accessible scale in the Disneyland
version of the alpine peak. The references to Fillmore and Custer bring into
ironic focus another mountain, Mount Rushmore, and its sculpted profiles
of the most illustrious U.S. presidents. That Fillmore was not illustrious
and that Custer was defeated by the Indians appears to be the poet's way of
reminding us that the most rustic setting of all, pristine America before the
European onslaught, has been desecrated and Mount Rushmore is equivalent to a Disneyland Matterhorn on a tourist's map.

Just as whimsical and edged in political cynicism is section 12 which is
constructed around the familiar verse of a popular song.

> There are smiles that belong to Mademoiselle
> from Armentières, the leader of Israel. . . .
>
> There are smiles that belong to Alabama,
> home of the Statue of Liberty.
>
> There are smiles that belong to America,
> the shoeless England. (15)

Cárdenas means to jolt our complacency about such familiar places as Israel,
Alabama, and America by combining them with odd, unexpected images.
In addition, he undercuts the blithesome quality of the easy "smiles" by
linking them with serious, even solemn subjects. Less whimsical in its
treatment of place is section 21 in Book Two. Dedicating the section to
Chicano frontier hero Joaquín Murriéta, the poet alludes to several different
loci to demonstrate the folk hero's universality.

> *Your {Murrieta's} heart blooms in the streets*
> *of Germany.*
>
> *Your blood is a river like the Mississippi*
> *of Viet Nam.*
>
> *Your land isn't Pancho Villa's land*
> *but your revolution is the same.*
> *You are the bandit of California.*
>
> *You are the Virgin of Guadalupe, you*
> *are my life.* (19; my translation)

The tone of sincere celebration above for the most part typifies the Spanish-language books of "La Autobiografía," and the tonal and thematic shifts matched with the codeswitching communicate the poet's earnest *chicanismo*. Ultimately, the strikingly various facets of Cárdenas' poem combine into a multiplicitous mosaic of *mestizaje*.

Another poet who writes of place to articulate his *chicanismo* is Ricardo Sánchez, who subtitled his most recent chapbook, *Brown Bear Honey Madnesses*, with reference to *hay: Alaskan Cruising Poems*.[7] The chapbook opens with homages to "The Royal Chicano Air-Force," to the poet's loss of "innocence in a Juarez Congal," and to the concept of "Entelechy" which is the cornerstone of Sánchez's *chicanismo* (4–5). Appearing throughout his poetic corpus, *entelechy* (or *entelequía*, also the title of a short independent film about Sánchez) refers to the actualization of one's true existence and to the vital force immanent in life. For Sánchez that force has consistently derived from his Chicano identity, whether manifested in his *pinto* poems, in his poignant verses to his "Jefito," who died without "the chance to read my works" (11), or in his neologistic excesses which occasionally achieve their intent (as in the bilingual "Alaskaztlán" and "entre corbatas/de JayCee Penny,/ . . . d'yves St./ L'Orient Expressed hopes" [37, 19]). Comparable to the Buddhist idea of enlightenment, entelechy is sought through life's journey, and it also reflects the journey itself.

As if to disclose the progress of his individual entelechy, in *Brown Bear Honey Madnesses* Sánchez provides a geographical and chronological epigraph to each of the pieces in the volume. He prefaces "interminable," for example, with the following epigraph: "capitol city, waterfront town, behemoths roam venting frustrations . . . Juneau, Alaska 17 June 79" (13, poet's ellipsis). The poem itself describes the poet's acute awareness of himself in a place foreign to his experience with its long "nightless/ moonless" days and "pre-fabricated food" (13). Sánchez discovers the Alaska of "oil boomtowns" marked by the "festooned fantasies" of artificial "j. wayne frontier[s]" and the "hordes of neo-beats/hipsters . . . escapees/ from an impacted/main-/ land" (14). By cataloguing the artifice that characterizes the "lifestyles" of this "denativized/disjointed Alaska" (15), the poet builds to his central theme, the way a frigid, uncaring sensibility produces an inability

> . . . to emote . . .
> bound in
> by bay, glacier,

    & awesome
isolation,
    S P A C E . . .
Alaska,
native land
of non natives . . .
brutally reliving
past centuries,
    methodically
committing genocide,
yes, deny
the eskimos,
aleuts,
athabaskans,
haida & tlingits (16)

In other words, Sánchez finds in Alaska the same cold "collective manifest destiny mentality" that killed Indians, Blacks, and Mexicans throughout "Amerika's" history (17). He can only shudder about "all that is interminable/ about the USA" (17).

A striking contrast to "interminable," Sánchez's "& would that I could" locates the poet in Mexico "waddl[ing] in heat, humidity,/ unlike [the] glacial realities" of Alaska (26). In this place, "this ancient capitol/ of the Nahuatl peoples," Sánchez finds intellectual and artistic stimulation "in the entourage of writers" being féted by the Mexican government. "I stoke my mind," he tells us, "at Tlatelolco" (27). And yet he cannot ignore the "beggars cry[ing] out/ for bread" and the Mexican "sovereignty" that was "sepulchred in San Jacinto," for Mexico's past explains why "Chicanos cry and lament" about being culturally "dismembered" like "shards of clay figurines" by First World attitudes that "unceremoniously" disparage *mexicanidad* (26). The poem's title expresses the poet's wistful yearning

    that I could
sing you, Mexico,
songs
that might waft
on mariachi strains,
that I could feel comfort
in all that you should be (26)

It is as if by singing the genuine spirit of Mexico he might lessen his sadness at all the frivolous "anti-mejicano doings" making a caricature of the "ancient capitol" (27). In any event, as in "interminable" Sánchez comprehends geographical space in terms suggesting both personal and cultural identity, what it was, is, and ought to be.

Lorna Dee Cervantes' "Visions of Mexico . . . " in the volume *Emplumada* incorporates some of these same concerns enunciated by Sánchez. She, too, finds that the "sense of [Mexico] can only ripple through my veins/ like the chant of an epic corrido"—that is, a song—and she, too, is alert to the popular caricature that "Mexico is a stumbling comedy."[8] In addition, Cervantes uses a contrasting *hay* as backdrop for "that far south" just as Sánchez employed Alaska to place Mexico in topographical and cultural perspective. She uses "Port Townsend, Washington" as the dissimilar locus, a place too "far north" where she doesn't "belong" (46) and which lacks "pueblos green on the low hills" and "all those meadows: Michoacan/ Vera Cruz, Tenochtitlan, Oaxaca" (45). Although when she's "that far south" her "own words somersault naturally as my name," speaking her joyful ease there, she is not impervious to the privations of the people.

> I watch and understand. . . .
> Alone with the women in the adobe, I watch men,
> their taut faces holding in all their youth.
> This far south we are governed by the law
> of the next whole meal. (45)

Nor does she exaggerate her understanding of the land of her "antepasados" ("Oaxaca, 1974," 44) by "pretend[ing]" she "can speak all the names"— she "can't"—for she comes "from a long line of eloquent illiterates" whose "gesture[s]" are "utterance[s] more pure than word" (45). This line leads her to introduce the poem's controlling metaphor—life experience as poetic language—which she develops especially effectively in the poem.

> We are not animals
> but our senses are keen and our reflexes,
> accurate punctuation.
> All the knifings in a single night. . . .
> We hear them
> and the poet within us bays . . .
> there are songs in my head I could sing you . . .
> songs that could tell you what I know
> or have learned from my people
> but for that        I need words

```
simple black nymphs between white sheets of paper
obedient words          obligatory words          words I steal . . .
I come north
to gather my feathers
for quills (46–47)
```

Cervantes thus transmutes her experience of places, her recollection of them from a distance, and her sense of herself feeling the total *hay* of her surroundings, into the very genera of poetry—its words, sounds, and rhythms. By doing so, she both reifies and gives meaning to the undifferentiated flow of time and experience.

In a different vein, her treatment of place in "Poema para los Californios muertos" (Poem for the Dead Californios) recalls the us/them polarity of Phase I protest poetry. Reminiscent of her early freeway poems, this one opens by stating the fundamental conflict between technological progress and historical traditions which urbanism brings: "these older towns die/ into stretches of freeway" (42). The poet likens the concrete and asphalt to a "cesarean across belly valleys and fertile dust," and she is "stir[red]" to wonder "[w]hat refuge did you find here, ancient Californios?" (42). The source of her wonderment is a "brass plaque" she encounters "outside a restaurant in Los Altos, California, 1974"; the plaque bears the inscription, "Once a refuge for Mexican Californios" (42). Serving as a mnemonic stimulus to the primal "memory" of *"her fertile blood,"* the plaque brings to mind her *"dead ancestors"* (42, my translations). That recollection elicits her resentment about the forced changes brought by time and the *"white phantasms"* of the new "high-class"—that is, U.S. material affluence (42). With the same anger that fueled the earliest Chicano protest poets, "Poema" concludes with Cervantes "see[ing] nothing but strangers . . . [and] bitter antiques,/ yanqui remnants," and the bitterness permeates all her senses.

```
A blue jay shrieks
above the pungent odor of crushed
eucalyptus and the pure scent
of rage. (43)
```

Even nature's creatures and plants are transformed by her rage.

Like Cervantes, Alberto Ríos experiences place as an extension of feeling, but he mutes his description of the experience in a way that buries emotion under a surface sangfroid which ultimately increases the darkness and vulnerability pervading his descriptions. "Wet Camp," for instance, offers

a straightforward evocation of *hay*, even though the speaker is "lost" and
seems strangely distant from the scene.

> We have been here before, but we are lost.
> The earth is black and the trees are bent
> and broken and piled as if the game
> of pick-up-sticks were ready and the children
> hiding, waiting their useless turns.
>                           (*Whispering to Fool the Wind*, 52)

The omniscient description gives a tone of assurance to the poem, one that
suggests that the speaker's feelings are detached from this place where
"ponds sit like dirty lilies in the black" (52). Everything seems distant—
the "children hiding," the "afternoon . . . gone grazing," and the "lost"
observers. With the last line, however, we recognize that the tone of
objective equanimity is a thin façade, just like the "thin mountains" and
"broken" trees in the horizon: "The night is colder here without leaves./
Nothing holds up the sky" (52). Initially hidden by the speaker/observer's
declarative assurance, the fear and loneliness nonetheless emerge clearly at
the end just as Cervantes' "rage" surfaced at the end of "poema para los
Californios muertos." In both poems, the actual places become projections
of the speakers' emotions.

Another Ríos poem, "Sonoita Burn," is especially suited to conclude
this section of the Epilogue, for it focuses simultaneously on the way
places affect us directly and on the means we use to escape them. Ríos
describes how "the wind . . . brings" the distant "town" near, blowing
the town's "ashes" indiscriminately as "[s]moke fills" the speaker's "eyes/
making tears" (31). Comparable to Molina's discomfort in Gary Soto's
"The Map," the real place here is both unpleasant and the source of the
speaker's distress. The "town fires far off/ are the last thing" the speaker
sees "before I curl to sleep," but like Molina he can "dream" an escape,
and he does, finding "a new sky covering me/ whose million sparks are
more alive" than the real fires of Sonoita. Accordingly, like the other poets encountered in the *hay* cluster of Phase III Chicano poetry, Ríos captures the way the reality of a place affects human consciousness and how
that same consciousness can elude the ever-present realities of one's
environment.

Individually, each of these poets renders place according to the requirements of his/her own aesthetics, but considered together they furnish a
rich and varied landscape of experience and outlook. Whether Soto's nos-

talgic reminiscences about his childhood home, or his and Cárdenas'
ironic treatments of place as exponent of classist inequities, or Cárdenas'
absurdist combinations of place to jolt one from expected responses, or
Sánchez's and Cervantes' employment of place to express identity and,
with Ríos, personally felt emotions— whatever the point of departure or
destination, the places toured in these poems are recognizable, if sometimes enigmatic, models of places that are as well traveled as a pathway
to an *ojito de una cueva* in the Southwest desert.

The third line of the song "Cielito Lindo" is

> Ay, Ay, Ay, Ay, Canta y no llores
> ( . . . Sing, don't cry).

The line conveys the thought that weeping—that is, the physical expression of sadness and suffering—is as common as the "beautiful sky" of the
title, a thought that lies at the center of Mexican balladry and popular song.
Along with the guitar and trumpets, the *llanto* or piercing cry is a *sine qua
non* of the familiar mariachi musical performance in both Mexico and the
United States. The cry functions as emotional punctuation, as spontaneous
interjection, and as emblem of the primal scream that gives us life and that
accompanies its end, either in the dying person or the grieving survivors.
Clustered under *¡ay!*, the third homophone of "eye" considered here,
sadness and suffering bind this set of poems. With or without exclamation
points, *ay* is a nearly universal expression of distress and anguish, thus
offering an appropriate rubric for poems in which pain constitutes the
thematic root and stem. Needless to say, agony, of whatever degree and
extent, is such a fundamental part of life experience that a large percentage
of the work already examined in *Chicano Poetry: A Critical Introduction* deals
with it in some way. The distinguishing characteristic at work in this
cluster is that pain as subject or theme is central and inexorable, not
necessarily as a condition to be overcome but simply as a ubiquitous
condition that must be acknowledged. Like the classical descent into the
underworld or the modern teetering on the edge of the existential abyss,
pain is manifest, and these poems address its essential being.
    "The Men in Dreams" by Alberto Ríos offers a cogent example of *¡ay!*
acknowledged—even if, as the poet asserts at the end of the piece, "no one
acknowledges anything" (*Whispering . . . Wind*, 56). Written as a profile of
a "stranger" who, "like the odd men in dreams," is instantly familiar, the
poem tells of a stranger who is "so terminally sad" that for him it is

"like . . . disease" (55). Ríos offers several overt sources for the sadness—
"relatives," "death," the poverty of "pants a little too short," and the
loneliness of strangers accosting each other as a means of human connection.
In visualizing the scene, however, another source of sadness emerges, that
of the speaker's response to the stranger dressed in "black" even to his
"nails . . . a little too long, [and] dirty black" (55). After listening to the
"thin man" explaining his "disease," the speaker

> . . . learns that he is sad for me, too,
> sad for anything sorrowful that might have happened
> ever, that is how far his disease has gone.
> I wait, and then he leaves. I have not said
> a word, but the man is not upset, or he has left
> so quickly I couldn't tell, and I am left wondering
> like those curious moments when something is said,
> or a noise made, and no one acknowledges anything. (56)

Silence appears to be the only possible response to such an encounter, but
it is a silence pregnant with "wondering" and faintly ironic regret at having
so mute a reply to "a stranger" who is "real," but haunting as "dreams."
By connecting dreams with waking experience, Ríos emphasizes melancholy's persistent power to adapt and flourish in any environment, conscious or subconscious. The poem thus articulates the palpable quality of
sadness—and also of dreams, which themselves produce and derive from
experience.

Sharing a number of motifs with the previous poem is Ríos' "The Man
I Cannot Talk To," describing how the poet's "hunger" in the present reminds him of "a group of fieldworkers . . . [w]hen I was younger" (52).
The shared motifs include mention of "dream things," of men as "strangers," and of "silence" in response to experiences that are etched indelibly
on the mind. Although "sadness" is not mentioned directly, "The Man I
Cannot Talk To" evokes melancholy sadness in its depiction of "a man"
who begins to feel "[f]orgiveness" when "[f]ood run[s] short" (57). The
suffering caused by hunger produces a penitential need to suffer even
more ("I refuse . . . the homemade bread") as if in atonement for suffering "hunger for the wrong reasons," unlike those who, like "fieldworkers," suffer the "primal . . . feeling" because of their social station (57).
The speaker's youthful projection of sympathy ends abruptly when his
hunger-induced memory is interrupted by thoughts of "the splash of
falls,/ of trees, of big cities and/ shopping malls, of movies" (58). The
interruption causes him to "eat/ carefully and slowly" and to realize "that

I am not those fieldworkers,/ each one is a stranger" (58). With this realization disclosed, the reader, too, suddenly realizes that the "man" the
speaker "cannot talk to" *is himself*. That man he becomes when he is so
preoccupied with the feelings of others that his *self* momentarily disappears "to dream/ things that will spawn/ *no* contempt in the hearts/ of decent women" (57, my italics). In other words, his state of mind at these
times is so egoless and unselfish that even "decent women," the proverbial nurturers of others, would approve. Thus, when he returns to him-
*self*, he must admit with mixed irony and sad resignation—

> . . . I have hunger
> also for the wrong reasons,
> but I am not a smart enough
> animal to cover my tracks
> with a thin and quiet tail. (58)

Hunger and its effects provide the subject of Gary Soto's "Salt" in *Where
Sparrows Work Hard*. Unlike Ríos' piece, however, Soto's speaks of actual
hunger felt and worried over by two boys sent for food like Stone Age
hunters, "a sack in our hands,/ A stone in each pocket" (65). Theirs is the
kind of hunger that is too real and all-consuming for tears because it
depletes all energy, even that of the imagination: "The day/ Was clear, and
what the wind turned over/ We took in our hands and imagined it bread"
(65). But the poet evokes tears nonetheless in his poignant closing image
of the "salt rock" which produces "bleeding . . . tongues," an emblem of
salt tears.

> . . . We ran
> Toward some cows, fenced but moving.
> I wrung their ears, as I might the wash,
> But nothing was squeezed into our hands.
> They were licking salt rock . . . [We] chipped
> A piece off and we sucked until our tongues
> Were stropped raw and bleeding.
> What was lost, the salt gave back. (65)

The "Salt" of the title thus resonates with the multiple significations
developed in the poem, including an elliptical allusion to the term "salt of
the earth," designating the abject poor. Moreover, the poem's final line
(cited above) holds an ambiguous richness as it refers to the loss of the stones
and sack ("what was lost"), to the failure to fetch the meat requested by

"mother," and to the possibility that even the boys' youth was lost in the hunger. By sustaining a matter-of-fact tone and oblique pattern of imagery throughout the description, Soto captures the *¡ay!* of the children's salt-rubbed "bleeding" wounds more effectively than had he chosen overtly intense emotional diction.

Similar suffering dominates two other Soto poems, "The Wound" and "Mission Tire Factory, 1969," and they too shun sentimental diction to more subtly convey pain and anguish. Like the previous piece, "The Wound" focuses on the experience of (in this case) one child, a "five-year-old" coping with fever-causing "bites" (*Tale of Sunlight*, 16). The poet deliberately leaves unstated the origin of the sores that "puffed like braille" on the boy's body, for he seeks to capture the way that pain alters consciousness and transforms sight from ordinary perception to an uncommon pellucidity. He does this by cataloguing the sights, sounds, and sensations the boy passes or feels as he "ran home" to safety:

> Past the yards
> Frisked clean
> The TV antennas
> That buzzed with a voice
> From beyond this barrio . . .
> You passed the old *Tejanos*
> Porched in shade,
> Watching the sky
> For a blimp
> To haul in the night
> Or a miracle (16)

The pain gives Soto's child persona a clarity of vision that culminates in his greater awareness of himself in relation to All-Other—"That night/ . . . You lay awake,/ Thinking of your body/ Unruffling to earth" (16–17). Like the miracle in the minds of the "old *Tejanos*," the boy, too, thinks of possible transcendence, of "what prayer/ could raise you, slowly,/ From one dark place into another" (17). In a word, pain alters consciousness in "The Wound" by shifting it from the mundane "wisdom of light bulbs" to the hope of metaphysical transformation.

Similarly, in "Mission Tire Factory, 1969" pain nigh unto death transforms the attitudes of the factory workers to a clearer realization of the value of life. The sonnet-length piece opens with a description of the quotidian trivia of the "tire factory"—"All through lunch Peter pinched at his crotch,/ And Jesús talked about his tattoos,/ And I let the flies crawl my arm, undisturbed" (*Where Sparrows Work Hard*, 10). But what at first seems inconsequential trivia is quickly revealed in its true aspect; "through lunch" the men are acutely conscious of the ordinary and routine because one of them almost lost both permanently.

> . . . earlier in the day Manny fell
> From his machine, and when we carried him
> To the workshed (blood from
> Under his shirt, in his pants)
> All he could manage, in an ignorance
> Outdone only by pain, was to take three dollars
> From his wallet, and say:
> "Buy some sandwiches. You guys saved my life." (10)

Just as the five-year-old in "The Wound" suddenly discovers the world around him with sharper sensitivity, so too the factory workers discover the specialness of mere "tattoos" and "flies," for they were pushed close to death. Like the "wash of rubber in our lungs," the fact of death hovering close brought sharply home to them the knowledge that life is as precarious and tenuous as the life of the fly crawling on someone's arm.

Life's precarious tenuity is the subject of Lorna Dee Cervantes' *¡ay!* poems, "Lots: I" and "Lots: II" in *Emplumada*. However, where the previous poems locate the antithesis to pain outside the self, these find it inside, within the resolute will of the victims. Although the poems differ in point of view— "Lots: I" is presented from a third person viewpoint and "Lots: II" through the first person—they share subject matter and theme. Subtitled "The Ally," the first "Lots" describes a violent attack on "a child" who becomes "more than a child" as a result of the attacker's "fist" (8). Her cowering fear is suddenly transformed by "the glint/ of steel at her throat/ that cut through/ to her voice" which, we assume, will shout her plea for help (8).

> She would not be
> silent and still.
> She would live,
> arrogantly,
> having wrestled
> her death
> and won. (8)

Her "ally" appears to be her powerful will not only to live but also to combat those aggressors who would have her "shut up and die" (8). Pain in this and the next poem partake of the universal fears shared by women because of their preponderant number as victims of violence.

More cryptic and thus more enigmatic than its companion poem, "Lots: II" subtitled "Herself," begins *in medias res* with the first person speaker "pick[ing] myself up" as if from an attack or scuffle (9). She does not describe what preceded the "picking up" because what is important in this poem is her finding the appropriate response to suffering. In finding that response, she considers "all the names who could help me" in the present situation and then "meticulously" eliminates "each one" as a potential protector because *"they won't hear me burning/ inside of myself"* (9; Cervantes' italics). This lonely realization that the separateness of self produces a fundamental isolation yields the mature but poignant image that ends the poem: "my used skin glistened/ my first diamond" (9). From the blows that knocked her down and left her externally "used," the narrator discovers the latent strength and beauty that lies within "herself," intact and hard and shining, like a diamond inside a nugget of coal. Here, victimization produces a proud self-reliance that, we assume, will outlast the suffering.

The same sort of affirmation that grows out of pain in the "lots" pieces weaves through "To My Brother," but in this poem the poet locates the center of "ay" agony in socioeconomic deprivation. Even the sun under- scores the absence of money in "that dreary setting" of barrio poverty through the speaker's description of the round, copper "sun" as "scarcely a penny" (38). Nevertheless, the "smog-strewn avalanche" of their squalid lives cannot destroy their minds and imagination.

> We were so poor.
> The air was a quiver
> of thoughts we drew from . . .
> I could work my mind's way
> out of there, out of needing
> a dime bag of uppers for the next
> buzzing shift. We paid our bills.
> We were brilliant at wishing.
> Our dreams wafted over the sullen skyline (38)

Just as the poet cannot understate the misery of their poverty, she cannot exaggerate the importance of thought and imagination in helping them— and, possibly, other poor—escape "the sullen skyline" of their objective reality. What saves the speaker and her brother from being overwhelmed by despair is the light of their "dreams" like "flying embers" which "glow

in the heart all night" (38). Thus, Cervantes matches the diamond
brightness which closes "Lots: II" with the fire brightness at the end of "To
My Brother." The affirmation produced out of agony at the end of these
pieces reveals an essentially biblical interpretation of suffering. It is biblical
in its view of human pain as a prerequisite for growth and, possibly,
transcendence (for example, Job 42: 10–17; Psalms 22 and 23; and the
New Testament belief in resurrection after death). While Cervantes does
not make the biblical ethos explicit, it is implicit in her poetry's phoenix-
like transformation of agony into affirmation.

Quite oppositely, Reyes Cárdenas in *Survivors of the Chicano Titanic* views
suffering as *suffering*, a condition whose source he usually traces to the greed
of the powerful, especially those whose vast abuse of power pollutes social
environments through the exploitation of masses of people. Some of
Cárdenas' poems depict pain in generalized terms that speak of "man's
inhumanity to man," as he writes in "Of Man" (57; also see "Grail," 51).
On the other hand, a number of his "ay" poems address a specific suffering
in terms associated with particular individuals. For instance, the eight-line
"In Kubla Khan" opens with an unlikely figurative comparison: a telephone
that "rings/ like a campesina/ tired from a hard day" (54). The unexpected
comparison of the "phone" with a "campesina" reminds us that our
bourgeois comforts depend directly on the underpaid labor of large masses
of farmworkers. After this Cárdenas moves quickly to climax the brief poem
with a reference to the murder of Santos Rodríguez, the twelve-year-old
boy killed by policeman Darrell Cain in Dallas, Texas, in 1973.[9] Because
of its irrationality, its clear abuse of power, and the light sentence Cain
received, the case led to a national protest by the Hispanic community.[10]
The poem's title, "In Kubla Khan," tells us that the boy's murder occurred
in a U.S. setting with identical abuses of power as those historically
attributed to the tyranny of the ruler Khan who founded the Chinese Yuan
dynasty. Hence, just as the poet forces us to wonder at the odd connection
of phone ring with campesina, so, too, does he force a subtle interpretation
of the title and the poem's succeeding eight lines. Moreover, through his
allusion to "Kubla Khan" and "little Santos," Cárdenas makes explicit a
logic of aesthetics that is fundamentally metonymic. That is, his allusions,
figures of speech, and indeed, much of his subject matter, are metonyms
of—in his ideological worldview—the injustice of the larger whole with its
racism, avarice, oligarchies, and oppression of the powerless.

"Elegy for Joe Campos Torres" repeats Cárdenas' metonymic perception
of pain and again relies on a specific actual case of injustice to transmit his

central message that "There's really/ no place for this pain,/ it doesn't even/ belong here" (15). The subject of his elegy was a young man left to drown after being beaten to unconsciousness by three policemen in Houston, Texas, in 1977.[11] As in the Santos Rodríguez case, the policemen received shockingly light sentences—one-year jail terms in Federal Court *after* the lower court's all-white jury released them to freedom. Incongruously roaming from "[t]his Houston Acropolis" to "it never was an Astrodome," then from "a Jack-in-the-Box Restaurant" to an "aloof political Mona Lisa," and from "pancakes" to "justice," Cárdenas indulges his typical style of free-association. But that style fails to work consistently in the elegy, for one is ill-at-ease with the poet's seeming whimsy in the context of the tragedy of Torres' murder. What, for instance, is one to make of stanzas like the following?

> This Houston Acropolis
> in the pit
> lionized into
> likenesses. . . .
> It was, after all,
> pancakes not justice.
> Just enough of them
> dinosaur out to us somehow. (14)

Nevertheless, starting with the title, the poet offers enough precision of image to eventually evoke an appropriately elegiac tone. The ending is particularly effective in its keen sensitivity to "a pain that we/ try to put in the trash . . . in the swimming pool/ if we can. . . . There's really/ no place for this pain,/ it doesn't even/ belong here" (15). As a result of the poet's treatment of the title subject, Joe Torres, the poem becomes a metonym of all victims who suffer the violence of racism.

Agony—whether the private pain of the individual psyche or the public suffering of populations in unrelentingly abject poverty or any of its other myriad lyric forms—is universal and has been universally described. This section shows how Chicano poets have contributed to the description of the universal "Ay, Ay, Ay, Ay." Ríos focuses on pain as loneliness in poems that delineate it as a psychic condition of individual consciousness. Even hunger in Ríos' "The Man I Cannot Talk To" serves as a metaphor dramatizing the agony of private suffering, for though hunger in the poem begins as an actual physical deprivation, it evolves in the course of the poem into a catalyst, first of memory and then of imagination. Hunger also appears in some of Soto's poems of suffering. In them he portrays pain as a step both to greater consciousness of the world and to a keener sensitivity to the precariousness of our life-hold on it. Similarly, Cervantes views pain as an awful and terrifying teacher from which one learns strength and determination. In "To My Brother" she also registers the way socioeconomic suffering can be transcended through the exercise of the imagination. Of these writers only Cárdenas employs pain literally as a metonym of the world's larger suffering. His poems, grounded in his Marxist politics, are descriptions of unrelenting suffering intended to demonstrate the urgency of doing something revolutionary about the originators and perpetrators of the global, historical experience of misery.

Having begun with the homophonic "ay" of the *eye*, emblem of the visionary artist, and continued to the *hay* of place, real and imagined, and then to the *¡ay!* of suffering, we turn now to *I*, the English-language first person pronoun which is often used as a synonym of the word *"self."* The possibilities of meaning in "I" are endless, vast, and varied because self-definition is a variable with *at least* three and one half billion different forms. This fact introduces a related feature: the *I* is one of the most particular, most unitary symbols, and yet it is also one of the most general, most universal as well. It can refer to the public individual as in Milton's Satan or to the private as in Eliot's J. Alfred Prufrock; it applies equally to Whitman's everyman "I" in "Song of Myself" and to the personal self in Dickinson's corpus, to the anonymous "I" of the Old Testament psalms, to the celebrated "I" of Byron's Don Juan. This paradoxical universality through individuality applies to the representations of self found in Chicano poetry. These representations apply not only to the "I" poems considered in this chapter, but also to those in earlier chapters— notably those of Inés Tovar in *Con razón corazón*, Elizondo's *Perros y antiperros*, Salinas' *Un Trip Through the Mind Jail*, and Zamora's *Restless Serpents*.

Another compelling aspect of "I" derives from its functional role as narrative voice and point of view, particularly, of course, in poems presented through the first person. In such poetry the speaker functions both as an identified character and as the very means by which we apprehend the text. Where the speaker is not clearly delineated or developed as a character, the "I" usually functions as the poet's persona, the stylized observer who sees, feels, experiences, and narrates the poetic record of experience or observation. Even in third person narration, an "I" is implicit in the deep structure as the source of the omniscient narrator. All the poetry examined in this chapter is told in the first person. As we would expect, the "selves" behind the I's vary from poet to poet and even from poem to poem within a poet's work. Gary Soto, for example, frequently creates characters to serve as the tellers of his verses, whereas Lorna Dee Cervantes employs surrogates of herself who self-consciously explore the nature of identity. In the poems discussed in this section, Ricardo Sánchez shares his retrospective journey through time, space, and self to expose the basic core of his being. Cervantes, on the other hand, also explores the self retrospectively but keeps it veiled in ambiguity. Gary Soto's "I" shifts from poem to poem, but he like the other two poets ultimately places its identity firmly within his art.

Probably the most well-known poem in Lorna Dee Cervantes' *Emplumada*, a volume of mostly lyric poetry, is "Beneath the Shadow of the Freeway," a dramatic poem that has been widely anthologized and reviewed. Its eighty-seven lines are sectioned into six parts told in the first person by a narrator who describes her environment and her place in it but who withholds direct information about her private self until the end of the poem. Critics usually interpret the poem as a feminist broadside against the vile consequences of machismo as well as an assertion of the emergent writer's need to express herself through literature. One reviewer comments that the poem "describes" a world where women have "learned to survive without and despite men,"[12] whereas another sees the poet's writing in general as "confessional . . . from a warm, female perspective."[13] Regarding the emergent writer's voice, one critic's observations are representative: "The ambiguity [the speaker] feels in deciding between action and romantic consciousness forces her into another occupation, that of writer, an occupation she can do only by herself."[14]

These discussions thus underscore both the feminism and the aesthetics of the poem's subject matter, but they do not explain the narrator's identity. At once the teller and the subject of the piece, the narrator seems to be wondering how, despite differences of generation and experience, she came to be just like her grandmother. Moreover, that she veils her intimate self from straightforward disclosure requires us to probe more carefully into her character. Thus, my reading of "Beneath the Shadow of the Freeway" hinges on an analysis of the I's subjective self.

In the first part of the poem, the speaker sets the scene both on a macro level ("the valley up from Los Altos to Sal Si Puedes") and a micro level (on her "porch") in a way that establishes a contrast between the speaker's restricted life and the boundlessness of the "freeway,/ blind worm, wrapping the valley up" (11). Through the reference to "[e]very day at dusk . . . the shadow of the freeway lengthened," the contrast between the freeway's vast power and the speaker's family's lack of power anticipates some of the ugliness and violence that surfaces later (11). In part two the speaker expands the scenic description by introducing her "woman family" consisting of herself, her mother, and her grandmother. To describe her relatives the speaker employs fairytale language—"Queen," "Princess," "knight," and so on—but only observes about "Myself: I could never decide" (11). This uncertainty appropriately captures the important fairytale motif of ambiguous origins and confused self-identity, as in "Cinderella" and "The Frog Prince." Resolution of the ambiguity and confusion typically involves a major transformation in the tale, as, for example, the frog becoming a prince or the servant becoming a princess.[15] A thorough reading of Cervantes' poem must thus address what, if any, transformation(s) occur in it. In the context of its particular section, the fairytale references stress the difference between the mother's escapist tendencies— "Even now she dreams of taffeta/ and foot-high tiaras"—and the speaker's resolute practicality—"I became Scribe: . . . interpreting letters from the government, notices of dissolved marriages . . . I [also] paid the bills, did light man-work, fixed faucets" (11). Later in the poem, when the speaker grows up, these traits appear to be reversed with the mother aging into a hard, cynical realist and the speaker transformed into a "soft" idealist (sections 4 and 6).

Shifting away from description, the poem's third section presents a more lyrical personal reminiscence. With its emphasis on nature, especially on the winged freedom "of birds," this part places the narrator's family within a larger, more salutary and natural matrix than that represented by the freeway.

> In California in the summer,
> mockingbirds sing all night. . . .
> [Grandma] likes the ways of birds. . . .
> She believes in myths and birds.
> She trusts only what she builds
> with her hands. (12)

The grandmother offers the child another role model, not necessarily an alternative to her mother but an additional adult example to both emulate and, eventually, to rebel against when she spreads her adolescent wings. If the mother's escapist fantasies spark the girl's imagination, then the grandmother's interest in "myths" and "birds," a conventional symbol of the "singing" poet, encourages her literary creativity. Furthermore, the last two lines in the passage above hint at the solitary nature associated with individual craftsmanship in a way that foreshadows the eventual solitariness of the speaker's life as a writer.

Section 4 provides the transition from the "woman family," alone in the macrocosm of the freeway and nature, to a glimpse at the three women in relation to men. Simply put, it is a relationship defined by violence and fear. Grandma, described by her daughter as "soft," lived "twenty-five years/ with a man who tried to kill her" (12). Although not explicitly stated, the mother, too, seems to have been mired in a similar battering relationship with a man (section 5). Unlike the poem's other parts, section 5 is written in a stream-of-consciousness that works to intensify the narrator's fear.

> in the night I would hear it
> glass bottles shattering the street
> words cracked into shrill screams
> inside my throat a cold fear
> it entered the house in hard
> unsteady steps   stopping at my door (13)

We assume that "Mama" is the victim here with the speaker feeling the nearby threat as well. To indicate how the speaker's indomitable will saves her in the face of domestic violence, section 5 closes with six brief lines that weave together significant images from art and nature.

> a grey kitten   a touchstone
> purring beneath the quilts
> grandma stitched
> from his suits
> the patchwork singing
> of mockingbirds (13)

The "kitten" and "mockingbirds" evoke nature's resilient power, while the "quilts" remind us of the crafter's power derived from her skill in transforming "his suits" into a "patchwork singing of mockingbirds." These interwoven images create a symbol of the artist transmuting objective reality, however unpleasant, into art, and they remind us that that same artistic transmutation is at work in "Beneath the Shadow of the Freeway."

The poem's last section brings us face to face with the speaker, now grown up and struggling to survive without loss of her own "soft" (i.e., compassionate) interior. Although she has "grown more silent [and] cynical/ on the outside," she insists about others, especially men, that " . . . 'if you're good to them/ they'll be good to you back'" (14). To end the poem, Cervantes returns in the last two stanzas to a scenic replica of the opening section with "[t]he freeway across the street," the "geraniums" like her grandmother's, and the "summer" (14). But even though it looks the same, life has changed for the speaker who, like a fairytale protagonist, has been transformed.

> Back. The freeway is across the street.
> It's summer now. Every night I sleep with a *gentle* man
> to the *hymn* of mockingbirds,
>
> and in time, I plant geraniums.
> I tie up my hair into *loose* braids,
> and trust only what I have built
> with my own hands. (14; my italics)

The transformation occurs on two levels. She is, first, no longer either the kittenish girl or the uncertain "handyman." Instead—wearing braids, planting geraniums, and trusting only her own work—she has become as strong and self-assertive as her grandmother. The second transformation itself has a twofold aspect: she has left her "woman family" for a relationship with a man, but she has not followed either mother or grandmother in her choice of men, for she lives with someone "gentle," and the hymnal music of love, not the frightening sound of violence, fill her life. In one sense, then, the "frog" has become a princess, and that has helped diminish "the shadow of the freeway" which is still "across the street." The narrator's transformation into a mature adult capable of coming to terms with her past by comprehending it through poetry ultimately reflects the artist's identity, and the poem can be seen as a portrait of the poet's consciousness developing from girl to woman.

Another Cervantes portrait of "I" appears in "Beetles," a poem that examines and subtly challenges conventional notions of feminine beauty. The piece is written in three movements, each of which offers a variation on the theme of beauty. In the four-line stanza of the first movement, the speaker encounters beauty as an asserted, unquestioned principle presented by a "man who once loved me" and who had "loved a double/ more beautiful than I" (54). The second movement shifts abruptly to the speaker's point of view which is marked by the self-deprecation often associated with ostensibly homely women.

> I'm hexed by a girl of pale heart,
> a dove who wouldn't circle in day.
> The thighs of her jeans are speckled with mustard.
> Her hands are in her pocket too much of the time . . . (54)

This middle movement appears to sing two tunes: that of the "hexed" persona of the wistful plain Jane and that of the unabashed tomboy whose "hands" are like "birds, fragile, humming" and who chooses to be "a farmer" because "[s]he loves the land," even "its ugliness" (54). But Cervantes does not leave us clouded in ambiguity about her self-assessment, for in the last movement of "Beetles" she describes herself with unflinching precision and objectivity.

> I'm an ugly woman, weedlike
> elbowing my way through the perfect
> grass. The best of what I am
> is in the gravel behind the train yard
> where obsidian chips lodge
> in the rocks like beetles.
> I burrow and glow. (54)

Without denying her "ugliness" she paradoxically evokes a subtler beauty. Like her literary forebear Emily Dickinson, her self-effacement and nature images of lowly creatures actually combine to form a picture of loveliness that tongue-in-cheekily emphasizes the maxim that beauty is indeed in the eye of the beholder—especially when the eye is male and the object is female. The poem argues for an acknowledgment of the beautiful quite apart from the hackneyed conventions of beauty.

The discrepancy between appearance and essence or between what one is and what others think one to be suggested in "Beetles" forms the basis of Cervantes' "For All You Know." Like the homely beetle that surprises with its "glow" despite its lowliness, the speaker in this poem surprises by presenting a series of seemingly unrelated self-descriptions whose bizarre nature teases the imagination. "I could call myself Lilith,/ or Edith or Ed," she begins, lodging the theme of identity in the freedom to choose to be whatever she desires (55). "I would not change/ the way I look to you," but, she suggests, that would not mean that "[y]ou know me" (55). To explain who she really is the speaker selects discrete "facts" about herself and family

as if to reveal herself through random bits and pieces of her past and
experience.

> . . . I have an aunt
> who murdered her husband in bed,
> drew a target in lipstick, then
> punctured the bull's-eye with methodical
> whimsy. My mother gave birth
> to a blue doll struck dumb
> from the start. I've seen whales
> leaping, rattlers give up the ghost. (55)

Such information, although not specifically about her, tells as much about
the speaker, the poet implies, as anything more specific could. The last
third of the poem shifts to simpler, more straightforward and homelier
items:

> I could be simple,
> cook a fine meal,
> hike without sweating,
> carve Christ figures in secret.
> For all you know
> I could let you cry out in front of me.
> I wouldn't say a word
> and say everything. (55)

Here especially (but also in the previous two poems) Cervantes employs the
self as a perfect metaphor of the paradox of human existence, the all in the
one that embodies the mystery of *the I-All*.

Sharing the paradoxes but through a more explicit statement of theme,
Ricardo Sánchez, in Part VI of his seven-part "Triangle Club," writes of the
"many me's" that describe him (*Brown Bear Honey Madnesses . . .* , 33). He
describes those selves as irrevocably altered by time and experience, and
although the tone of the section is nostalgic, it is pensive, not sad or
sentimental. Unlike the hortatory pitch of much of his verse, the poet's
voice here is soft—subdued by the knowledge of all the "years [that] have
passed" (33). Adding texture to his reminiscence is the symbolic thread of
imprisonment images woven through the section. As discussed earlier in
*Chicano Poetry*, Sánchez began his writing career as a *pinto* poet, and
enclosures understandably hold a particularly powerful hold on his imagination. The poem contains references to "my chains," to "my ex-barriered
existence," to "enclosing spaces," and to other images of confinement, all
in the service of the theme concerning

> our human fragility,
>        cloaked by insecurity
> and the knowledge
> that life is transient,
> no promises, pledges nor clinging,
> just strong feelings,
>        caresses, cariño (33)

The poem's challenge to the ceaseless, inexorable march of time lies within the power of each "I" to have and to share "strong feelings." This is a vital, crucial power, for whether "darting" or "lasting," they are the most important and "unequivocal imprints" that remain impervious to change (34). As such they provide intermittent glimpses of eternity.

In most of his poetry, Gary Soto lacks Sánchez's explicit self-reference; yet Soto nonetheless writes of the multifaceted "I" throughout his corpus. One poem that contains an unusually straightforward reference to himself is "Mexicans Begin Jogging" in *Where Sparrows Work Hard*, a poem that won the Pushcart Prize in 1982. The title's irony establishes the poem's tone of gently mocking humor. Relying on the American jogging craze as a well-known part of popular culture, Soto employs jogging as a metaphor for the various forms of escape forced on Mexican workers, both the undocumented *and* legal citizens, by the U.S. Immigration Service, *la migra*.

> At the factory I worked . . .
> Until the border patrol opened
> Their vans and my boss waved for us to run.
> "Over the fence, Soto," he shouted,
> And I shouted that I was American.
> "No time for lies," he said, and pressed
> A dollar in my palm, hurrying me
> Through the back door. (24)

By humorously addressing the serious subject of government harassment in this poem (elsewhere he treats it more solemnly), he generates a wonderful warmth of feeling in his audience that powerfully communicates the indignity suffered and that also inspires a tender empathy for the "Mexicans" who "[r]an past the amazed crowds that lined/ The street" (24). Soto concludes with an ironic wink that reinforces the bond between him and his audience:

> What could I do but yell *vivas*
> To baseball, milkshakes, and those sociologists

> Who would clock me
> As I jog into the next century
> On the power of a great, silly grin. (24)

The conclusion simultaneously emphasizes the smallness of the one, the "I," in the face of the ubiquity of U.S. culture and officialdom, at the same time that it demonstrates the individual's power to legitimately laugh at, and therefore undermine, that awesome cultural dominance. Like the light-hearted whimsy pervading "La Autobiografía de Reyes Cárdenas," the humor here enriches the poem.

Warmth of feeling also characterizes "Angel," another poem in *Where Sparrows Work Hard*, though its subject is the more private one of an expectant father's meditation as he anticipates the birth of his child. The sensitive speaker of the piece, a keen observer of odd details, describes "my woman asleep,/ Legs pushed up to/ Veined breasts, heavy/ And tilting with child" (59). Conveying an intimate tenderness that suggests the vital underpinning of love shared by the couple is the speaker's mind as it roams from her "belly rising" to "that good day" when their "child will kick/ His joints into place" and will "slide . . . [f]rom his life to ours" (59–60).

An especially interesting aspect of "Angel" is the way the speaker travels back and forth from the general to the particular, from a public, shared reality to the private, individual reality of his consciousness. The first six lines place the situation within the broad temporal and spatial expanses of all-time everywhere.

> Tonight I find the
> Calendar with its days
> Marked like targets.
> It has to do with
> The rationed water
> Falling from the north (59)

From this acknowledgment of the universal, Soto shifts to the particular moment and space of his bed described in the previous paragraph, and although he concentrates on the specific meaning of the pregnancy and awaited childbirth, he integrates into his meditation images from beyond the couple's privacy. For example, he describes her "belly" as "not pure and rubbed white—/ But tangled in TV/ and telephone poles" (59), thereby incorporating elements from public life into his private world. Similarly, he pictures the just born child opening his/her eyes not to the eager parents but "circl[ing]" around "an opening room" (59), the image stressing the

child's place within society and the world. Toward the end of the poem—
in a final reinforcement of the connectedness of the individual to the
surrounding universe—the speaker returns to the calendar image that
opened "Angel," referring to "July,/ Weeks before our dark/ One slides
from water/ And blood, his blue hands/ Tightening on air,/ And turns,
beyond knowing,/ From his life to ours" (60). The poet gives us a glimpse
into a common life process, and in doing so elevates the event from the
mundane to the spiritual.

The understated trace of mystical union or transcendent integration between the solitary "I" and the manifold Whole which is hinted at in
"Angel" appears more clearly in two works in Soto's *The Tale of Sunlight*—"The Cellar" and "The Tale of Sunlight." Both poems focus on a
solitary figure suspended in a moment of keen sense perceptions in which
place (the *hay*)—its immediacy and particularity—dominates the I's
awareness. In "The Cellar" the speaker descends alone into "the cellar's
cold,/ Tapping my way deeper/ Than light reaches," and although he is
literally concerned with the errand of locating a specific something
"[d]iscarded some time back" (24), his descent takes on the emblematic
quality of probing the unknown (as in Dante's *Inferno* or Paz's *Labyrinth of
Solitude*). Attentive to concrete details like a "Hat rack and suitcase" and
a "Tire iron and umbrella," the speaker's mind and imagination wander
beyond the "fine dust" of the cellar to "the rented rooms" upstairs and,
in a marvelous image, to a "radio" saying "What was already forgotten"
(24). Thus, what begins as a casual errand becomes a magical journey
through time that partakes of mythic dimensions. In this way the poet
captures precisely the power of memory and imagination to transform the
present.

In the same vein, "A Tale of Sunlight" focuses on Manuel Zaragoza,
Soto's earthy persona and subject of one cluster of poems in this volume.
In this title poem, gregarious Manuel is uncharacteristically alone in the
process of opening up "the cantina" for a day's business. But like the "I"
in "The Cellar" Manuel's mundane activity is momentarily arrested by
his sudden awareness of "A triangle of sunlight . . . stretched out/ On
the floor/ Like a rug/ Like a tired cat" (59). Mesmerized by the patch of
light that does "not vanish" even when its source at the window is covered, Manuel becomes preoccupied with the "pyramid/ Of whiteness"
(59). He ignores his customers "knock[ing]/ To be let in," and instead
pours himself "a beer" and keeps watch as the light crosses the floor to
"Hang on the wall/ Like a portrait/ Like a calendar/ Witnout numbers"

(59–60). Transfixed by the strange illumination and distracted from quotidian reality by it, Manuel has a magical experience.

>      . . . a fly settled
> In the sunlight
> And disappeared
> In a wreath of smoke,
> I tapped it with the broom,
> Spat on it.
> The broom vanished.
> The spit sizzled.
> It is the truth . . .
> And by misfortune
> This finger
> This pink stump
> Entered the sunlight,
> Snapped off
> With a dry sneeze,
> And fell to the floor (60)

The bartender's "tale of sunlight" is thus a tale about the ordinary become extraordinary, the natural overcome by the supernatural. As such, it is as much about Manuel Zaragoza's glorious imagination and the artist residing in his peasant eye and experience as it is about faith and metaphysical belief.

Just as "The Tale of Sunlight" builds from the speaker's rapt concentration on the light to a rapturous climax, "The Cellar" also moves from the ordinariness of the cellar to a transcendence of time and place. Soto accomplishes this through a particularly effective figure that is textured dramatically in several layers of imagery.

> I imagined the sun
> And how a worker
> Home from the fields
> Might glimpse at it
> Through the window's true lens (24–25)

Despite its simplicity and compactness, the passage discloses five layers of figurative imagination and perception. First, there is the level of the speaker's imagination perceiving both "the sun" and "a worker," which leads to the second level of the imagined worker's "glimpse" of the sun. However, because this perception occurs through "the window's true lens," the window offers a third—framing—level of perception. The fourth layer of consciousness captured in these lines consists of the image of the sun as emblem of universal power, and the fifth derives from the reality of the poet, Gary Soto's consciousness which is responsible for the entire piece. From this dramatic multilayered figure, the poem shifts to the speaker himself, now transformed into a buoyant source of energy and power by his descent and consequent discoveries.

> I imagined I could climb
> From this promise of old air
> And enter a street . . .
> Where, if someone
> Moved, I could turn,
> And seeing through the years,
> Call him brother . . . (25)

These lines convey the limitless power of the "I"—its awareness, its imagination, and its inclusive consciousness—to shape experience, whether lived in the flesh or, equally real, lived in the mind. Thus, the speaker's descent into the cellar triggers a parallel retreat into the self, into memory and imagination, out of which he conjures the image of his "brother," not as a ghost from the past but as hauntingly real in the present, the present that is the poem. Similarly, the speaker Manuel Zaragoza in "The Tale of Sunlight" experiences a private demonstration of magic that is both real as "the ants/ Who know me/ For what I gave" (60) and real as the poem in the eyes and ears of the audience.

This final exploration of the homophonic figure, eye/hay/ay/I, focused on the "I" as universal emblem of both *self* and of poetic *voice*. As this section indicates, Lorna Dee Cervantes's I reveals the multifold dimensions of feminine identity and pointedly includes within those dimensions the writer's vocation, for it is as irrepressibly within her as it was within her Golden Age *tocayo, the* Cervantes. Ricardo Sánchez also portrays an I composed of "many me's," one looking back upon past experience with a nostalgia that is sufficiently well-seasoned to avoid effusive sentimentality. On the other hand, unlike Cervantes or Sánchez, Soto's I appears in masks, in personae of the self, to convey a range of deeply felt emotions and to showcase an imagination that is at once strikingly original and notably conventional in its *chicanismo*. Regardless of their approach or narrative viewpoint, these poets reaffirm the quintessential truth that literature consists of parables of the writers' selves. All three poets discussed in this section—like all the poets included in this book—also suggest the myriad number of forms, types, essences, and labels of the "I" existing in Chicano poetry and which—like their Latin American literary *hermanos/as*—enrich world literature as importantly as any contemporary literature.

It is because of this important enrichment that another "eye" emerges out of the "ay/ay/ay/ay" of Chicano poetry: the *aye!* of affirmation inherent in the artistic process. Mexican American writers share with other artists the transparent fact that to create is to affirm, for art is not a simple reflexive or mindless act occurring at random. Born of inspiration, idea, imagination, talent, and discipline, the crafting of art speaks a resounding *yes!* even when its content tells of pain, defeat, or even nihilism. In this sense, then, the work discussed in this book, like the flower of the desert cactus whose roots reach deep to a primal source, evinces the aye! of affirmation that has sustained it and the life of *el pueblo* for centuries.

## NOTES

1. Author unknown [*American Favorite Ballads*, edited by Irwin Silver and Ethel Raim (New York: Oak Publications, 1961), 23].

2. Ríos, "Belita," *Whispering to Fool the Wind* (New York: Sheep Meadow Press, 1982), p. 9; subsequent references to this book will be made parenthetically in the text.

3. Cárdenas, "Oracles," *Survivors of the Chicano Titanic* (Austin, Tex.: Place of Herons Press, 1981), p. 33; subsequent references to this book will be made parenthetically in the text.

4. Soto, "The Point," *The Tale of Sunlight* (Pittsburgh: University of Pittsburgh Press, 1978), p. 5; subsequent references to this book will be made parenthetically in the text.

5. Soto, "There," *Where Sparrows Work Hard* (Pittsburgh: University of Pittsburgh Press, 1981), p. 56; subsequent references to this book will be made parenthetically in the text.

6. Cárdenas, "La Autobiografía de Reyes Cárdenas," *El Grito*, 7:3 (1974), p. 10; subsequent references to this book will be made parenthetically in the text.

7. Sánchez, *Brown Bear Honey Madnesses: Alaskan Cruising Poems* (Austin, Tex.: Slough Press, 1981); subsequent references to this book will appear parenthetically in the text.

8. Cervantes, "Visions of Mexico," *Emplumada* (Pittsburgh: University of Pittsburgh Press, 1981), 45–46; subsequent references to this book will be made parenthetically in the text.

9. *Rolling Stone* (May 18, 1978), p. 52.

10. *Newsweek* (April 17, 1978), p. 122.

11. Larry Trujillo, "Police Crimes in the Barrio," *History, Culture, and Society: Chicano Studies in the 1980s* (Ypsilanti, Mich.: Bilingual Press, 1983), p. 235.

12. Sylvia Madrigal, "*Emplumada*: A Female Pen in Flourish," *Imagine: International Chicano Poetry Journal*, 1:1 (Summer, 1984), p. 138.

13. Francisco A. Loméli and Donaldo W. Urioste, *Chicano Perspectives in Literature* (Albuquerque, N. Mex.: Pajarito Publications, 1976), p. 104.

14. Tey Diana Rebolledo, "Witches, Bitches and Midwives: The Shaping of Poetic Consciousness in Chicana Literature," *The Chicano Struggle* (Binghamton, N.Y.: Bilingual Press, 1984), p. 166.

15. Padraic Colum, "Introduction," *The Complete Grimm's Fairy Tales* (New York: Pantheon Books, 1972 [1944]), p. xi. Also, Joseph Campbell, "Folkloristic Commentary," pp. 857–864, in the aforementioned book.

# Bibliography

## PRIMARY SOURCES

### Chicano Poetry

Alarcon, Justo, Juan P. Aldape, and Lupe Calderon. *Canto al Pueblo*. Phoenix, Arizona: Canto al Pueblo, 1981.

Alurista. *A'nque*. Albuquerque, New Mexico: Pajarito Publications, 1979.

——. *Dawn*. *El Grito* 7, no. 4 (June-August 1974): 55–84.

——, ed. *Festival de Flor y Canto: An Anthology of Chicano Literature*. Los Angeles: University of California Press, 1976.

——. *Floricanto en Aztlán*. Los Angeles: Chicano Studies Center of UCLA, 1971.

——. *Nationchild Plumaroja*. San Diego: Toltecas en Aztlán Publications, 1972.

——. *Spik in glyph?* Houston, Texas: Arte Publico Press, 1981.

——. *Timespace Huracán*. Albuquerque, New Mexico: Pajarito Publications, 1976.

Anaya, Rodolfo and Simon Ortiz, eds. *Ceremony of Brotherhood, 1680–1980*. Albuquerque, New Mexico: Academia, 1981.

Arellano, Anselmo F. *Los pobladores nuevo mexicanos y su poesía, 1889–1950*. Albuquerque, New Mexico: Pajarito Publications, 1976.

Bornstein, Miriam. *Bajo Cubierta*. Tucson, Arizona: Scorpion Press, 1976.

Bruce-Novoa, Juan. *Inocencia perversa/Perverse Innocence*. Phoenix, Arizona: Baleen Press, 1977.

Burciaga, José Antonio. *Cultura*. San Jose, California: Mango Publications, 1972.

Candelaria, Cordelia. *Ojo de la Cueva/Cave Springs*. Colorado Springs, Colorado: Maize Press, 1984.

Cárdenas, Margarita Cota. *Noches despertando inconsciencias*. Tucson, Arizona: Scorpion Press, 1975.

Cardenas, Reyes. *Survivors of the Chicano Titanic*. Austin, Texas: Place of Herons Press, 1981.

Carillo, Leonardo, et al. *Canto al pueblo*. San Antonio, Texas: Penca Books, 1978.

Castro, Carrie A., et al. *Morena*. Santa Barbara, California: Francisco A. Loméli, ed./publ., 1980.

De Hoyos, Angela. *Arise, Chicano, and Other Poems*. Bloomington, Indiana: Backstage Books, 1975.

——. *Chicano Poems for the Barrio*. Bloomington, Indiana: Backstage Books, 1975.

——. *Selecciones*. Xalapa: Universidad Veracruzana, 1976.

De Leon, Nephtalí. *Chicano Poet*. Lubbock, Texas: Trucha Publications, 1973.

——. *Chicanos: Our Background & Our Pride*. Lubbock, Texas: Trucha Publications, 1972.

——. *Coca Cola Dream*. San Antonio, Texas: Trucha Publications, Inc., 1975.

——. *5 Plays*. Denver, Colorado: Totinem Publications, 1974.

——. *Hey Mr. President, Man!* San Antonio, Texas: Trucha Publications, Inc., 1976.

——. *I Color My Garden*. San Antonio, Texas: Trucha Publications, Inc., 1974.

——. *I Will Catch the Sun*. San Antonio, Texas: Trucha Publications, Inc., 1974.

——. *Poems: With Illustrated Woodcuts by Nephtalí*. Trucha Publications, 1977.

——. *Tequila Mockingbird*. San Antonio, Texas: Trucha Publications, 1980.

Delgado, Abelardo Lalo. *Bajo el sol de Aztlán: 25 soles de Abelardo*. El Paso, Texas: Barrio Publications, 1973.

——. *Chicano: 25 Pieces of a Chicano Mind*. Denver, Colorado: Barrio Publications, 1969.

——. *It's Cold: 52 Cold Thought-Poems of Abelardo*. Salt Lake City, Utah: Barrio Publications, 1974.

——. *Reflexiones*. N.p., n.d.

——, et al. *Los cuatro*. Denver, Colorado: Barrio Publications, 1970.

Elizondo, Sergio. *Libro para batos y chavalas chicanas*. Berkeley, California: Editorial Justa, 1977.

——. *Perros y antiperros*. Berkeley, California: Quinto Sol, 1972.

Empringham, Toni, ed. *Fiesta in Aztlán: Anthology of Chicano Poetry*. Santa Barbara, California: Capra Press, 1982.

Festival Committee, eds. *Flor y Canto IV and V*. Albuquerque, New Mexico: Pajarito Publications, 1980.

Garcia, Ricardo. *Selected Poetry*. Berkeley, California: Quinto Sol, 1973.

Gonzales, Rodolfo. *I am Joaquín*. Denver, Colorado: Crusade for Justice, 1967; New York: Bantam Books, 1972.

Herrera, Juan Felipe. *Rebozos of Love*. San Diego: Toltecas en Aztlan Publications, 1974.

Kopp, Karl and Jane, eds. *Southwest: A Contemporary Anthology*. Albuquerque, New Mexico: Red Earth Press, 1977.

Loméli, Francisco A., ed. *Nuevos Horizontes de 15 Mundos*. Santa Barbara, California: Chicano Studies Creative Writing UCSB, 1979.

Mirandé, Alfredo, ed. *Alma Abierta, Pinto Poetry*. Riverside: University of California Chicano Studies, 1980.

Montoya, José. *El sol y los de abajo and other R.C.A.F. poems*. San Francisco: Ediciones Pocho-Che, 1972.

Pereira, Teresinha. *Hey Mex! & Andale, Rosana!* Boulder, Colorado: Backstage Books, 1978.

———. *Poems of Exile & Alienation*. Robert Lima, transl. Boulder, Colorado: Anvil Press, 1976.

Perez, Reymundo "Tigre." *Free, Free at Last*. Denver, Colorado: Barrio Publications, 1970.

———. *Phases*. N.p., 1971.

———. *The Secret Meaning of Death*. Lubbock, Texas: Trucha Publications, 1972.

Quintana, Leroy V. *Hijo del pueblo: New Mexico Poems*. Las Cruces, New Mexico: Puerto Del Sol Press, 1976.

———. *Sangre*. Las Cruces, New Mexico: Prima Agua Press, 1981.

Ríos, Alberto. *Whispering to Fool the Wind*. New York: Sheep Meadow Press. 1982.

Rivera, Tomás. *Always and Other Poems*. Sisterdale, Texas: Sisterdale Press, 1973.

*Riversedge*. Vols. 2:2 (1978) and 5:3 (1981), Special Chicano Numbers.

Rodríguez, Esteban A., ed. *Agua Fresca: An Anthology of Raza Poetry*. Tucson, Arizona: Oreja Press and Pajarito Publications, 1979.

Romano-V., Octavio, and Herminio Ríos C., eds. *El Espejo/The Mirror: Selected Chicano Literature*. Berkeley, California: Quinto Sol Publication, 1969; 2nd ed., 1972.

Romero, Leo. *Agua Negra*. Boise, Idaho: Ahsahta Press, 1981.

———. *During the Growing Season*. Tucson, Arizona: Maguey Press, 1978.

Romero, Lin. *Happy Songs, Bleeding Hearts*. San Diego: Toltecas en Aztlán Publications, 1974.

Salinas, Luís Omar. *Crazy Gypsy*. Fresno, California: Origenes Publications, 1970.

———. *I Go Dreaming Serenades*. San Jose, California: Mango Publications, 1979.

Salinas, Raúl R. *Un Trip through the Mind Jail y Otras Excursions*. San Francisco: Editorial Pocho-Che, 1980.

———. *Viaje/Trip*. Providence, Rhode Island: Hellcoal Press, 1973.

Sánchez, Ricardo. *Brown Bear Honey Madnesses*. Austin, Texas: Slough Press, 1981.

———. *Canto y grito mi liberación*. El Paso, Texas: Mictla Publications, 1971.

———. *Hechizo/Spells*. Los Angeles: Chicano Studies Center of UCLA, 1976.

———. *Milhuas Blues and Gritos Norteños*. Milwaukee: Spanish Speaking Outreach Institute, University of Wisconsin, 1978.

Shular, Antonia C., et al., eds. *Literatura Chicana, Texto y Contexto*. Englewood Cliffs, New Jersey: Prentice-Hall, 1972.

Somoza, Joseph. *Olive Women*. Los Cerrillos, New Mexico: San Marcos Press, 1976.

Soto, Gary. *Black Hair*. Pittsburgh: University of Pittsburgh Press, 1985.

———. *The Elements of San Joaquín*. Pittsburgh: University of Pittsburgh Press, 1977.

———. *Father is a Pillow Tied to a Broom*. Pittsburgh: Slow Loris Press, 1980.

———. *Living Down the Street*. San Francisco: Strawberry Hill, 1985

———. *The Tale of Sunlight*. Pittsburgh: University of Pittsburgh, 1978.

———. *Where Sparrows Work Hard*. Pittsburgh: University of Pittsburgh, 1981.

Tafolla, Carmen, et al. *Get Your Tortillas Together*. San Antonio, Texas: S/A Publications, 1976.

Tovar, Inés. *Con razón corazón*. Austin, Texas, 1977.

———— and Margarita Cota Cárdenas, eds. *Siete Poetas*. Tucson, Arizona: Scorpion Press. 1978.

Vento, Arnold, et al., eds. *Floricanto II: An Anthology of Chicano Literature*. Albuquerque, New Mexico and Austin, Texas: Pajarito Publications and the Center for Mexican American Studies, University of Texas at Austin, 1979.

Villanueva, Tino. *Hay otra voz Poems*. Staten Island, New York: Editorial Mensaje, 1972.

Zamora, Bernice. *Restless Serpents*. Menlo Park, California: Diseños Literarios, 1976.

## Other Literature

Arias, Ron. *The Road to Tamazunchale*. Reno, Nevada: West Coast Poetry Review, 1975.

Duran, Cheli. *The Yellow Canary Whose Eye Is So Black*. New York: Macmillan, 1977 [contains the poetry of Ruben Darío, Jose Martí, and Páblo Neruda, et al.].

Hesse, Hermann. *Siddhartha*. New York: New Directions, 1957.

————. *Steppenwolf*. New York: Holt, Rinehart and Winston, 1961.

Jeffers, Robinson. *The Double Axe*. New York: Liveright, 1977.

————. *Roan Stallion, Tamar and Other Poems*. New York: Modern Library, 1953.

————. *The Selected Poetry of Robinson Jeffers*. New York: Random House, 1938.

Poulin, A., Jr. *Contemporary American Poetry*. Boston: Houghton Mifflin, 1971.

Ríos, Alberto. *The Iguana Killer: Twelve Stories of the Heart*. San Francisco: Confluence Press, 1983.

Roethke, Theodore. *Collected Poems*. Garden City, New York: Doubleday, 1975.

## SECONDARY SOURCES

### Books

Acuña, Rudolfo. *Occupied America: A History of Chicanos*, Second Edition. New York: Harper & Row, 1981.

Alonso, Amado. *Poesía y estilo de Páblo Neruda*. Buenos Aires: Editorial Sudamerican, 1968.

Blessing, Richard A. *Theodore Roethke's Dynamic Vision*. Bloomington: Indiana University Press, 1974.

Bruce-Novoa, Juan. *Chicano Authors: Inquiry by Interview*. Austin, Texas: University of Texas Press, 1980.

_____. *Chicano Poetry: A Response to Chaos*. Austin, Texas: University of Texas Press, 1982.

Chacón, Felipe Maximiliano. *Obras de Felipe Maximiliano Chacón, El Cantor Neomexicano: Poesía y Prosa*. Albuquerque, New Mexico: Self-published, 1924.

Coffin, Arthur B. *Robinson Jeffers: Poet of Inhumanism*. Madison: University of Wisconsin Press, 1971.

de Costa, René. *The Poetry of Pablo Neruda*. Cambridge, Massachusetts: Harvard, 1979.

Creeley, Robert. *Was That a Real Poem & Other Essays*. Bolinas, California: Four Seasons Foundation, 1979.

Cardenas de Dwyer, Carlota. *Chicano Voices Instructor's Guide*. Boston: Houghton Mifflin, 1975.

Davis, Walter A. *The Act of Interpretation: A Critique of Literary Reason*. Chicago: University of Chicago Press, 1978.

Del Pino, Salvador. "La poesía chicana: una nueva trayectoria" in *The Identification and Analysis of Chicano Literature*, Francisco Jimenez, ed. New York: Bilingual Press/Editorial Bilingüe, 1979.

Duran, Cheli., ed. *The Yellow Canary Whose Eye is So Black*. New York: Macmillan, 1977.

Eger, Ernestina N. *A Bibliography of Criticism of Contemporary Chicano Literature*. Berkeley: University of California, 1980.

_____. "A Selected Bibliography of Chicano Criticism" in *The Identification and Analysis of Chicano Literature*, ed. Francisco Jimenez. New York: Bilingual Press/Editorial Bilingüe, 1979.

Evans, David A., ed. *New Voices in American Poetry*. Boston: Little, Brown, 1973.

Franco, Jean. *A Literary History of Spain: Spanish American Literature Since Independence*. London: Ernest Benn, 1973.

Galarza, Ernesto. *Merchants of Labor: The Mexican Bracero Story*. Santa Barbara, California: McNally & Loftin, 1964.

Galbraith, John K., *Economics and the Public Purpose*. Boston: Houghton Mifflin, 1973.

Garvin, Paul., ed. *A Prague School Reader on Esthetics, Literary Structure, and Style*. Washington, D.C.: Georgetown University Press, 1964.

Gonzales, Rafael. *Proceedings: National Conference on Bilingual Education*. Austin, Texas: Dissemination Center for Bilingual Education, 1972.

Gottesman, Ronald, et al., eds. *The Norton Anthology of American Literature*, Volume I. New York: W. W. Norton, 1979.

Hall, Donald. *Contemporary American Poetry*. Baltimore, Maryland: Penguin Books, 1962 [rev. 1971].

Hinojosa-Smith, Rolando. "Literatura Chicana: Background and Present Status of a Bicultural Expression," in *The Identification and Analysis of Chicano Literature*. New York: Bilingual Press/Editorial Bilingüe, 1979.

Hoil, Juan José. *The Book of the Chilam Balam of Chumayel*, Ralph B. Roys, transl. Norman: University of Oklahoma Press, 1967.

Holman, C. Hugh. *A Handbook to Literature*. Third Edition. Indianapolis, Indiana: Odyssey Press, 1972.

Jimenez, Francisco, ed. *The Identification and Analysis of Chicano Literature*. New York: Bilingual Press/Editorial Bilingüe, 1979.

Johnson, Thomas H. ed., *Final Harvest, Emily Dickinson's Poems*. Boston: Little, Brown and Co., 1961.

Juhasz, Suzanne. *Metaphor and the Poetry of Williams, Pound and Stevens*. Lewisburg, Pennsylvania: Bucknell, 1974.

Keller, Gary, ed. *Return: Alurista Poems Collected and New*. Ypsilanti, Michigan: Bilingual Press, 1982.

Léal, Luis. "Mexican American Literature: A Historical Perspective" in *Modern Chicano Writers*, Joseph Sommers and Tomas Ybarra-Frausto, eds. Englewood Cliffs, New Jersey: Prentice Hall, 1979.

Leon-Portilla, Miguel. *Aztec Thought and Culture: A Study of the Ancient Nahuatl Mind*. Norman: University of Oklahoma Press, 1963.

————. *Pre-Columbian Literature of Mexico*. Norman: University of Oklahoma Press, 1969.

Loméli, Francisco and Donaldo Urioste. *Chicano Perspectives in Literature: A Critical and Annotated Bibliography*. Albuquerque, New Mexico: Pajarito Publications, 1976.

Maldonado, Jesus. *Poesía chicana: Alurista, el mero chingón*. Seattle, Washington: Centro de Estudios Chicanos Monograph Series, 1971.

Malkoff, Karl. *Crowell's Handbook of Contemporary American Poetry*. New York: Thomas Y. Crowell, 1973.

Mariani, Paul. *William Carlos Williams: A New World Naked*. New York: McGraw-Hill, 1981.

Mazzaro, Jerome. *William Carlos Williams: The Later Poems*. Ithaca, New York: Cornell, 1973.

McWilliams, Carey. *North from Mexico*. New York: Greenwood Press, 1968.

Meier, Matt S. and Feliciano Rivera. *Dictionary of Mexican American History*. Westport, Connecticut: Greenwood Press, 1981.

Meyer, Michael C. and William L. Sherman. *The Course of Mexican History*. New York: Oxford Press, 1983.

Mileck, Joseph. *Hermann Hesse: Life and Art*. Berkeley, California: University of California Press, 1978.

Mirandé, Alfredo and Evangelina Enríquez. *La Chicana*. Chicago: University of Chicago Press, 1979.

Monegal, E. R. *El viajero inmovil*. Buenos Aires, 1967.

Nogales, Luis. *The Mexican American: A Selected and Annotated Bibliography*. Stanford, California: Stanford University Press, 1971.

Ortego, Philip D. *New Voices in Literature*. Edinburg, Texas: Pan American University, 1971.

Padden, R. C. *The Hummingbird and the Hawk: Conquest and Sovereignty in the Valley of Mexico, 1503–1541*. New York: Harper Colophon Books, 1967.

Paredes, Américo. *"With His Pistol in His Hand": A Border Ballad and Its Hero*. Austin, University of Texas Press, 1958.

Paz, Octavio. *The Labyrinth of Solitude*. Lysander Kemp, transl. New York: Grove Press, 1961 [1950].

Quirarte, Jacinto. *Mexican American Artists*. Austin: University of Texas Press, 1973.

Rocard, Marcienne. *Les Fils du Soleil: La Minorité Mexicaine á travers la Littérature des États-Unis*. Paris: Maison-neuve et Larose, 1980.

Rothenberg, Jerome. *Pre-Faces & Other Writings*. New York: New Directions, 1981.
———. *Shaking the Pumpkin*. New York: Doubleday, 1972.

Samora, Julian and Patricia Simon. *A History of the Mexican American People*. Notre Dame, Indiana: Notre Dame Press, 1977.

Silver, Irwin and Ethel Raim, eds. *American Favorite Ballads*. New York: Oak Publications, 1961.

Sommers, Joseph and Tomás Ybarra-Frausto, eds. *Modern Chicano Writers*. Englewood Cliffs, New Jersey: Prentice-Hall, 1979.

Soustelle, Jacques. *Daily Life of the Aztecs on the Eve of the Spanish Conquest*. Stanford, California: Stanford University Press, 1961.

Swadesh, Frances L. *Los Primeros Pobladores: Hispanic Americans of the Ute Frontier*. Notre Dame, Indiana: University of Notre Dame Press, 1974.

Tijerina, Reies López. *Mi lucha por la tierra*. México, D. F.: Fondo de Cultura Economica, 1978.

Tréjo, Arnulfo D. *Bibliografia Chicana: A Guide to Information Sources*. Detroit: Gale Research Company, 1975.

Trujillo, Larry. "Police Crimes in the Barrio" in *History, Culture, and Society: Chicano Studies in the 1980's*. Ypsilanti, Michigan: Bilingual Press, 1983.

Turner, Alberta T., ed. *Fifty Contemporary Poets*. New York: David McKay, 1977.

Valdez, Luis. *Actos*. San Juan Bautista, California: Cucaracha Press, 1971.
———. Introduction to *Aztlán: An Anthology of Mexican American Literature*. New York: Alfred A. Knopf, 1972.

Vallejos, Tomas. "Mestizaje: The Transformation of Ancient Indian Religious Thought in Contemporary Chicano Fiction." Boulder: University of Colorado Dissertation, 1980.

Vasconcelos, Jose. *Vasconcelos: Prologo y Seleccion de Genaro F. MacGregor*. México, D.F.: Ediciones de la Secretaria de educación publica, 1942.

Villanueva, Tino, ed. *Chicanos: Antología historica y literaria*. México, D.F.: Fondo de Cultura Economica, 1980.

Vinson, James, ed. *Contemporary Poets*. New York: St. Martins Press, 1980.

Weigle, Marta. *The Penitentes of the Southwest*. Santa Fe, New Mexico: Ancient City
    Press, 1970.
Williams, Raymond. *Marxism and Literature*. Oxford, England: Oxford University
    Press, 1977.
Ybarra-Frausto, Tomás. "Alurista's Poetics: The Oral, the Bilingual, the Pre-
    Columbian," in *Modern Chicano Writers*. Englewood Cliffs, New Jersey:
    Prentice-Hall, 1979.

## Articles

Bornstein, Miriam. "The Voice of the Chicana in Poetry," *Denver Quarterly*, 16:3
    (Fall, 1981), 33–34.
Bruce-Novoa, Juan. Review of *Restless Serpents* in *Latin American Literary Review*,
    5:10 (1977), 153.
———— and C. May-Gamba. "El Quinto Festival de Teatros" in *De Colores*, 2:2
    (1975).
Candelaria, Cordelia. "Anahuac Again and the Influence of Chicano Writers,"
    *American Book Review*, 4:5 (July, 1982) [review of Daniel Peters' *The Luck of
    Huemac*].
————. "Another Reading of Three Poems by Zamora," *MELUS*, 7:4 (Winter,
    1980).
————. "Hang-Up of Memory: Another View of Growing Up Chicano," *American
    Book Review*, 5:2 (April, 1983) [review of Rodriguez's *Hunger of Memory*].
————. "*Los Ancianos* in Chicano Literature," *Agenda: A Journal of Hispanic Issues*,
    10:5 (November, 1979).
————. Review of *Fiesta in Aztlán* and *Flor y Canto IV and V* in *La Red/The Net*, 61
    (December, 1982).
Castillo, Rafael. *Imagine: International Chicano Poetry Journal*, 1:2 (Winter, 1984).
Castro, Donald. "Chicano Literature: A Bibliographical Essay." *English in Texas*,
    7:4 (Summer, 1976).
Cooley, Peter, "I Can Hear You Now," *Parnassus*, (Fall/Winter, 1979).
Cortés, Carlos E. Review of Bruce-Novoa's *Chicano Poetry: A Response to Chaos* in
    *Southeastern Latin Americanist*, 27:2 (September, 1983).
Elizondo, Sergio. "Myth and Reality in Chicano Literature," *Latin American Literary
    Review*, 5:10 (Spring, 1977).
Fallis, Valdés Guadalupe. "Code Switching in Bilingual Chicano Poetry," *Hispania*,
    59:4 (December, 1976).
Grajéda, Rafael. "The Pachuco in Chicano Poetry: The Process of Legend-
    Creation," *Revista Chicano-Riquena*, 8:4 (Otono, 1980).
Hancock, Joel. "The Emergence of Chicano Poetry: A Survey of Sources, Themes,
    and Techniques," *Arizona Quarterly*, 29:1 (Spring, 1973).

Jimenez, Francisco. "Chicano Literature: Sources and Themes," *Bilingual Review/ Revista Bilingue*, 1:1 (January–April, 1974).

Kermode, Frank. "Modernism," *Modern Essays* (London: Collins, 1970).

Kopp, Karl. Review of *Hijo del Pueblo, American Book Review*, 1:1 (December, 1977).

Kuykendall, Mabel M. "Road to Tres Piedras," *The Taos News*. (March 24, 1971).

Leal, Luis. "In Search of Aztlán," *Denver Quarterly*, 16:3 (Fall, 1981).

Loméli, Francisco, and Donaldo Urioste. Review of *Restless Serpents, De Colores*, 3:4 (1977).

Madrigal, Sylvia. "*Emplumada*: A Female Pen in Flourish," *Imagine: International Chicano Poetry Journal*, 1:1 (Summer, 1984).

Moreno, Joseph A. Clarke. "A Bibliography of Bibliographies Relating to Studies of Mexican Americans," *El Grito*, 5 (Winter, 1971–72).

Olvera, Joe. Review of *Restless Serpents, American Book Review*, 2:2 (October, 1979).

Ortego, Felipe. "The Chicano Renaissance," in Livie I. Duran and H. Russell Bernard's *Introduction to Chicano Studies*. Second Edition. New York: Macmillan, 1982 [1971].

Padilla, Ray. "Apuntes para la documentación de la cultura Chicano," *El Grito*, 5 (Winter, 1971–72).

Ramirez, Arthur. Review of *The Tale of Sunlight, Revista Chicano-riqueña*, 9:3 (Verano, 1981).

Rebolledo, Tey Diana, "Witches, Bitches and Midwives: The Shaping of Poetic Consciousness in Chicana Literature," *The Chicano Struggle* (Binghamton, New York: Bilingual Press, 1984).

Rodríguez, Alfonso. Review of Alurista's *A'nque: Collected Works, 1976–79* in *La Palabra*, 3:1–2 (Primavera, 1981).

Rodríguez, Juan. Review of *The Elements of San Joaquín, New Scholar*, 6 (1976).

Sánchez, George I. "Pachucos in the Making," *Common Ground*, 4:1, (Autumn, 1943).

Sánchez, Marta E. "Inter-Sexual and Intertextual Codes in the Poetry of Bernice Zamora," *MELUS*, 7:3 (Fall, 1980).

Segade, Gustavo, "Chicano *Indigenismo*: Alurista and Miguel Mendez M.," *Xalman*, 1:4 (Spring, 1977).

Soto, Gary. "Notes on Creative Writing," *Revista Chicano-riqueña*, 7:4 (Otono, 1979).

Tatum, Charles. "Toward a Chicano Bibliography of Literary Criticism," *Atisbos*, 2 (Winter, 1967–77).

Wagner, Maryfrances. Review of *The Tale of Sunlight* in *New Letters*, 46:1 (September, 1979).

Zamora, Bernice. "Archetypes in Chicana Poetry," *De Colores*, 4:3 (1978).

# Glossary

*abajo* [adverb]: under, underneath, below; down; often used as adjective signifying oppressed as in "los de abajo," the downtrodden.

*abuela, -o* [noun, masc./fem.]: grandmother, grandfather; diminutive form common in the U.S. is "abuelita, -o."

*alabado, -a* [adjective]: praised, honored; [noun, masc.]: hymn in praise of the Sacrament.

*aliento* [noun, masc.]: breath, spirit, courage; enterprise; scent.

*alma* [noun, fem.]: soul, spirit; human being.

*amigo, -a* [noun, masc./fem.]: friend, companion.

*ánimo* [noun, masc.]: spirit, will, courage; mind, thought; intention; encouragement.

*a tirones*: see *tirón*.

*Aztlán* [noun]: place of origin of the Aztecs; at the height of the Chicano Movement, many referred to the U.S. Southwest as "Aztlán"; now sometimes used to refer to any place where Chicanos live.

*barrio* [noun, masc.]: neighborhood; inner city ghetto.

*bronce* [noun, masc.]: bronze; bronze colored.

*cabron, cabrones* [noun, masc.]: male goat, buck; (slang) obscenity for bastard or cuckold.

*campo, campesino* [noun, masc.]: field, agricultural land; camp; farmworker.

*carnal, carnalismo* [noun, masc.]: (slang) brother, brotherhood.

*cebolla* [noun, fem.]: onion.

*chicanismo* [noun, masc.]: concept referring to entire range of elements, beliefs, values, characteristics of Mexican American culturalism.

*chingar* [verb]: to violate obscenely (profanity). *Chingado, -a* [noun, masc./fem.] signifies one who is violated.

*con* [preposition]: with.

*con safos* [colloquial expression]: same to you; often abbreviated C/S following graffiti to signify "same to you."

*congal* [noun, masc.]: (slang) small business, grassroots project.

*corbata* [noun, fem.]: necktie, cravat; streamer (of flag); ribbon, insignia.

*cuento* [noun, masc.]: story, tale; yarn; tall-tale.

*curandero, -a* [noun, masc./fem.]: healer, lay medical person; quack, witch-doctor; *curanderismo* [noun, masc.] refers to the practice of healing with remedies and prayer.

*de* [preposition]: of.

*desesperación* [noun, fem.]: despair; desperation.

*dicho* [noun, masc.]: maxim, proverb, folk saying.

*el* [definite article, masc.]: the [plural: *los*]; *él* [personal pronoun; plural: *ellos*]: he, him, it [they].

*en* [preposition]: in, into; at; on, upon; for.

*entre* [preposition]: between, among.

*escamado, -a* [adj.]: scaly; (slang) wary, afraid; [noun, masc.]: work wrought with designs of scales; [noun, fem.]: embroidery, usually with scale designs.

*familia* [noun, fem.]: family.

*frente* [noun, masc.]: front; face (of a bastion); blank space at beginning of a document; obverse side of coins.

*frijol, -es* [noun, masc.]: bean, bean seeds, bean dishes; (slang) derogatory term for Mexican or person of Latino origin.

*gaba, gabacho, -a* [noun, masc./fem.]: (slang) Anglo or North American origin person, sometimes derogatory, depending on context.

*grito* [noun, masc.]: yell, shout; loud cry. *El Grito de Dolores*: cry of independence made by Father Hidalgo on September 16, 1810, on church steps of Dolores which led to the revolution by Mexico against Spain.

*guerrero, -a* [noun, masc./fem.]: soldier, fighter, revolutionary.

*hay* [adv.]: (slang, especially in New Mexico) there, diminutive of *allá*.

*hermano, -a* [noun, masc./fem.]: brother, sister.

*huelga* [noun, fem.]: strike (labor).

*jodido, -a* [noun, masc./fem.]: (slang) obscenity meaning abused, violated; *jodiendo*: obscene violation of someone or something.

*la* [definite article, fem.]: the (plural: *las*).

*llano* [noun, masc.]: flat terrain, plain; [adj.]: straightforward, plain.

*loco, -a* [noun, masc./fem.]: crazy, demented; (slang) foolish; carefree.

*los de abajo* [noun]: the downtrodden, oppressed, poor.

*lo ser chicano*: (philosophical) Chicano being.

*madre* [noun, fem.]: mother; (slang) obscenity used in combination with other words.

*maestro, -a* [noun, masc./fem.]: master, teacher; conductor.

*manito, -a* [noun, masc./fem.]: diminutive form, little brother; little sister; (slang) person from New Mexico.

*manos morenas* [noun, fem.]: brown hands.

*mero, -a* [adj.]: mere; pure; simple; (slang) number one, the best.

*mí* [pers. pronoun]: me, myself; [possessive]: mine, my.

*migra* [noun, fem.]: (slang) U.S. Immigration and Naturalization Service.

*nada* [adv.]: not at all; [noun, fem.]: nothing, nothingness.

*obscura* [adj.]: dark; obscure (also spelled *oscura*).

*ojito (de una cueva)* [noun, masc.] diminutive form, little spring (of a cave), small pond.

*ojo* [noun, masc.]: eye; hole; spring or springs (as in cave springs).

*ombligo* [noun, masc.]: navel, belly button; hub.

*orgullo* [noun, masc.]: pride; haughtiness, arrogant pride.

*pachanga* [noun, fem.]: (slang) party, celebration, festivity.

*padre* [noun, masc.]: father.

*penitente* [noun, masc.]: member (usually male) of a fanatical religious sect that practices self-flagellation and other forms of masochism in emulation of the crucifixion of Jesus Christ.

*pinche* [noun, masc.]: scullion, kitchen help. (slang) obscenity.

*pinto* [noun, masc.]: (slang) prisoner, jail inmate.

*poblador, -es* [noun, masc.]: pioneer, pioneers, first settlers.

*poeta* [noun, masc.]: poet.

*pueblo* [noun, masc.]: village, town; the people, the folk, community; often used synonymously with *la raza* to refer to the Mexican culture.

*que* [relative pronoun]: who, whom, that, which; [interrogative]: what? how?

*remedio, -s* [noun, masc.]: remedy, home remedies; natural healing, homeopathy.

*ruco, -a* [noun, masc./fem.]: (slang) old man or woman, usually derogatory.

*sangre* [noun, fem.]: blood; gore. *sangrienta* [adj.]: bloody, blood-stained. savage.

*santero* [noun, masc.]: woodcarver of religious figurines (i.e., *santos*).

*sapo* [noun, masc.]: frog, toad.

*siguir* [verb]: to follow; *nos sigue*: it follows us.

*si se puede*: yes, it can be done; slogan from the Chicano Movement serving as an inspiration to farmworkers and others.

*su* [possessive pronoun, masc./fem.]: his, her, its, one's, their, your.

*tierra* [noun, fem.]: earth; land; dirt; real estate.

*tirón* [noun, masc.]: pull, jerk, tug; *a tirones* [adverb]: intermittently.

*tlamatinime* [noun, masc.]: Nahuatl term for wise man, sage, teacher.

*tocayo (also tocallo)* [noun, masc.]: namesake, person for whom one is named.

*todo está bien*: all's well.

*tortillero, -a* [noun, masc./fem.]: tortilla maker.

*trenza* [noun, fem.]: braid, plait.

*triste* [adj.]: sad, morose; *tristeza* [noun, fem.]: sadness, melancholy.

*vato* [noun, masc.]: (slang) guy, dude (sometimes spelled "bato"); *vatos locos*: crazy (or cool) dudes; *vatito*: diminutive form.

*viaje* [noun, masc.]: trip, journey.

*vida* [noun, fem.]: life.

*viejo, -a* [noun, masc./fem.]: old person, senior citizen; *viejito, -a*: diminutive form used usually as an endearment.

*Virgen*: the Virgin Mary, often *la Virgen de Guadalupe* referring to the Virgin of Guadalupe, patron saint of Mexico (and many Chicanos).

*vivir* [verb]: to live; *vivimos*: we lived.

*y* [conjunction]: and.

# Index

**About the Author**

CORDELIA CANDELARIA, Associate Professor of English, University of Colorado at Boulder, serves as a consulting editor to *Frontiers: A Journal of Women's Studies*. She has contributed to *Chicano Literature: A Reference Guide* (Greenwood Press, 1985), *A History of the Mexican American People*, *Midwest Quarterly*, the *Dictionary of Literary Biography*, and *MELUS*. Her volume of poetry, *Ojo de la Cueva*, was published in 1984, and her poems have appeared in *Revista Chicano-riqueña, Rocky Mountain Review, Grito del Sol*, and *Riversedge*, among others.